Books should be returned on or before the
last date stamped below.

15. JUL. 1981	−1. AUG. 1983	15. NOV. 1990
16. AUG. 1981	26. SEP. 1983	1 1 NOV 1991
11. SEP. 1981	10. OCT. 1983	− 5 MAR 1992
−8 OCT. 1981		
26. OCT. 1981	28 NOV. 1983	2 0 JUL 1992
16. NOV. 1981		
30. NOV. 1981	12. MAR. 1984	−7 SEP 1992
	24. SEP. 1984	
10. DEC. 1981		9 JUN 1998
15. JAN. 1982	30 JUN 1986	
15. MAR. 1982	15. JUN. 1987	− 2 MAY 2006
14. FEB. 1983	−7. DEC. 1987	
28 APR 1983	−7. APR. 1988	
23 JUN 1983	28 ... 1988	3 0 MAR 2010
	−7. ... 1990	

DONALDSON, William <u>and</u> Young, Douglas <u>eds</u>.

Grampian hairst

10.   X6

GRAMPIAN
HAIRST

GRAMPIAN HAIRST

AN ANTHOLOGY OF NORTHEAST PROSE

Edited by
William Donaldson
and Douglas Young

With a foreword by
Cuthbert Graham

and an essay on Northeast Scots by
David Murison

ABERDEEN UNIVERSITY PRESS

First published 1981
Aberdeen University Press
A member of the Pergamon Group
© Grampian Regional Council 1981

X6

10.

982056

British Library Cataloguing in Publication Data
Grampian Hairst
1. Scottish literature—19th century
2. Scottish literature—20th century
3. English literature—Scottish authors
I. Young, Douglas   II. Donaldson, William
828'.808'08094121   PR8643

ISBN 0 08 025747 X (hard)
ISBN 0 08 025748 8 (flexi)

Design and illustrations by AUP Graphics

PRINTED IN GREAT BRITAIN
AT THE UNIVERSITY PRESS
ABERDEEN

Contents

CITY, TOWN AND VILLAGE

MOUNTAIN AND MOORLAND

Contents

SHOD AGAIN FOR SCHOOL

A MAN AND A MAID

THE SOCIAL HOUR

APPENDIX

Foreword

Quarter of a century ago, David Ogston, a small farmer's son in a Buchan farm-house, "looked in the dresser and discovered Lewis Grassic Gibbon" among the books which his mother had borrowed from the County Library. Looking back now from the mid-point of his career as a parish minister to what then happened to him at the age of ten he writes (in *White Stone Country*, a work-in-progress on a Buchan boyhood):

> "Reading *A Scots Quair* was like entering a new territory, exploring a land at once excitingly unknown and yet unerringly familiar. The story seemed to come from somewhere very close at hand, the characters from somewhere deep within myself: they said things I heard in conversation and exchanges between grown-ups in my world. They said out loud some things that I myself had thought and felt.
>
> Gibbon's descriptions of people and fields and work were so real and so direct that when I left off reading about the Howe of the Mearns, and went outside into the sun and all the sights and sounds and smells of the close, I felt that Gibbon had taught me to see what was all around me for the first time. He heightened for me the awareness of life I lived unwittingly. He showed me how the things I took for granted—earth, bushes, trees, rain-water, glaur—were the raw material of poetry.
>
> And Grassic Gibbon talked of poetry and of pure feeling, of innocence being lost, of passion and the meeting of men and women in their serious joys . . . some of it was beyond me, but I read and re-read the passages where he talked of these mysteries. It was quite one thing to know of such remote realities, but seeing them in print imbued them with new and vibrant meaning."

The case is made there, I think, for an anthology of Northeast literature for the people of the Northeast, both young and old. It gives the shock of *recognition* that comes upon us when the flesh of everyday reality is made word. To me *Grampian Hairst* is full of such thrills. This is because it contains well-selected samples of the masters of our imaginative regional literature, men like John R. Allan, William Alexander, George MacDonald, David Grant and Ian Macpherson, as well as contemporary story-tellers who have, beyond a peradventure, something of the creative fire: like David Toulmin and Jessie Kesson.

It is one of the great advantages of a book like this that in it we can check the vision of a prose writer against our local knowledge. I shall never be able to read the last part of the extract from Gibbon's *The Land* without remembering an exchange of letters I had with him about vegetarianism. I had met at the YMCA hostel in Aberdeen a very ardent vegetarian who took very seriously the idea of not eating animal flesh. I suggested to LGG that if his Gay Hunters, the early men who were said to be gentle, kind and innocent, yet lived by hunting, killing and eating animals, really examined their behaviour they must have guilty dreams. The answer came in *The Land,* where he remarks that the cattle he has been watching "abandoned playfulness and took to grazing, remembering their mission was to provide fat carcasses for the slaughtershed"—

> We balk from the thought of our strange unthinking cruelties, the underpit of blood and suffering and intolerable horror on which the most innocent of us build our lives. I feel this evening that never again will I eat a dead animal . . . But that resolve will be gone tomorrow; the Horror is beyond personalism, very old and strange and terrible. Even those hunters all those millenia ago were eaters of flesh.

As this book is intended for use in upper schools, as well as for the general public, I can imagine some sixth-former choosing as his thesis for critical exposition the development and survival of spoken and written Scots for well over a century, as illustrated in these pages. From George MacDonald's "Mischief in Glamerton", through the amusing rustic courtship in *Johnny Gibb,* and Councillor Ettershank's unfailing Doric eloquence, we come with side glints from Gavin Greig and William Robbie's *Heir of Glendornie,* to the Scots of well within living memory, as reflected in "Chris's Wedding" and Hunter Diack's Kemnay folk, until finally we arrive at the living tongue as it is still exercised in David Toulmin's "Playing Truant".

Behind this inextinguishable, stubborn survival of the language is the sense of community—a special form of community centred on the family farm or the hillside and moorland croft, yet echoed in the town by craftsmen and fishermen. It is my hope that this book, in which the Northeast of Scotland manifests an identity in all its diversity, will give pleasure to all who pree its contents. I hope it will rouse wonder and interest by the unexpected shock of recognition—a recognition equally potent in city, burgh, village, and rural parish, in the mountain lands at the Back of Gairn, in the corn-rich lowlands of the Garioch, in the wind-fretted coastline of Buchan and the Moray Firth with all their fisher havens. For there is enough here to reanimate that slogan, culled from a verse by Sir Alexander Gray, by which I have lived for so long:

> This is my country,
> The land that begat me,
> These windy spaces
> Are surely my own.
> And these that here toil
> In the sweat of their faces
> Are flesh of my flesh
> And bone of my bone.

Cuthbert Graham

Introduction

In 1976 a collection of Scottish verse was published, at the behest of Grampian Regional Council, under the title *Poetry of Northeast Scotland.* In his introduction, the editor, James Alison, expressed a wish that the book would meet an important need in the schools of Grampian Region, as well as giving pleasure to a wide general public. His hopes were amply justified by the event. The committee who planned the present volume wish to extend the process of exploration and re-discovery to the equally rich field of prose literature in the Northeast. They look in the first instance to the classroom, but hope to interest those of all ages and airts for whom the first qualification of a good book is that it should contain good writing.

Grampian Hairst is made up, therefore, of extracts from longer prose works, chiefly fictional, and dating in the main from the middle of the nineteenth century to the present. In order to achieve the greatest possible coherence, it was decided to dispense with a chronological arrangement and group the passages around a number of central themes, reflecting at once the main preoccupations of the writing, and life of the Region itself.

A major difficulty was created by the sheer quantity and quality of the material available. The editors confess that prior to undertaking this project they were unaware of how rich and extensive a prose tradition existed in the Northeast of Scotland. Economic considerations, however, placed a severe restriction on the size of the book that could be produced. There was a limit, for the same reason, upon the number of writers who could be included. The major figures clearly required substantial representation, but we have also tried to include some lesser-known writers, so that our readers may combine the pleasure of renewed acquaintance with the excitement of fresh discovery. Nonetheless we are very conscious that a number of good writers and a very great deal of good writing have had to be left out.

Indeed the book makes no pretence at being a comprehensive survey of the prose writing of the Northeast. It is more in the nature of an appetiser, and we hope that it will encourage the reader to explore the local prose tradition more fully for himself. In this matter he will probably find useful, as the editors have done, the bibliographies contained in Joyce Philip Collie's unpublished thesis *A*

Introduction

Study of the Treatment of the Life of Northeast Scotland by Scottish Novelists, which is available in the King's College Library at the University of Aberdeen.

As *Grampian Hairst* is intended to be a popular work, we have excised and condensed to suit our purpose, but not so as to alter what in our view was the spirit, intention, or texture of the original. Longer omissions have been indicated in the conventional way. Glossing has been kept to a minimum, because we believe that the context should as far as possible be allowed to supply the meaning.

We have received generous help and advice from enthusiasts too numerous to mention, but we must express our particular indebtedness to our advisory committee—Messrs Robert Erridge, Bruce Finlayson, Ronald Garden, William Hall, Colin MacLean, Dr. Cuthbert Graham—and its convener Mr. Charles King, Adviser in English in Grampian Region. We are doubly indebted to Dr. Graham, who not only made available to us his wide knowledge of Northeast life and literature but also graciously agreed to write a foreword to the book.

Equally invaluable has been the support of the Director of Education, Mr. James Michie, his Senior Depute, Mr. James Graham, Grampian Regional Council, and Aberdeenshire Educational Trust. Without this support and personal interest the publication of the book would not have been possible.

Responsibility for the final selection and for any error the book may contain rests, however, with the editors.

William Donaldson
Douglas Young

THE LIFE OF THE LAND

The Life of the Land

THE LAND
Lewis Grassic Gibbon *Scottish Scene*

I *Winter*

I like the story of the helpful Englishman who, when shown a modern Scots Nationalist map with "Scotland Proper" stretching from John o' Groats to the Tweed, and "Scotia Irredenta" stretching from the Tweed to the Mersey, suggested "Scotland Improper" in place of the latter term. The propriety of Northern England to rank as a section of Scotland may have political justice; it certainly has no aesthetic claim. If I look out on the land of Scotland and see it fouled by the smoking slag-heaps of industrialism rightwards and leftwards, a long trailing rift down the eastern coast and a vomiting geyser in Lanarkshire, I feel no stirrings of passion at all to add those tortured wastes of countryside, Northumbria and Lancashire, to the Scottish land. I like the grey glister of sleet in the dark this night, seen through the unblinded window; and I like this idle task of voyaging with a pen through the storm-happed wastes of Scotland in winter; but I balk at reaching beyond the Border, into that chill land of alien geology and deplorable methods of ploughing. This paraffin lamp set beside me on the table was lit for the benefit of myself and Scotland Proper: I shrink from geographical impropriety to-night as my Kailyard literary forerunners shrank from description of the bridal bed.

And now that I bend to the task and the logs are crackling so cheerfully and the wind has veered a point, and there's a fine whoom in the lum, it comes on me with a qualm that perhaps I have no qualifications for the task at all. For if the land is the enumeration of figures and statistics of the yield of wheat in the Merse or the Carse of Gowrie, fruit-harvesting in Coupar-Angus, or how they couple and breed their cattle in Ayrshire, I am quite lost. And if the land is the lilting of tourist names, Strathmore, Ben Lomond, Ben Macdhui, Rannoch, Loch Tay and the Sidlaw Hills, I confess to bored glimpses of this and that stretch of unique countryside, I confess that once (just such a night as this) I journeyed up

3

to Oban; and the train was bogged in a snow-storm; and I spent shivering hours in view of Ben Cruachan; and once an Anglo-Gaelic novelist took me round Loch Lomond in his car and we drank good whisky and talked about Lenin; and an uncle once dragged me, protesting, up Lochnagar, in search of a sunrise that failed to appear—the sun hid that morning in a diffusion of peasoup fog; and I've viewed the Caledonian Canal with suitable commercial enthusiasm and recited (as a small boy at concerts) verse about the Dee and Don, they still run on (a phenomenon which elicited complacent clappings of commendation from my audiences); and I've eaten trout by Loch Levenside. But I refuse the beetling crags and the spume of Spey; still I think they are not The Land.

That is The Land out there, under the sleet, churned and pelted there in the dark, the long rigs upturning their clayey faces to the spear-onset of the sleet. *That* is The Land, a dim vision this night of laggard fences and long stretching rigs. And the voice of it—the true and unforgettable voice—you can hear even in such a night as this as the dark comes down, the immemorial plaint of the peewit, flying lost. *That* is The Land—though not quite all. Those folk in the byre whose lantern light is a glimmer through the sleet as they muck and bed and tend the kye, and milk the milk into tin pails, in curling froth—they are The Land in as great a measure. Those two, a dual power, are the protagonists in this little sketch. They are the essentials for the title. And besides, quite unfairly, they are all so intimately mine that I would give them that position though they had not a shadow of a claim to it.

I like to remember I am of peasant rearing and peasant stock. Good manners prevail on me not to insist on the fact over-much, not to boast in the company of those who come from manses and slums and castles and villas, the folk of the proletariat, the bigger and lesser bourgeoisies. But I am again and again, as I hear them talk of their origins and beginnings and begetters, conscious of an over-weening pride that mine was thus and so, that the land was so closely and intimately mine (my mother used to hap me in a plaid in harvest-time and leave me in the lee of a stook while she harvested) that I feel of a strange and antique age in the company and converse of my adult peers—like an adult himself listening to the bright sayings and laughter of callow boys, parvenus on the human scene, while I, a good Venriconian Pict, harken from the shade of my sun circle and look away, bored, in pride of possession at my terraced crops, at the on-ding of rain and snow across my leavened fields. . . .

How much this is merely reaction from the hatreds of my youth I do not know. For once I had a very bitter detestation for all this life of the land and the folk upon it. My view was that of my distant cousin, Mr. Leslie Mitchell, writing in his novel *The Thirteenth Disciple*:

Lewis Grassic Gibbon

A grey, grey life. Dull and grey in its routine, Spring, Summer, Autumn, Winter, that life the Neolithic men brought from the south, supplanting Azilian hunger and hunting and light-hearted shiftlessness with servitude to seasons and soil and the tending of cattle. A beastly life. With memory of it and reading those Catholic writers, who, for some obscure reason, champion the peasant and his state as the ideal state, I am moved to unkindly mirth . . . unprintably sceptical as to Mr. Chesterton or his chelas* ever having grubbed a livelihood from hungry acres of red clay, or regarding the land and its inhabitants with other vision than an obese Victorian astigmatism.

Not, I think, that I have gone the full circle and have returned among the romantics. As I listen to that sleet-drive I can see the wilting hay-ricks under the fall of the sleet and think of the wind ablow on ungarmented floors, ploughmen in sodden bothies on the farms outbye, old, bent and wrinkled people who have mislaid so much of fun and hope and high endeavour in grey servitude to those rigs curling away, only half-inanimate, into the night. I can still think and see these things with great clarity though I sit in this warm room and write this pleasant essay and find pleasure in the manipulation of words on a blank page. But when I read or hear our new leaders and their plans for making of Scotland a great peasant nation, a land of little farms and little farming communities, I am moved to a bored disgust with those pseudo-literary romantics playing with politics, those refugees from the warm parlours and lights and policemen and theatre-stalls of the Scots cities. They are promising the New Scotland a purgatory that would decimate it. They are promising it narrowness and bitterness and heart-breaking toil in one of the most unkindly agricultural lands in the world. They are promising to make of a young, ricketic man, with the phthisis of Glasgow in his throat, a bewildered labourer in pelting rains and the flares of head-aching suns, they are promising him years of a murderous monotony, poverty and struggle and loss of happy human relationships. They promise that of which they know nothing, except through sipping of the scum of Kailyard romance.

For this life is for no modern man or woman—even the finest of these. It belongs to a different, an alien generation. That winter that is sweeping up the Howe, bending the whins on Auchindreich hill, seeping with pelting blasts through the old walls of Edzell Castle, malagarousing the ploughed lands and swashing about and above the heavy cattle-courts where in darkness the great herds lie cud-chewing and breath-blowing in frosty steam, is a thing for most to

chelas disciples

5

be stared at, tourist-wise, endured for a day or a week. This night, the winter on the countryside, the crofter may doze contentedly in the arm-chair in the ingle-neuk and the mistress yawn with an equal content at the clock. For you or I or young Simon who is taking his girl to the pictures it is as alien and unendurable in permanance as the life of the Kamtchatkan.

II *Spring*

Going down the rigs this morning, my head full of that unaccustomed smell of the earth, fresh and salty and anciently mouldy, I remembered the psalmist's voice of the turtle and instinctively listened for its Scots equivalent—that far cooing of pigeons that used to greet the coming of Spring mornings when I was a boy. But the woods have gone, their green encirclement replaced by swathes of bog and muck and rank-growing heath, all the land about here is left bare in the North wind's blow. The pigeons have gone and the rabbits and like vermin multiplied—unhappily and to no profit, for the farmers tell me the rabbits are tuberculous, dangerous meat. Unshielded by the woods, the farm-lands are assailed by enemies my youth never knew.

But they are fewer and fewer, the cultivated lands. Half of them are in grass—permanently in grass—and browsed upon by great flocks of sheep, leaving that spider-trail of grey that sheep bring to pastures. We are repeating here what the Border men did in Badenoch and the Highlands—eating away the land and the crofter, killing off the peasant as surely as in Russia—and with no Russian compensation. If the little dykes and the sodden ditches that rivuleted in the Springs of bygone times with the waters hastening to the Forthie—the ditches that separated this little farm from that—were filled and obliterated by a sovkholz* with tractors and high enthusiasm and a great and tremendous agri-cultural hope, I at least could turn to the hills and the heath—that other and older Land—with no more regret than the sensitive felt in the passing of the windjammers and the coming of the steamboats. But instead there has come here only a brainless greed, a grabbing stupidity, the mean avariciousness and plan-lessness of our community in epitome. I do not wonder that the rabbits are tuberculous: the wonder is that they are not jaundiced as well.

It was then that I thought what a fine and heartsome smell has rank cow-dung as the child with the graip hurls it steady heap on heap from the rear of his gurling cart. They sell stuff in Paris in little bottles with just that smell, and charge for it handsomely, as they may well do, for it is the smell that back-grounds existence. And then (having come to the end of the rig and looked at the rabbit-snare and found it empty and found also a stone whereon to sit) I fell into

sovkholz Soviet state-farm

another meditation: this dung that backgrounded existence, this Autumn's crops, meal for the folk of the cities, good heartsome barley alcohol—would never be spread, never be seeded, never grounded to bree, but for the aristocracy of the earth, the ploughmen and the peasants. These are the real rulers of Scotland: they are the rulers of the earth!

And how patient and genial and ingenuously foul-mouthed and dourly wary and kindly they are, those self-less aristos of Scotland. They endure a life of mean and bitter poverty, an order sneered upon by the little folk of the towns, their gait is a mockery in city streets, you see little waitresses stare haughtily at their great red, suncreased hands, plump professors in spectacles and pimples enunciate theses on their mortality and morality, their habits of breeding and their shiftlessness—and they endure it all! They endure the chatter of the city salons, the plannings of this and that war and blockade, they endure the pretensions of every social class but their own to be the mainspring and base of human society—they, the masters, who feed the world! . . . And it came on me that all over Great Britain, all over Europe this morning, the mean fields of France and fat pastures of Saxony and the rolling lands of Roumania those rulers of the earth were out and about, bent-backed at plodding toil, the world's great Green International awaiting the coming of its Spartacus.

There are gulls in from the sea this morning, wheeling in comet tails at the heels of this and that ploughman, a dotting of signatures against the dark green of the Bervie braes. Here the land is red clay, sour and dour, but south, by Brechin, you come to that rich loam land that patterns Scotland like a ragged veil, the lovely land that even here erupts in sudden patches and brings tall corn while the surrounding fields wilt in the baking clay. The clay is good for potatoes in the dry years, however—those dry years that come every decade or so for no reason that we know of here in the Howe, for we are beyond the "mountain-shadow" that makes of Donside and Braemar the tourist's camping-ground. . . .

In the sunlight, down by Kinneff, the fog-horn has begun its wail, the sun has drawn great banks of mist out of the North Sea and now they are billowing over Auchendreich like the soft, coloured spume from a washing-tub. But left-wards the sun is a bright, steely glare on the ridged humps of the Grampians, hastening south into the coming of Summer, crowned with snow in their upper haughs—much the same mountains, I suppose, as the Maglemosians looked on that Spring day in the youth of the world and the youth of Scotland when they crossed the low lands of the Dogger Bank and clambered up the rocks of Kinneff into a still and untenanted Scotland. The great bear watched them come, and the eagle from his Grampian eyrie and scattering packs of wolves on the forest fringes saw that migration of the hunters seven thousand years ago. They came over Auchendreich there, through the whins and heath, and halted and stared at the billowing Howe, and laughed and muttered and squatted and stared—dark men, and tall, without gods or kings, classes or culture, writers or artists, free and happy, and all the world theirs. Scotland woke and looked at them from a hundred peaks and stared a shy virgin's amaze.

All winter the cattle were kept to the byres. This morning saw their first deliverance—cows and stirks and stots and calves they grumphed and galumphed from the byre to the park and squattered an astounded delight in the mud, and boxed at each other, and stared a bovine surprise at the world, and went mad with delight and raced round the park, and stood still and mooed: they mooed on a long, devilish note, the whole lot of them, for nearly two minutes on end and for no reason at all but delight in hearing their own moo. They are all of mixed breed, except one, a small Jersey cow of a southron coldness, who drops her aitches, haughtily, and also her calves. The strains are mostly shorthorn, with a dash of Highland, I suspect: a hundred years of mixed pasturing and crop-rotation weeded out the experimental breeds and left these satisfying mongrels. Presently (after racing a grocer's cart for the length of the field and all but hamstringing themselves on the boundary fence) they abandoned playfulness and took to grazing, remembering their mission was to provide fat carcases for the slaughtershed. . . .

We balk from such notions, in Spring especially, in especial as the evening comes with that fresh smell all about it, impregnating it, the kind of evening that has growth and youngness and kindliness in its essence—balk from the thought of our strange, unthinking cruelties, the underpit of blood and suffering and intolerable horror on which the most innocent of us build our lives. I feel this evening that never again will I eat a dead animal (or, I find myself guarding the resolve with the inevitable flippancy, a live one). But that resolve will be gone tomorrow: the Horror is beyond personalism, very old and strange and terrible. Even those hunters all those millenia ago were eaters of flesh.

It is strange to think that, if events never die (as some of the wise have supposed), but live existence all time in Eternity, back through the time-spirals, still alive and aware in that world seven thousand years ago, the hunters are *now* lying down their first night in Scotland, with their tall, deep-bosomed sinewy mates and their children, tired from trek. . . . Over in the west a long line of lights twinkles against the dark. Whin-burning—or the camps of Maglemose?

JOHNNY GIBB DISCUSSES THE SITUATION

William Alexander *Johnny Gibb of Gushetneuk*

To Johnny Gibb, the autumn of 1847 had been a season of varied and engrossing business. There was first the erection of Mr. MacCassock's new manse. So long as the project had remained a matter merely to be talked about and resolved upon, there had been no lack of people to express their ideas and give their advice, but when it had assumed the practical aspect of settling contracts for the building, some of those who had talked most fluently became remarkably vague, and did not seem in haste to commit themselves to any specific action. Johnny Gibb's course was precisely the reverse of this; the erection of the manse was not his proposal, but once it had been resolved upon, Johnny declared that it must be carried out forthwith. "We maun hae the wa's up, an' the reef on immedantly, an' lat 'im get marriet, an' win in till 't fan simmer comes roon again." Everybody admitted that this was expedient and desirable, and everybody felt how naturally it fell to Johnny Gibb to push the necessary operations on. And Johnny pushed them accordingly, taking no end of pains in getting materials driven, and kept to the hands of the workmen. Then there were the private arrangements at Gushetneuk, in view of Johnny Gibb ceasing to be "tacksman". The general belief was that Johnny would flit down to the Broch, buy half-a-dozen acres of the unfeued land, and settle down in a sort of permanent attitude as a small laird, cultivating his own land. Johnny meditated much on the point but said little, until one day, addressing his wife on the question of their future arrangements, he ran over one or two points that had come up to him, and, without indicating any opinion, abruptly finished with the query, "Fat think ye, 'oman?"

"Hoot, man," replied Mrs. Gibb, "fat need ye speer at me? I've toitit aboot wi' you upo' this place naar foorty year noo, an' never tribbl't my heid the day aboot fat ye micht think it richt to dee the morn; an' aw sanna begin to mislippen* ye noo at the tail o' the day."

"Weel," said Johnny, with an air of more than his ordinary gravity, "I've been thinkin 't owre, a' up an' doon. It's a queer thing fan ye begin to luik back owre a' the time byegane. The Apos'le speaks o' the life o' man as a 'vawpour that appeareth for a little, and than vainisheth awa';' an' seerly there cudna be a mair nait'ral resem'lance. Fan we begood the pilget* here thegither, wi' three stirks, an' a bran'it* coo't cam' wi' your providin', the tae side o' the place was ta'en up

---

mislippen mistrust *pilget* struggle *bran' it* brawny, sturdy

wi' breem busses an' heather knaps half doon the faul'ies,* and the tither was feckly a quaakin' bog, growin' little but sprots* an' rashes. It luiks like yesterday fan we hed the new hooses biggit, an' the grun a' oon'er the pleuch, though that's a gweed therty year syne. I min' as bricht 's a paintet pictur' fat like ilka knablich* an' ilka sheugh an' en' rig was."

"An' ye weel may, man, for there's hardly a cannas breid* upo' the place but's been lawbour't wi' yer nain han's owre an' owre again to mak' it."

"That's fat aw was comin' till. Takin 't as it is, there's been grun made oot o' fat wasna grun ava; an' there it is, growin' craps for the eese o' man an' beast—Ou ay, aw ken we've made weel aneuch oot upon't; but it's nae i' the naitur' o' man to gang on year aifter year plewin', an' del'in', an' earin,* an' shearin' the bits o' howes an' knowes, seein' the vera yird, obaidient till's care, takin' shape, an' sen'in' up the bonny caller blade in its sizzon, an' aifter that the 'fu' corn i' the ear,' as the Scriptur' says, onbeen a kin' o' thirled to the vera rigs themsel's."

"Weel, a bodie *is* wae tae think o' lea'in 't."

"Ay, ay; but that's nae a'. Gin fowk war tae luik at things ae gate we wud be wae to pairt wi' onything 't we hae i' the wardle. But here's oorsel's noo 't 's toil't awa' upo' this place fae youthheid to aul' age, an' wi' the lawbour o' oor nain han's made it's ye may say—Gushetneuk the day's nae mair fat Gushetneuk was fan we cam' here nor my fit's a han' saw. Sir Seemon ca's 'imsel' laird o 't; but Sir Seemon's deen nae mair to the place nor the man o' France. Noo, you an' me can gae roon an' roon aboot it, an' wi' a' honesty say o' this an' that—'Here's the fruit o' oor lawbour—that'll bide upo' the face o' the earth for the eese o' ithers aifter we're deid an' gane.' Noo, this is fat I canna win at the boddom o' ava. I'm weel seer it was never the arreengement o' Providence that the man that tills the grun an' spen's the strength o 's days upon 't sud be at the merciment o' a man that never laid a han' till 't, nor hardly wair't a shillin' upon 't, to bid 'im bide or gyang."

"Hoot, man, ye're foryettin seerly 't Sir Seemon gae ye an offer o' the tack yersel', an' that it's ta'en to oor young fowk," said Mrs. Gibb.

"Vera true," answered Johnny. "Sir Seemon, peer man, 's made little o 't, ae gate nor anither. He's jist as sair in wunt o' siller the day as he was fan the aul' factor gat the first hun'er poun 't ever we scraipit thegither in a quate wye to len' till 'im. But it's nae oorsel's nor Sir Seemon't aw'm compleenin aboot in particular. It's the general run o' the thing. Fat for sudna lawbourin the rigs in an honest wye for beheef o' the countra at lairge gi'e a man a richt to sit still an' keep the grip, raither nor lat the haill poo'er o' traffikein wi' the grun, for gweed

faul'ies folds   *sprots* coarse grass   *knablich* stone   *cannas breid* canvas breadth
earin ploughing

or ill, be leeft wi' a set o' men that nae only never laid a han' till't, but maybe never hardly leet their een see't.''

"Is that the lairds?"

"Ay, ay."

"Eh, but ye ken they gat it fae their forbears."

"An' fat aboot it! Fa gyau 't to their forbears, aw wud like to ken? A set o' reivin' scoonrels that tyeuk it wi' the strong han', an' syne preten't to han't doon fae ane till anither an' buy 't an sell 't wi' lawvyers' vreetin on a bit sheep's skin. Na, na; there's something clean vrang at the boddam o 't. We're taul that the 'earth is for the use o' all: the king 'imsel is served by the field.' The Government o' the countra sud tak' the thing i' their nain han' an' see richt deen; an' the best teetle to the grun sud be the man's willin'ness to lawbour 't, and grow corn an' cattle for the susteenance o' man.''

In this high flight Mrs. Gibb did not attempt to follow Johnny. She merely smiled and said, "Weel, aw'm seer, man, ye div tak' unco notions i' yer heid. . . .''

"That's nedder here nor there. Fowk canna mak' owre seer that there's a richt an' a vrang in a'thing; an' lang eesage'll never gar oonjustice be richt nae mair nor it'll mak' black fite, say fat they like. Only we wus speakin' aboot oor nain sma' affair—I div not think that there wud be muckle thrift in you an' me gyaun awa' buyin' a twa three rigs o' grun an' sittin' doon wi' a'thing unco aboot's to fecht upon't for a fyou years. Fan ance fowk's at oor time o' life they sud be willin' to lat the theets* slack a bit; an' gin they've ta'en up their yokin' straucht an' fair, they can luik back wi' a kin' o' contentment upo' the wark that's deen, min'in' a' the time that ithers sud be layin' their shooders to the draucht, raither nor themsel's hingin' i' the heid o' things as gin this wardle wud laist only as lang as they keepit fit wi 't. Noo, I'm fell sweir to think o' a cheenge fae this place, an' I'll tell ye foo."

"Loshtie man, ye're seerly gyaun gyte—"

"Na, na. I see fat ye're ettlin at. I'm nae foryettin 't the place is set to the young fowk, 's ye ca' them; nedder wud I wunt to stan' i' their road a single hair's-breid, nor to meddle wi' them ae gate nor anither. For ance *they're* waddit *we're* sooperanniwat, that's a doon-laid rowle. But there sudna be nae gryte diffeekwalty aboot gettin' hoose-room for twa aul' fowk. The hoose is a byous* size for length; an' yer neebour 'oman, ye ken, 's taul ye a dizzen o' times owre that it wud be a spawcious hoose for a genteel faimily gin it hed a back kitchie wi' a lang chimley biggit. It winna be in oor day that Willie M'Aul an' the lassie'll be so far up b'cairts* as be needin' a castell to haud their braw company, an' wi'

---

theets traces, reins *byous* unusual *up b'cairts* prosperous, originally winning at cards

little contrivance an' nae muckle biggin' we mith get a snod aneuch beil' by partitionin' aff the wast en' an' makin' a sin'ry* door to oorsel's.''

"Weel, fa wud 'a minet upo' that but yersel', noo,'' exclaimed Mrs. Gibb, lost in admiration of her husband's inventive genius. She was not in the habit of ever seriously disputing his will, yet Johnny was evidently gratified to find that his project was not merely acceptable to Mrs. Gibb, but that the prospect it opened up, as the good woman phrased it, "liftit a birn aff o' her min','' and would, she was sure, be welcomed by all concerned.

"Weel, we'll see,'' said Johnny, "we maun jist a' leern to ken that the wardle can dee wuntin's. We 'a get oor day, an' oor day's wark; the time slips bye like the mist creepin' seelently up the howe. 'What thy hand findeth to do, do with thy might' is the lesson we ocht aye to bear in min', though we af'en, af'en foryet it; an' fan we luik back fae a point like this o' the lang track o' years streetchin into the saft mornin' licht o' oor days, an' a' croon't wi' blessin's, it's like a dream, but a pleasant dream tee, an' foreshaidowin' a better time to come to them that's faithfu' to their trust. But, ye ken, an' aul' tree disna seen tak' reet again, nor yet haud the grun weel fan it's liftit. An' aw'm thinkin' gin they're to get ony mair gweed o' me, they'll hae maist chance o 't by lattin 's stick faur we are. An' though Sir Seemon may ca' the rigs o' Gushetneuk his, I'm maistly seer gin the rigs themsel's cud speak they wud ca' me maister raither nor him. But it mak's na muckle back or fore. They'll be mine to the sicht o' my een maybe as lang's I'm able to see the sproutin' blade or the yalla corn sheaf; and Sir Seemon's lairdship cann gi'e 'im mair.''

sin'ry separate

MAINS GOES TO WAR

W. P. Milne *Eppie Elrick*

Kirstan Elrick stood at the gate that gave entrance to the "closs" one evening in the harvest time of 1715, awaiting the return of her lord from his day's labours.

"Hech Sirs'', she cried as she saw him approaching, "faar hae ye been hiterin aboot tull ur noo, Mains? It's lang by yer usual supperin time, an' 'e brose watter's been aff an' on 'e bile a hunner times sin' A begoot tae expeck ye hame.''

"Yea, yea,'' answered Mains in an off-putting sort of way.

"A suppose it's been 'at weety wadder i' the hicher pairts o' the lan sin' we got clyack* 'at ye hinna been able tae won forrit wi the leadin.* Gin't dinna come some drucht seen, 'e stuff'll be rottin i' the stook."

"Lickly, lickly," replied her husband somewhat abstractedly.

"Faar mith ye hae been than, Mains?"

"Oh maybe up by o' the back hull near han e' pumfle.* Ye see it cam on a fine blyaavy win' i' the aifterneen, sae A thocht A wid jist tak a bit dander roon amo' the stooks an' turn 'e shaves tae lat 'em dry an' won."

"Hae ye seen onybody?"

"Maybe that than."

"Fa?"

"A widna say bit 'at A mith hae seen 'e Laird o' Tullymachar 'imsel."

"Gweed guide's an' keep's, Mains, bit A doot ye've been keepin company wi the gintry. Hid ye a news wi' 'im?"

"A wudna say No tae that aider maybe."

"Fat wis 'e Laird sayin tull't, Mains, an' fat airt cam 'e fae?"

"Aa weel, umman, A hid turnt a' the shaves an' wis gidderin puckles o' lowsse steens an' biggin 'em up in hullockies for cairtin awa fin we'd a meenit's time, an' maybe files layin an antrin muckler een o' the dike. An' forbye that, A wis maybe ruggin oot a fun reet here an' 'ere kiss A've aye been intennin as ye ken tae tak in 'e haill o' the back hull faar it mairches upo the Moss o' Rora an' faar ye can see the Midder Tap o' Bennachie teetin up fae far awa on a clare day."

"A ken 'e place fine, bit fat aboot 'e Laird?" said Kirstan with a note of impatience in her voice.

"Aa weel, A wis jist comin tae that," replied Mains obviously anxious to postpone arriving at his main communication for as long as possible.

"A hid jist steed up tae strachen ma back fin fa sud A see bit 'e Laird 'imsel comin scoorin oot ower 'e taps o' the stooks at a maist yaafu rate an' nae badderin tae gae roon 'em; fleein like tae redd fire, like."

"Gweed preserve a' livin crater. Fat sorra wis garrin a man at his time o' life gang binnerin oot ower 'e stooks at siccan a lick's 'at, loupin like a five 'ear aal?"

"Ye mith weel say that," answered Mains.

"Fat said 'e tull ye?" asked Kirstan. "Canna ye tell ma fair furth 'e gait?"

"A'm comin tae that tee, gin ye wid jist gie me a mamen," replied her husband. "'Ay, Ay, Mains, some airish 'e day,' he begoot fin 'e'd gotten back 'is win', 'sae here A've gotten ye i' the lang rin tyaawin awa amo the fun reets.'

"'Dyod Ay, Laird,' says I back tull 'im like, "e fyower o' that gintry i' yer lan, 'e better.'

---

clyack last of the cutting corn   *leadin* carting   *pumfle* enclosure for cattle

13

"'Aa weel, Mains,' says he, 'hing in amo the fun reets for a day or twa yet, an' dinna lat yer back heat amo them, for A rackon it'll be a gey file ur ye won back amo them again.'

"A didna tak up richt fat 'e wis wonnin at.

"'Weel,' A said, 'we'se tyaave awa at 'e fun reets ur 'e wadder fairs an' lats 'is back tae the hairst. An' gin we cud bit only get a wee pirrie o' drucht tae dry the stooks, things mith be meevin again wi the leadin. Bit, stull an' on, we'se aye be ruggin oot a fun reet tae clean 'e lan' an' get mair o't teen in.'

"Seen, 'e lyookit at ma gey sairious like.

"'Mains, it's dyaan tae be a lang pitten aff hairst for some folk.'

"'Foo that think ye, Laird, gin 'e wadder wis dyaan tae clear up?'

"'E Laird shook 'is heid a gait 'at gart ma winner.

"'There'll be a cyarn o' folk in Buchan nae able tae get in 'eir hairsts 'is 'ear, Mains. An' 'ey'll be pitten aff 'eir eggs in idder rodds forby ur a' be said an' deen.'

"'Fat upo this earth gars ye think that, Laird? Is 'ere ony wurd aboot 'e eyn o' the wardle ur something waar nur 'at?'

"'There's dyaan tae be fechtin, Mains. We're dyaan tae get wir aal Keengs back again.'

"'Dyod, Laird, 'at's an aal sang seerly. 'at's been soochin i' the win' near sin iver I can min'. Div ye railly think 'at onything's dyaan tae come o't?'

"'E haill rickmatick o' the Buchan Lairds his gotten 'eir orders tae mairch, an' you an me maan tak 'e rodd tee, an' nae be ahin han. A've jist come eence eeran tae tell ye. Fat say ye tae that, Mains?'

"'A wid jist say 'at 'e haill thing's bein deen ower hurriet, Laird.'

"'Bit we've been plannin't for a quarter o' a cintry an' mair, Mains.'

"'Maybe that, Laird, bit tae cowp ae Keeng aff 'is throne an' dowp anidder Keeng doon in 'is place needs some speakin ower.'

"'Weel, Mains, A doot 'e time for speakin ower thing is by, an' we hae tae tak the rodd.'

"'Sae that's the lang an' the short o't, is't, Laird?'

"'Ay, Mains, the lang an' the short o't. We canna be ahin 'e lave.'

"'Fan got ye wurd o' a' this, Laird?'

"'Oh, nae time seen, Mains. Wir muckler neeporin Lairds fae a' ower 'e cuntraside, wi the Earl o' Mar at 'e tap o' them his been haadin a' kin-kine o' meetins an' collieshangies forby great muckle huntin pairties at 'e Hielan eyn o' wir shire. 'Ey've hid a' thing throwe han' an' 'ey've sint doon wurd tae Buchan tae be ready at a mamen's nottice.'

"'I've come here tae tell ye that 'ere's nae hilp for't bit ye maan gird yer soord upo yer thigh, as 'e Scripter says, an' gae forth tae slachter 'e Keeng's innimies.'

"'Weel, weel 'an, Laird, fat maan be maan be, sae be 'at 'ere's nae idder rodd oot o't. Bit deil a bit o' me can see fat's vrang wi the new German Keeng 'at we hae, gin 'e warst come tae the warst, though we maybe girn a gweed hantle aboot 'im an' lay faats at 'is door 'at maybe him nur nae idder boddy cud hilp. A boddy hardly kens ony odds here in Buchan fa's Keeng.'

"'Mains, Mains,' he said near greetin like, 'faar's yer sowl? Wir vera ain aal Keengs, man. Neen o' yer foreign dirt. Keengs o' Scotlan sin 'e Flood, man. It gars ma vera hert dunt tae think upo't.'

"'Weel, weel an', Laird. Sae be't. 'E heft an' blade's in your han an' nae in mine. Sae that sattles 'e haill queyston. Here's me tenan in Eynriggs, an' ma faader, an' ma granfaader an' ma great-granfaader afore ma, an' a lang strip o' Elricks afore 'em, sin 'e beginnin o' time an' maybe afore't, an' 'e haill clan-jamfery o' them haadin their lease upo the precunnances 'at fin 'ere's ony fechtin tae be deen, Mains o' Eynriggs maan aye be steppin oot nae far ahin e' Laird. We've black upo fite for 'at iver sin laird ur factor kint foo tae sign 'eir name tull a dokkymint. Sae we dinna argy-bargy aboot 'at. Fin fechtin his tae be deen, 'e laird's wull's 'e tenan's pleezher, an' 'at's a' that's tae be said aboot it.'

"'E Laird lyookit doon upo the grun a mamen, an' shook 'is heid a thochtie disappintit like, maybe.

"'Nae doot, Mains, nae doot,' he said aifter a wee filockie, 'that's 'e Laa without a doot, bit A wuss A saa ye mair haill-hertit for 'e aal Keengs.'

"'As A said afore, Laird, fa's Keeng's nae doot a maitter o' muckle concern in Lunnon bit disna maitter a preen-heid in Ugiehaach. Bit, gin 'at be the set o't, we'se awa hame an' see aboot gettin some aal kin' o' a wappin riggit tae the rodd. Fan div we set oot?'

"'Vera seen, Mains. A'm settin oot masel 'is vera nicht, bit A've left orders at 'e Castle fat ye're a' tae dee.'

"'Weel, weel, 'an, Laird. Sae be't.'

"Sae he badd's gweed nicht, an' A antert awa hame."

When Mains had finished, Kirstan remained silent for a short space, contrary to her wont. He had unfolded a totally unfamiliar situation and she was not ready.

"Weel, weel 'an, Mains, 'at cowes cock-fechtin," was all she could say.

"Dyod, Ay, umman. A daft like prottick a'thegidder."

"You a sodger, Mains, sheetin an' killin folk. A canna believe ma sinses."

"Weell A rackon it'll be new ploy tull a lot o's," answered Mains.

"'Ey've spoken for lang aboot Keengs over 'e Watter, bit A hid growen tae think it wad niver come tae onything," meditated Kirstan.

"A hantle o's hid come tae think the same, gweedwife."

"A' the same, Mains, A wuss ye cud jook an' let 'e jaa gae by an' bide at hame. A'm nae sae browdent upo this fechtin idaea."

Mains goes to war

"Faar wad ye hae ma bide at hame an' hide, gweedwife? I' the strae soo?* Gin I wis tae jook an' bide at hame, you an' yer faimily wid be sittin upo a kist i' the cornyard witin for 'e roup."

"Ay, Ay, Mains, an' seen gweed day an' gweed nippin tae Eynriggs."

"Jist 'at, umman, jist 'at."

"The Lairds his't a' i' their ain hans," pursued Kirstan.

"There's nae twa wyes aboot 'at," said Mains.

The facts being proven, Kirstan began to envisage what had to transpire.

"Fat sorra wye wull ye manage tae sleep 'e furth i' the caal nichts, Mains, you 'at's aye been tennit like a bee on a brod, an' aye been eest sleepin wi seyven blankets abeen ye i' the winter an' sax i' the simmer, forbyes a het pig a' throwe the deid o' the 'ear."

"A suppose we'se jist hae tae eese wuntin 'em, replied Mains taking a 'lang draa' at his 'cutty' and emitting a volume of smoke.

"Haith Ay, Mains, 'at'll tak a pike o' ye. A've niver cuddamt masel wi a' that blankets mair espeecially i' the simmer time. Mony a plottin simmer's nicht hae A turnt three-fower faal o' them aff o' masel on o' you, an' winnert i' the mornin fat rodd ye didna waaken a splairge o' miltit creesh i' the boddom o' the bed."

"Nae doot, nae doot," answered Mains blowing forth another cloud of smoke.

"Fan wid ye be settin oot, said ye Mains?"

"Vera seen, gweedwife. We're tae get wir orders fae the Castel."

"Gweed preserve a' livin crater. In a jiffy like 'at. A wunner fat 'e wardle's comin tull. A'll niver hae yer sarks gotten mennit wi sae little warnin."

There was silence for a moment or two.

"An aafu wardle fin ye canna shiv yer finger throwe a steen," Kirstan soliloquized in the spirit of the philosopher, appealing to the old aphorism.

They both gazed around the landscape.

"Ay, Mains man, an 'e bonny lans o' Enyriggs'll be the weers o' bein naething bit skellach* an' chucknart* an' grunsel* afore ye be hame again."

And so it was all over Buchan.

The men were getting ready to march and their womenfolk were planning how they would carry on the labours of the farms in their absence, and what extra habiliments their menfolk would require to take with them on this great enterprise which was none of their seeking.

---

soo a stack *skellach* wild mustard *chucknart* chickweed *grunsel* the herb groundsel

THE LIFE OF THE PLOUGHMEN

John R. Allan *Farmer's Boy*

There was one community on the farm who had little chance of grace and desired less. I mean the ploughmen. They lived in the bothy, a one-roomed house across the yard from the cart-shed. Unlike most of its kind this bothy was pleasant enough, for its back window looked west to the valley and the hills. The furniture was of the simplest —two big double beds filled with chaff, a wide open fireplace for burning peats, a tin basin to wash in and a roller towel behind the door, and a spotty mirror in one of the windows. Pitch-pine walls and a cement floor looked almost as cold as they were, but they had the necessary merit of being clean. Cold and clean but never a home, you might have said if you had seen it at Whitsunday weekend when the old men had left and the new ones were not yet home, and after Sally had spent a day in scrubbing it out with soap, soda and ammonia. If you had seen it a fortnight later, when the new boys had moved in, you would have found it neither cold nor clean nor any more like home. The farm servant in those days—and I suppose there has been little change—had only two possessions—a kist and a bicycle. So, if you had looked into the bothy, you would have seen the kists set out against the walls and the bicycles in a recess at the foot of the bed. Sunday suits, shirts and long woollen drawers hung from nails on either side of the windows, each man having a bit of the wall for wardrobe. Boots, ranging from stylish browns for Sunday to great tacketty boots all glaur and dung, huddled beneath the beds where they had been lightly thrown off their owners' feet. A strange collection of things littered every shelf—bits and pieces mostly broken, collar studs, screw nails, jews' harps, cogs, flints, gas burners, ball bearings, old knives, corkscrews, cartridges, bicycle clips—everything for which you might find a use if you kept it seven years. Anything they really valued they kept locked in their kists. But you must not think that they left only rubbish about or that they made no attempt at decoration. Most of them had photographs nailed up beside their beds—photographs of relations, very self-conscious in Sunday blacks or white elbow-length cotton gloves; photographs of horses in gala trim on the way to a show or a ploughing match; or photographs of ample ladies in a state of frilly *déshabillé* who must have been left over from the Gay Nineties. These last were real art and treasured as such. Sometimes the reverent owners enclosed them in wreaths of strawplaiting, such as they used in horses' tails, and I suppose the Gaiety Girls must have looked strangely bucolic enclosed in 'long and short' and peeping coyly from under a head of corn. Still I thought they were lovely ladies and so, I am sure, did their owners.

The life of the ploughmen

The etiquette of the bothy and stable was equalled in rigidity only by that of the Court of Louis XIV. Each man had his place and was taught to keep it. For the second horseman to have gone in to supper before the first horseman would have created as much indignation as an infringement of precedence at Versailles. The foreman was always the first to wash his face in the bothy at night; it was he who wound the alarm clock and set it for the morning, and so on and so on. The order of seniority was as strictly observed between the second horseman and the third, while the halflin always got the tarry end of the stick. The cattleman's status was indeterminate; I rather think he was on his own; but, as he tended cows while the others worked that noble beast the horse, he was always regarded as inferior, whether he admitted it or not. But the foreman had pride of place in everything. He slept at the front of the first bed—that is, nearest the fire; he sat at the top of the table in the kitchen; he worked the best pair of horses; and he had the right to make the first pass at the kitchen maid. His character had a considerable influence on the work of the farm; if he was a good-tempered fellow he kept the others sweet, and if he could set a fast pace at the hoeing he could save pounds for his master.

The ploughmen usually rose at five in summer and half-past five in winter. They went to the stable at once, fed their horses and then came into the kitchen for breakfast. Yoking time was six from March onwards, and from daylight in winter. They stopped for dinner at eleven, then yoked at one and lowsed for the day at six, or dark. In harvest they might work on till ten or eleven, if the dew did not fall heavily, and I remember two autumns at least when the binder worked till midnight under the great red harvest moon. As soon as they had fed their horses they came into the kitchen for supper and in winter used to remain at the fireside till nine o'clock, telling stories or playing cards, when they looked to their horses and retired to the bothy for the night.

Sometimes a few of the boys from the neighbouring farms came to see them. We would all go out to the bothy then and lie on the beds while somebody played the melodion and we sang the traditional songs of the countryside with variations to suit our mood. I enjoyed those parties. The peat fire glowed with an intense smouldering heat; the paraffin lamps burned dimly, for there was always a black comet on the glass; the bothy was warm and smelled of hard soap and human kind. I lay on the foreman's half of the bed, three parts asleep, and listened to the melodion, or joined in leisurely songs where the beat was held up interminably for romantic effects. But, no matter how hard I tried to keep awake, the sleep overcame me, and I sank down into the deeps of bliss, troubled only by the gales of laughter that saluted some hardy tale. Then the foreman carried me into the house—and morning came in a long moment.

THE FEEIN MARKET

Alexander Gordon *The Folks o' Carglen*

In most of the country towns in the north of Scotland there are certain days known as "feein Friday", "hairst Monday", and such like. In the town of Kail, the little urban centre adjoining our parish, there were three great hiring markets for farm-labourers in the course of the year. These were the "feein Friday", immediately before Whitsuntide, "hairst Monday", occurring about four weeks before the anticipated commencement of the local harvest; and "feein Friday" again, the week before Martinmas. Thither flocked all the male and female farm-labourers who were desirous of obtaining fresh engagements, and by ten or eleven o' clock a huge concourse of people anxious to be "feed", and a very large number of employers in need of hands for the farmwork during the coming season, had assembled in the town's square and in the main adjoining thorough-fares.

The men generally take their stand in the street, or along the square in little companies of twos and threes; the women in similar dispositions; and in the big throng there may be observed not a few fathers keeping watchful eyes on the movements of certain awkward youths whose services they are eager to dispose of for the next six months—or for the period of harvest, as the case may be; several mothers, likewise, with strong red-cheeked girls bent on obtaining a similar market; but one and all noisy, hearty, laughter-loving beings; rude of manner, and ruder still of speech; quarrelsome to a degree; yet on the whole brimming over with the milk of human kindness. Hiring and feeing are, however, serious matters, and it is not until this, the chief business of the day, is over, that the mirth and fun grow fast and furious. . . .

When the main business of the day is over, the period of saturnalia sets in with a vengeance. All over the Market Square there are numerous rickety stalls groaning under the weight of huge quantities of treacle candy, lozenges, and miscellaneous sweets made of the vilest compounds, and in the purchase of these articles (for the farm-labourer, whether male or female, is a very sweet-mouthed animal) the whole of the "arles"* speedily disappears, and a considerable portion of the hardly-earned half-year's wage to boot. The booth of the itinerant showman who exhibits the marvel of marvels in the form of a headless trunk, or a human head detached from the body, is also crammed with gaping spectators, whose feelings find vent in such expressions as "Saw ye ever onything like it," or "Weel, noo, wha wad hae thocht it", or such like. The young lads and the women imbibe unlimited quantities of lemonade and similar non-intoxicants; the

arles money paid to seal the contract when feeing.

men prefer a more potent liquor, and betake themselves to the public-house, where they sit over their glasses of whiskey—"critur", as they prefer to call it. By and by the centre of the little town becomes a scene of the wildest uproar. Drunken men rush hither and thither; dames shriek and children scream; quarrels are rife; stalls are crushed in the general hubbub; the noise of a babel of voices is carried on the breeze all over the town; and it is only the fall of evening that puts an end to the rustic revelry, merriment, and din. It is a somewhat delicate subject upon which to touch, but any description of "feein Friday" and its accompaniments which failed to include an allusion to the notorious immorality which usually attends it, would be lamentably incomplete. At the same time it will be enough to say, that while the county of Banff especially has an unenviable notoriety on account of the foremost place which it occupies in respect of its statistics of illegitimacy, one cannot err in tracing a large percentage of such cases, directly and indirectly, to the debasing orgies of the feeing market.

TERM DAYS AND TERM NIGHTS

Jessie Kesson *Glitter of Mica*

For most of his working life Hugh Riddel's father had known but two days off in the year. The "Term Days", at the end of May and November.

Golden days though. Hugh Riddel could recall them still with an uprising of excitement. The unfamiliar smell of bacon filling the kitchen, his mother clucking around the range, warning and worrying in the same breath.

"Dip your bread in the fat, Hugh. But the bacon's for Father. He's for the Town."

And his father big with the good humour that was over him.

"My best suit. The blue, the day. Pressed beneath the mattress three nights hard running. And how's *that* for a crease in my trousers, Hugh? It would just cut your throat, wouldn't it not now? It's as sharp as that! My bonnet, Hugh. Jump to it, son. Not *that* bonnet, you gowk! My Sunday bonnet. For I'm for the Town."

Even now, such excited preparation seemed just as it should be to Hugh Riddel. For it was a wild town, a wanton town, that farm-workers set out for on Term days, and wide-eyed on the watch for country men. Though blind, its nose could still have sniffed them out with sharn for sweat, and deaf, its ears could still have recognised their tackett-booted tread, and their laughter rising ribald in Dobb's Cafe, and Dobb's market too, where siren women lurked behind the stalls, big bosomed, blonde, and honey-mouthed, or so they seemed to farm-workers on Term Days, luring their hard-won penny Fees with tartan trinkets.

"Come on now, Jock. This pouch should hold your six months' siller. In your own tartan too. 'By Dand', and *up* the Gordons!'"

And teasingly, with bits of fripperies, would confront the lumbering red-faced men, whose hands had seldom fumbled anything finer than flannelette.

"This pair should fit your best lass, Jock. Think of the fun you'll have fitting them on her. Come, buy—for love's sake!"

Dobb's market was all for love's sake. Post-cards showing How. Books telling When. "The Chemist"—Quack—doing business all day long with herbs and pills and special advice in after hours. But dark and dear. And not for country men, grinning but stubborn, rejecting such abortive practices.

"We'll risk it yet. For the pill was never made would empty Bogie Bell of what Tom the Ternland gave her, six months come Friday, at Boynlie Ball."

Free of Dobb's market. Swerving to Baltic Cross—traditionally their own, and freemen of the Town for this one day. And down by Baltic Cross, teeming but islanded alien townsfolk caught in hurried passing the warm dissenting talk of cattle.

"We're tackling Ayrshires up our way."

"Dangerous vratches. Far too fond of hooking, Ayrshires. They rip each others' flanks to bits."

"For safety, give me a Red Poll."

"*Never*, man. Great fat hornless lumps, the Red Polls. Granted they don't hook each other, for they've got damn all to hook with. But, by God, they make up for that by lashing out. For a quiet-natured cow, now, give me the Guernsey."

"Too delicate a brute for this part of the country. A Guernsey needs as muckle care as a thoroughbred horse. Fair-weather beasts, Guernseys. No, no. For a good all-round cow there's just nothing to touch the Shorthorn. They're tough beasts and their yield's aye consistent."

And in the more exclusive haunts, the farmers talked of this and that. Of subsidies and costs, and how they were rising all the time. And never once, not even in trust amongst each other, confessed to profit. But down at Baltic Cross, made bold by beer and strengthened by each other, their workers claimed the leases of their lands by right of deed, and tenanted them with new ideas.

"If I was in Clayacre's shoes, I'd sell at Whitsun. For yon land's souring. It's fair worn out."

"High time too that Lower Ardgye grew less grain. Yon's not mixed farming. It's just grain forever up in yon place!"

"He'd need to let such land lie fallow for a while."

The last bus home. The thought of it ettling in their minds, like chaff that itched against their skins on threshing days. And all eyes cocked against the sky for a reprieve, or even extension. Then watches, turnip-faced, dragged out to check the stars; their minds would stray to that wild pub down by the docks, and linger there, where women were as bold as brass, offering you all they had for one and sixpence. Near forcing't on you. It was just such women's haste, and the price they put upon it, made it immoral in farm-workers' eyes. Since they preferred it given, just for the love of it. Or, for at most a dozen new-laid eggs, and that but hansel. And, though their thoughts might linger in such places, their feet invariably but unsteadily led them buswards, yet with a kind of virtue. "For, God Almighty! You never can tell. With women such as yon, you never know what you'll get left with."

★   ★   ★

But it was his father's homecoming on Term Nights that lay within Hugh Riddel's own remembrance, and still could move him in the minding of it.

God! But what a difference a drink and a day off had made to the man. Hard to reconcile the dour everyday father of the fields and byres with the huge genial man who stood swaying and singing in the doorway, flanked by his fellow farm-workers on Term Nights.

> Her brow 'tis like the snawdrift.
> Her neck 'tis like the swan.
> Her face it is the fairest
> That e'er the sun shone on.
>
> And dark blue is her e'e.
> And she's a' the world to me.
> And for bonnie Annie Laurie
> I wad lay me doon and dee!

That was another of the times when Hugh Riddel, the boy, had felt all the glamourie of manhood tugging at himself. The *Annie Lauries* and *Bonnie Peggies* of his father's songs had come across to him even then as something more than idylls of time gone past; they became the lush promises of his own future. Strange, though; strange that they should still have remained idylls when the future had become the present.

Jessie Kesson

Like dew on the gowan lying
Is the fa' o' her fairy feet.
And like wind in the summer sighing.
Her voice is low and sweet!

"Keep *your* voice down, then. And come on inside the house with you. For it will be the clash of the countryside that you couldn't stand on *your* fairy feet on Term Night."

Down all the years Hugh Riddel could still call up his mother's capacity for diminishing his father. Not even the presence of his father's fellow-workers had ever prevented her from putting on the hurt, white face of martyrdom. A right bad wife could ease a man's conscience, and so set him free. But a good wife could bind you prisoner forever, with the swaddling bands of her goodness. God! but I had to burst myself out and free, Hugh Riddel thought. His father had never brought himself to do likewise. For this, his son could pity but also envy him, and saw him still in all his huge, blustering futility.

"Well, well, woman. If everybody's tongues are clashing about *me*, it stands to reason that they will be leaving some other poor sinful bugger to a bit of peace. And *that's* surely something to be thankful for! Come in, about then, all of you. Come on, now. Draw your chairs up to the fire, and we'll have a bit of a crack and a song to ourselves."

That was another of the times when Hugh Riddel had felt insulated in a comfort of spirit. Curled up in the kitchen bed, in the dim flicker of firelight and lamplight. Within hand's touch of a world of men. Yet still safe onlooker, with the voices of his father and his father's friends droning over and round him.

Oh, never were harvests so wet and wild as those they recollected in their cups on Term Nights. And still miraculously ingathered. For they could see themselves in their young years, through such a space of time that personal identification left them altogether. And it was giants, immune to wind and weather, who rode the rigs; and scythed the "in-roads" to epic harvests.

But, despite all their exaggerations, and for all his own youngness at the time, Hugh Riddel had instinctively recognised their underlying truth. It was simply that words had caricatured their thoughts. And, by God, words could do *that*, right enough. Look and touch and feel should suffice to allow you walk wordless all your days. Hugh Riddel remembered one small such instance of his own, on the farm near Stonehaven, where the hill slopes had lain under grass through living memory, till one morning on his road to school he had stood arrested, staring at the sharp gleaming coulter of the plough cutting into the hill slope and leaving the first dark furrow. That had struck him with an almost physical sense of pain. And the image of the virgin land with the gash of a wound across it had lain unvoiced in mind for a long time. Small wonder, then, that with the nowhereness of words, his father and his father's friends had grabbed them and twined them and stretched them this way and that, in a kind of anger at their impotence.

But there was the other side of it. The times when threadbare words could cast a shadow, far greater than the substance of their meaning, across your mind, mantling it for the rest of your days. A small memory too, and gleaned on a Term Night.

"Oh, but he was a hard farmer to work for" God Knows had said. "You durst never be caught straightening your back when yon one came in sight of you. And God knows, many's the time I have seen myself, after ten hours' forking to the threshing mill, bend down just to pick up some straw, knowing that the wind would blow another in its place, when I'd hear the sound of his footsteps."

That was when Hugh Riddel had first known the true meaning of physical tiredness, even before experiencing it. And, ever afterwards, the ultimate weariness was indeed just to "pick up some straw, knowing that the wind would blow another in its place".

But he had been infatuated by the speak of the life on the land on those far-off Term Nights. For those nights were Hugh Riddel's initiation into a society to which one could only obtain membership by right of birth. A comparatively secret society too. One which had its being scattered unmarked on the teacher's map at school, where Scotland was made up of Highlands and Lowlands, mining and shipbuilding, cathedral towns and university cities, and all their world ending abruptly "over the Border".

It was his father and his father's friends who crammed the blanks of that map on Term Nights, till Scotland became a continent on their tongues and famous for things that never found their way into the Geography lesson at school. The fine tattie-growing soil of Easter Ross. South of the Mearns where the land was more mellow, the farmers easier, the darg lighter, and fees higher. Up Inverness way, where the last battle fought on British soil was forgotten, and only the democracy of the "folk" remembered.

"I kent a ploughman once," Dod Feary had pointed out, as impressive proof of this to his incredulous listeners, "who used to get blind drunk every Saturday night with the local Doctor, up Culloden way."

For nowhere was "Keeping one's proper place" so strictly adhered to as in our shire. Even his mother, Hugh Riddel remembered, had once commented on this:

"If the farmer's wife passes the time of day with the cottar wives, it just makes their day. Poor, silly bodies! You would think that the Lord above had looked down from Heaven, and greeted them personally, so overcome are they."

Hugh Riddel smiled at the recollection. But there was a kind of pain and protest at the heart of his amusement.

Jessie Kesson

... Oh, Burns. Was it to suit the fine sentiments of the Edinbro' Gentry, once cursed by you, and always half despised, that you wrote such smarm as *The Cotter's Saturday Night*?

> From scenes like these
> Old Scotia's grandeur springs . . . .

The lines grued in Hugh Riddel's mind. It was easily seen that such a poem was written by a man who ploughed his *own* furrows. Never by a fee'd ploughman. And although farm-workers' conditions had improved beyond all recognition now, Hugh Riddel's pain, though momentary, was ever recurring. It was just that no man could come into good estate free of that which and those who had preceded him.

Far more true of their way of life were the songs of his father and his father's friends on Term Night. Songs of their own countryside, composed by themselves for themselves; and having their origins in the very farms they worked on.

> When I gaed doon to Turra Market
> Turra Market for to fee
> I met in wi' a wealthy fairmer
> Frae the Barnyards o' Delgaty!
>
> He promised me the twa best horse
> That was in a' the country roon
> But when I gaed hame to the Barnyards
> There was nothing there but skin and bone!

It was when they reached the singing stage on Term Nights that they really tried his mother's patience. It was then that they sent her sighing "God be here" round the kitchen, and "there will be no word of this in the morning"; and, as the night advanced and the songs grew coarser, would set her redding up the kitchen. As if by the very act she could also redd up the dirt rising round her ears. For how the men loved dirt. That which his father had always protested was "*Clean* dirt, woman!" And Hugh Riddel himself had always been in alliance with the men over this.

> She let him in sae cannily
> To do the thing you ken, Jo!
> She chased him out syne cried him back
> To do it once again, Jo!
> But the bottom fell out o' the bed
> The lassie lost her maiden-head
> And her mither heard the din, Jo!

It always meant some other new song for Hugh Riddel to go racing school-wards with, the wind in his face; and a pack of loons panting behind him to hear the rest of it, syne flinging themselves face downwards on the grass with the exhaustion of their laughter, and laughing long after they had forgotten the cause. Pure laughter that, Hugh Riddel realised now, for it had needed no reason.

God! you could stand out here in the dark, and listen to the youngness of your life singing away past you there, as if it had been conceived in song. His mother had never realised it was like that with him, though. She was always protecting him from his father and his father's cronies, their songs and their talk.

That's fine language to be on you all! And the bairn Hugh there, lying in his bed."

"Well! Hugh's got to find out for himself one of these fine days," his father would defend. "For fine he knows that he wasn't found at the back of a cabbage plant, as you would like him to believe!"

And fine he did know. Ever since he could remember, Hugh Riddel had dis-covered that sex was the great topic and the huge laugh, the joke that the farm-workers seldom tired of, and rearing itself up at all odd times in all kinds of places. The bulls serving the cows. And the stallions serving the mares. And ill-favoured Annie Coultrie, whom no man had tried to tempt for years, drawing her cardigan fierce around her shoulders, like to protect her virtue, and screeching across the steading.

"There's the stallion man. Just coming up the road yonder, with that great muckle brute of a stallion. But I'm not going to put *him* up for the night. Not *me*! He can just go to the bothy for a bed, or to some woman that's his own like. For they're saying that the man has gotten as randy as that stallion he treks around the country with. They have it that no woman under sixty is safe with him now."

And the deep satirical laughter her indignation evoked in the men.

"You'll be safe enough then, Annie, for you'll not see sixty again. Though you was always safe enough, Annie. Even when you was sixteen!"

But there was always a quality of cruelty in the laughter evoked by sex. A quality which Hugh Riddel recognised in himself, and which was maybe con-tained to an even greater degree in men far beyond the parish of Caldwell. Take the war years, now, and the time when the Polish airmen were stationed over there at Balwhine. What a clash of tongues *they* had caused in the countryside. God Knows had been fair flabbergasted by their methods. His fiery denuncia-tion of the Poles still burned in Hugh Riddel's recollection.

"The Cottage Hospital is fair full of queans with festered breasts the now! For it seems that plain fornication is just not good enough for that Polish chields. Na. Na. They've got to bite as well. And that, mark you, with all their fine polite words and ways, their kissing hands and all the rest of their palaver. Surely to God a decent man can have a quean without wanting to take bites out of her."

Laughter shook Hugh Riddel at the recollection, and metaphorically flung him face downwards on a grassy bank, thirty years away in time. But, like laughter of that kind and quality, it left him empty enough for tears. *O! My love Annie's wondrous bonnie.* It was the idyll one's spirits always wept for.

"It's when there's neither lust nor liking," his father had once confided, "that a man's marriage has got nothing." Lust nor liking. He had never heard his father use the word "love", except in song.

But it was all going to be different with *him*. Hugh Riddel had made up his mind early about that.

THE LIFE OF THE SEA

The Life of the Sea

THE FISHER COMMUNITIES
John R. Allan *Northeast Lowlands of Scotland*

The fisher communities are unlike any others in Scotland, though the miners a generation ago might have had a near resemblance. There is that isolation which has cut them off from the country people round them. This is not a new thing. The minister of Cullen wrote of them a hundred years ago: "The almost invariable habit which prevails of intermarrying with those of their own craft, and the no less general practice which obtains of every fisherman's son following his father's occupation, prove serious drawbacks to the progress of this order of the community in the march of improvement, having the effect of rendering them a distinct class of society, with sentiments, sympathies and habits peculiar to themselves. Until some amalgamation shall take place between them and their brethren of terra firma, their advancement in the improvements of civilised life must necessarily be slow and partial." That is rather a mouthful but the fact remains today, although the fishermen may be well off without some improvements of civilised life. It would be interesting if some good reason could be found to explain an isolation so old as to seem inherent. Is it perhaps racial? I don't know; but that it still exists is certain.

There has been intensive inbreeding in the villages for many generations. Now inbreeding is a good thing if the stock is good, and it seems to have done no harm in this case, physically; though mental inbreeding has produced a certain narrowness. It has had one result that is rather confusing to a stranger—in one village there may be only a few surnames. Where everybody is a West or a Buchan or a May and there is no enterprise in choosing Christian names, there are bound to be many John Wests and Thomas Buchans. So there has grown up a system of tee-names. Let us suppose there was a man of Portallochy called Thomas Buchan. He would be called Tam. Now suppose he had a son called John and daughters Jean and Annie. Contemporary with those children there would be others with the same surnames and Christian names. So those three might be called Tam's Jock, Tam's Jeanie and Tam's Annie. Their children would require to be further distinguished. If Tam's Jock had a daughter Jean she

31

The fisher communities

might become Tam's Jock's Jeanie. And there might be Tam's Jeanie's Willickie and Tam's Annie's Mary. It is really most logical and gives a pedigree along with the name. There is a common tee-name "Pow" pronounced "Poo". A father may be called John Buchan "Pow". His son may be Pow's Sandy or Pow's Tam. He might be Willie Pow, and his son if he too were William by the use of one of our many diminutives might become Willockie Pow. Sometimes the fisherman gets the name of his boat—Seahorse or Heatherbell. There is no end to the combination of unlikely words. Even the house address may be used. One old man, the wisest of the fishermen, who has always been thinking a generation ahead of his time, is known from Wick to Lowestoft as Seven-and-a-half.

The result of this sequestered tribal life is that the fishermen live in a very narrow, very rigid family society, with a strict and narrow code of morals, offset by great heights and depths of emotion. Their religion is deeply felt and hardly at all a matter of intellectual persuasion. That is quite natural; as an observer who had lived a long time beside them once told me, "When you are accustomed to have nothing but the thickness of a plank between you and a watery grave, you do want to feel that the Almighty's hand is strong to save." Or, considering the age of some drifters—both hands. That may be a way in to the heart of the matter—the natural piety of the fishermen and the superstitious fear or caution with which they move among the dangers of the world.

They are superstitious, more than most people. If a fisherman meets a black cat on the way to his boat it troubles him. Pigs also are of evil omen. Recently while writing a radio script to illustrate how trawlermen send messages to their wives over the short-wave, and wishing to use a message that would interest children, for whom the programme was intended, I put down that the trawler skipper would say among other things, "Tell the bairns to be sure to feed the guinea-pigs." But the fishery expert to whom the script was referred said the guinea-pigs must come out, for no fisherman would speak the name of pig on his boat. The fishers used to be much concerned about the evil eye and persons liable to bring bad luck. There were in some of the villages women thought to be—if not witches, at least of evil omen. If one of them stepped across a fisherman's lines she would bring bad luck. Ministers of religion too, though sacred, had no place on the quay. Among the many stories of superstition there is none to beat that about the new minister of religion who did not understand the primitive beliefs of his parishioners. McPherson* says:

> Two or three years ago a minister was newly inducted to a church in the same town (Moray Firth). Soon after, taking a walk along the shore, someone told him that A.B.'s boat was about to set out for the

* Dr. J. M. McPherson (1875–1944), *Primitive Beliefs of the Northeast of Scotland.*

32

English fishing. Thinking he would greet his parishioner before his departure, he made for the harbour and hailed the skipper but found him surly, uncommunicative and lacking in ordinary courtesy. A.B. did not dare ask the new minister "Throw us good luck", in order to counteract the evil influence of his presence. The skipper was disturbed but not dismayed. At once he took the necessary steps to avert disaster. He ordered the loosening of the mooring ropes and followed this up with "Full steam ahead", as he grasped the steering wheel. Out into the bay the vessel sped. When about half a mile out it began to turn in a huge circle. Seven times round the bay went the vessel, always following the way of the sun. A.B. himself held the wheel, and during the whole performance had his hand on the cord of the siren which he kept blowing continuously. The townsfolk were somewhat alarmed at his behaviour, thinking that a man had fallen overboard, and that he was circling round the spot where the man had disappeared. They looked on the blasts of the siren as calls for assistance from shore. But no boat put out to sea. Those who went down to the sea in ships knew the cause. To the landsman they explained, "Oh, A.B. had the minister seeing him off. Somebody might tell the minister to bide at hame; it wad save a hantle o trouble." My informant saw and heard this effort to outwit the powers of darkness.

One must not deduce from the story that fishermen have no respect for kirk religion. But as McPherson has suggested somewhere, there are also the powers of the sea which must not be annoyed even though the Almighty is on your side. . . .

The fishermen do value religion of a more orthodox kind. They like the kirk services and join with great spirit in the singing. It is perhaps unfortunate from a purely musical point of style that the proof of power is the ability to sing higher than anybody else, so that a few competitive soprani assault the very courts of heaven; but, if the purpose of psalm-singing is to call attention to one's faith and hope, that style may serve very well. They have an old-fashioned taste for sermons and an old-fashioned ability to concentrate on a lengthy discourse, divided under three heads and argued out to a conclusion about sin and punishment. Some of them have a gift of extempore prayer and an enjoyment in using it. Better even than a closely reasoned discourse, they love declamation. A political speech full of fire and fury and pointed with Biblical texts is as good as an orgy to them and far more worth than any reasoned arguments. There are also in the fishing communities at least two sorts of Brethren and a varying number of the even more esoteric and evangelical sects. Some of those carry still further the isolation of fisher society. For instance, they take no part in public affairs: they do not vote in elections or offer themselves as any sorts of candidate. They confine themselves rigidly to their devotions in public and private, sparing just enough time to make a living, at which they are said to be rather successful.

The fishers used to be subject to intermittent bouts of revivalism. Now and then some evangelical spell-binder would run a campaign and work up an audience till all their inhibitions were relaxed in hallelujahs. People leaped up and confessed their sins; the light-witted got into a frenetical state, and the fever worked up to a bonfire of vanities. "Bring out your gauds. Bring out your trinkets. Throw your cigarettes and your pipes on the flames. Your mirrors and your powder puffs. Your song sheets and your musical instruments." As the fire blazed up, the preacher thus called on the sinful and the sinful responded. It was at least a fine scavenging of rubbish and no doubt it did the participants good; having some virtues of a good blind without the physical nausea of the morning after. Those orgies in the name of the Lord are in the past; and that there have not been any these last twenty-five years may be a sign that the tensions of life have been relaxed. Whether that is good or bad I am not called on to decide.

Having written so much about the fishermen I realise I have missed perhaps the most important thing. Among the best of them there is a simplicity and a dignified way of living and a complete integrity that is seldom found anywhere else. The wisest of them are very simple people who have come to an understanding of essential things; and, having broken out of the rigid confinements of the tribe, voyage through strange seas of thought alone, keeping an even course. They stand very square among all the confusions of the world and they have a power of greatness in them.

REVIVAL MANIA

Neil Paterson *Behold Thy Daughter*

In August of 1858 the North of Scotland was devastated by a religious revival which swept like a tidal wave over the fishing towns of the Moray Firth and left in its wake a great sense of piety and moral exaltation, a form of insanity known as mania, and a sharp rise in the birth-rate. In fanatical all-night rallies thousands of solid citizens of both sexes and all ages were converted and saved, hundreds were struck down dramatically in swoons, and there was hardly a family on the coast from Colliston to Clyth in which there was not at least one case of mental or physical prostration.

Kaysie did not escape unscathed.

On Thursday, August 17, a covered wagon with crimson lettering on its white tarpaulin hood, drawn by a pair of Shetland ponies and driven by an unsmiling gentleman in a dark frock-coat, entered Kaysie by the Banff Road, and, accompanied by a swirl of capering children and yapping dogs, proceeded to exhibit its slogans throughout the town. They read, in letters almost a foot high:

EZEKIEL FLEMING, MAN OF GOD. YE GENERATIONS OF VIPERS, HOW CAN YE ESCAPE THE DAMNATION OF HELL? FRIENDS, COME TO JESUS.

Supplementing these exhortations, Mr. Ezekiel Fleming, the driver, would raise his hat and announce from time to time in flat, conversational tones: "Nightly at 8 p.m. In the school."

The caravan paraded everywhere. It criss-crossed the main streets, explored the lanes, entered all openings big enough to take the ponies' heads. If you had taken a pencil and charted the course of that caravan you would have made a pretty mess of your map: you would have obliterated all the roads with your scribbles and covered almost every backyard in the town.

By late afternoon the news that Mr. Ezekiel Fleming was in town had reached Carmichael House, and the atmosphere became charged with tension as the servants gathered in groups to recall the glories of past revival meetings and to speculate on their chances of getting the night off to attend this one. Most of the excitement passed over Thirza's head. She was too young to remember the last revival, and, taking her cue from Manson, she affected to disapprove of the whole affair.

But she was much more interested than she pretended, and the following day, when the household was all a-twitter with reports of the first revival meeting, she searched out certain of the maids who had been there, and asked to be told all about it. She listened with rapt attention to their vivid, incoherent accounts, and she could not but see, as she studied their flushed faces and bright contented eyes, that these girls had undergone a great, a soul-stirring, experience.

When, at lunch-time, she brought up the subject of the revival and its effects on the maids, Manson, to her great surprise, snapped at her "Let's dinna ha'e nae mair aboot it. I've had enough brimstane and fire, an' mair than enough revival this mornin' to last me a lifetime. . . . Ask Mr. Spence".

Mr. Spence appeared to have no knowledge of the matter, however; and after an interval of silence, in which she ate herself into a better humour, Manson gave them an account of the affair.

Findlay was a parlourmaid. She was about thirty-five years old, but she could have been taken for fifty. She had small, smudged features in an indeterminate face, a topping of streaked, sandy-grey hair, and no more figure than a boy; and, all in all, she was so insignificant that the moment you took your eyes off her you forgot what she looked like. You could not have found a less heroic figure, and it was very hard for Thirza, listening avidly, to identify the Findlay she knew with the wild and reckless creature of the housekeeper's story.

It appeared that Findlay had been brought home from the Revival Meeting in a donkey cart and dumped in a heap at the servants' entrance. She had passively allowed Manson to undress her and help her into bed, and Manson had thought that a night's sleep would restore her to normal. But it hadn't. Findlay had wakened singing "Canaan" at the pitch of her voice, had dressed herself sketchily, and had come downstairs to the west wing to drive the buyers and sellers out of the temple. She had been restrained from overturning Mr. Carmichael's desk only by its weight, and had been removed by main force to the kitchen annex, where she had calmed down and eaten a good breakfast.

During the early part of the morning she was vague but docile, doing her work as usual, and content to express her new self only by pushing her face into other faces and saying with a fatuous smile "I've been saved, dearie. Have you?" But towards ten o'clock she had taken a turn for the worse. She stood on the stairs with an open Bible in her hand and declaimed to the maids in the hall. She declared that she had had four illegitimate children and that she had suffocated them all at birth. She was irrepressible. She had talked incessantly from that time on, shouting evangelical slogans and breaking into snatches of evangelist choruses. She had chased the other maids round the house, trapped Tweeny in the angle between two walls in the scullery, and so terrified that poor half-witted creature with her talk of pit and serpents and flaming cesspool that Tweeny was now as good as demented herself and was meantime in bed with hysterics. Finally, they had caught Findlay and locked her in her room, but she had dropped the fifteen feet from the window to the ground, and had marched back into the house—by the front door, if you please! Nobody could do anything with her. Mistress Carmichael herself had spoken to her, severely but not unkindly. It had been a waste of breath. Findlay had merely clasped her Bible to her breast and, shaking her head, said serenely "Poor sinner, I pity you."

Mistress Carmichael had naturally been shocked that a parlourmaid should talk to her in such a way, and she had sent MacGregor for the doctor.

But Dr. Grant had refused to come. MacGregor was sure that Dr. Grant could not have understood who he was, and he had gone to some trouble to explain that he was MacGregor, coachman to the Carmichaels of Carmichael House, and that he had been sent as a personal messenger by Mistress Carmichael herself.

"I don't care if you're the personal messenger of the Archangel Gabriel," Dr. Grant said. "If this woman's a revival case I won't attend her. Let her stew in her juice."

"What shall I tell Mistress Carmichael, sir?"

"Tell her I'm a busy man", the doctor said. "Tell her to get her ain fine doctor from Aberdeen."

No one else would have dared to send such a message to a Carmichael of Carmichael House, but Dr. Grant was a law unto himself.

At their wits' end to know what to do with Findlay, they had finally asked Mr. Carmichael, and Mr. Carmichael had given the answer. They were to lock Findlay in one of the boxrooms without a window, keep her there for forty-eight hours, and feed her only on bread and water. It was Mr. Carmichael's opinion that that would bring her to her senses, and if it did not, nothing would.

"And that's how I've spent my morning," Manson finished up grimly. "Chasin' that daftie. And I repeat"—she shot a hard glance at the hitherto insignificant Mr. Spence—"that I personally have, despite what some may choose to think, had mair than enough revival to last me for the rest o' my time. It'll be weeks—weeks before I get a decent day's work out o' the maids after this."

"Most regrettable", Mr. Sinclair said in his bland, high voice. "Most regrettable. Females should not be admitted to revival meetings. They lack emotional stability. It is a thing I have frequently commented on. They flock in thousands to hear these preachers, and come away seeing visions and bleating like sheep about them. Did you hear the maids singing as they came up the drive last night?"

"I did that," Manson said. "And I also heard a good few rams bleatin' among them. You needna be so superior, Mr. Sinclair. I hear that there were as many men at the meeting last night as there were women."

RELIGION AND SUPERSTITION

Peter F. Anson *Fishing Boats and Fisher Folk on the East Coast of Scotland*

There are two important factors which have always played a great part in the lives of the fisherfolk of the east coast of Scotland as in most other seafaring communities, i.e. religion and superstition. The two must be classed together since superstition is no more than credulity regarding the supernatural, a misdirected reverence due to ignorance, combined with an irrational fear of the unknown. The Scottish fisherfolk possess this inborn sense of the supernatural to a strong degree, but owing largely to the survival of pagan ideas among them, the want of instruction, the comparatively little hold which the Presbyterian Kirk seems to have had over their imaginations and emotions during the two centuries that followed the Reformation, however much they may have been afraid of disobeying its ordinances, we come across an amount of extraordinary superstitions, beliefs, and practices, which ruled the daily lives of the old fishing commmunities until almost within living memory. Traces of them survive today and even young fishermen are nervous of ignoring the superstitions of their forbears. Fisher life until quite recently was bound up with a hundred and one superstitions; many of these are still believed in by the older people. But a century ago, no matter where one went, either in Banffshire or Berwickshire, Caithness or Fife, superstition was rampant, haunting its victims day and night.

Buckie fishermen of fifty or sixty years ago, when they went out in the morning were convinced that a strange beastie, whom they referred to as the "cockie-coo", was on the look out for them in order to seize hold of their "bonnets".

Innumerable things might happen that would absolutely prevent a Buckie fisherman from going to sea of a morning. For instance, if anyone met him and asked where he was going, that was quite enough to make the man turn back home and not go to sea that day. Likewise it was equally unlucky to meet a red-haired person, or anyone who was flat-footed, or someone who was supposed to be "ill-fitted". In Portknockie, even dogs were looked upon as "ill-fitted". Stories are told of more than one fisherman who met a dog when going down to the harbour, pursued it, and killed it for fear that the same animal might cross his path another morning! To have found a hare, rabbit, or salmon on board a boat would have absolutely prevented a fisherman from going to sea that day.

If anyone should meet the minister on his way to the boat, that again was more than enough to cause a whole crew to remain in port, although some men maintained that ill luck could be averted by a timely appeal to "cauld iron". . . .

A queer superstition among the old Buckie fishermen was that of spitting upon a piece of "bent" or grass and throwing it overboard if their nets ever got entangled at sea. This mysterious act, it was supposed, unfastened the line!

The number of strange superstitions among the Nairn fisherfolk was amazing. It was unlucky to shoot nets on the port side, to taste food before any fish were caught, to leave a creel or "scull" uppermost, not to draw blood from the first fish caught. It was equally unlucky to take dead fish on to a boat before the lines were shot, to pick up a dead body at sea, and to clean fish scales off a boat before the end of a week's fishing.

No Morayshire fisherman would ever be induced to carry a parcel for a friend, or to go to sea at the beginning of the season, before blood had been shed. Very often a free fight would be started in order to arrive at the desired result! No fisherman's wife would venture to comb her hair after sunset if her "guid man" was at sea, and she knew there was good luck awaiting him if she dreamed of a white sea.

If a cock was heard to crow before midnight, it meant a death in the family.

Even the days of the week were bound up with various superstitions. On Tuesday, nobody would cut their nails for fear of witches. Wednesday was a most unlucky day for girls to enter service. Changes of weather were always expected on a Friday. Work begun on a Saturday was sure to "see seven Saturdays before completion", while any job started on a Monday was always likely to be finished quickly. Sunday was a lucky day, but no ship would ever put to sea "until a blessing had been pronounced", i.e. until after morning service.

The first Monday and the first Friday of every quarter were looked upon as being unlucky days, for some strange reason.

On New Year's day the Buckie fisherfolk of sixty years ago had the curious custom of going down to the seashore, filling a small jug with salt water, and taking home some seaweed. They sprinkled the water round the fire and put the seaweed over their doors. On New Year's Day no fire was ever allowed to be taken out of a house.

At Burghead there existed the superstition that a fisherman should never go to sea after the New Year until he had shed blood. The first person who should draw blood in a quarrel was held to have fulfilled this obligation. In regard to drawing blood, the Portessie fisherman would go so far as to beat anyone who should wish him good luck (a sure sign that he will not catch fish!), and to draw blood so as to turn the ill luck. . . .

Within the past hundred years the fisher folk of the east coast of Scotland have been greatly affected by more than one religious revival movement which has swept over them like a prairie fire. From a psychological point of view there is a marked temperamental difference between the fisher folk and the average cautious lowland Scot. The religion of the latter finds expression in moral action; that of the former in emotion. During the past sixty or seventy years great changes have undoubtedly come over the Scottish fishing communities. Taken as a whole, seventy or eighty years ago they were a race of rough, uneducated smugglers and drunkards, whose lives were ordered by superstition. In 1859 a change began with the revival movement which arrived in Scotland from America, via Ulster. It broke out in Peterhead, where its leader was James Turner, a cooper and herring curer, a remarkable character, who in two years was the means of converting more than eight thousand persons along the north-east coast of Scotland. This first revival was followed by an "invasion" of the Salvation Army, whose emotional appeal caught on among the fisher folk. A few years later another revival took place, this time under the direction of the Baptists, who opened "bethels" and meeting-houses of every description in almost all the fishing centres. In 1921, during the autumn fishing season, the Scottish fishermen and fisher lassies were suddenly moved by yet another religious revival of an equal if not greater violence than any other which had preceded it since 1859. Extraordinary scenes took place at Yarmouth and Lowestoft. Weather-beaten skippers, young lads and lassies, were swept off their feet by this sudden whirlwind of religious emotionalism. The leader was a young fisherman of about twenty-seven years of age, Dave Cordiner, tall, with jet-black hair, with a dynamic quality in his preaching. Strange legends grew up about him: that he had "heard the voice of God calling him to throw his packets of cigarettes into the galley-fire on board his drifter".

On those cold winter nights in November and December 1921, vast crowds of Scottish fishermen and lassies hung on his words as he preached to them in the open air. Groups of fishermen might be found gathered under a lamp-post at a street corner, singing hymns with intense fervour, or listening to some recently converted brother relating his spiritual experiences, while they interrupted him every few moments with ejaculations of "Amen" and "Hallelujah". Dave Cordiner, the converted fisherman, was soon followed up by Jock Troup, the converted cooper, and his friend, Wullie Bruce, who for several months carried on an evangelical campaign all along the east coast of Scotland that recalled that of Moody and Sankey in the previous century. Today the revival of 1921 is but a memory of the past, and the chief witness of its having taken place is the number of meeting-houses, and "bethels" belonging to rival sects of "brethren" which have sprung up in nearly all the fishing villages affected by this strange religious movement.

Religion counts for so much in the lives of the Scottish fisherfolk, that to understand them and their outlook on life this must never be forgotten. They belong to various Protestant denominations; perhaps the majority of them are Presbyterians, but it would seem that the greater number of those who are "converted" invariably go over to some other body where their emotional cravings will find satisfaction. Baptists of various kinds, "Strict," "Particular," etc., abound all along the Moray Firth coast. Methodists and Plymouth Brethren are also very numerous, while those who are not satisfied with any existing religious body split off and worship in a "gospel hall" of their own. . . .

TRAWLING

Burns Singer *Living Silver*

A trawler is such a special kind of generalised vessel that practically nothing that floats, except in the designer's mind, could be efficient at all the jobs she is expected to do. Almost any other kind of ship is designed specifically for one job, for carrying cargoes or for towing other vessels, for lying static among the big waters or for racing from port to port. But a trawler must be capable of doing half a dozen specific jobs and she is, therefore, seldom better than a most inadequate compromise between conflicting demands. In the first place, she must sail, and as quickly as possible; for her catch must be back to market before it has had time to decay; and must sometimes travel two thousand miles before it can be sold. Then again, speed is economic since lack of it means that she spends more time in going backwards and forwards between the grounds, and to and fro over them, than she spends in fishing. And all the time she is travelling. All the time she is using fuel, coal or oil, money. And a trawler must be able to tow. She must be like a tug, able to make an even course through a high swell. She must have stability. She must also have strength in the beam, be able to sit out long hours in a thwart sea, like a lightship. Then too, she must be capable of carrying a cargo. And that cargo must be easy to load; for the loading will not be done in the stillness of a dock backwater but, more probably, in the swell that follows a full gale; at least, in the open sea. On top of all this, she has a crew, much larger than that of a cargo vessel of similar tonnage, and that crew must be accommodated: so the trawler must be like a passenger vessel. How then could there be a perfect trawler?

Trawling

There were certainly none in Aberdeen when Jan first visited the fish-market. Occasionally a streamlined Icelandic vessel would unload, or an oil-burning Norwegian, or one of the new Belgian trawlers. They too had their disadvantages but they still set a standard of design that should have shamed the owners of the home fleet. Most of it was over forty years old and had long since been reduced to units of scraggy rust as obsolete as the *Caroon,* uncomfortable, dangerous, inefficient ships that threatened continually to ruin their owners and drown their crews. They were known as scratchers and they sailed out once or twice a week to the near and middle waters of the North Sea, going as far as the Gut to the south and the Viking Bank in the north, and returning promptly with a small catch covered in its own weight of ice. And just because they were so unseaworthy, because they had to come back to port after such a short time at sea, their fish was better preserved and sold for higher prices than the catches of the more efficient long-distance trawlers of other ports, like Hull and Fleetwood. It was almost as though a premium had been put upon a niggardly lack of any economic imagination. At least, for a time. In the long run, the diesel would win. The rust slums would rot out and the richer resources of the far north would leave the owners of the scratchers impoverished. But, in the late forties, when Jan first saw them, these ancient sea-bitten junk heaps were still helping to make Aberdeen a prosperous city. . . .

The men who lived and worked on them could take almost anything. If they couldn't then they didn't sail twice; for it was the crew's accommodation that had been most skimped by the builders and that had suffered most with the ageing of the vessels. The tiny fo'cs'le of a scratcher, with its double tiers of bunks arranged in a bent triangle, the anchor groaning overhead, its chain rumbling with rust as the whole room soared clear of a wave or slapped back down like a fist on the water, the mugs swaying until they had broken from their little iron hooks, the fug of eight sweating bodies, each screwed to a pipe or a cigarette, all this Jan could imagine; but not until he had made a trip on one of them did he really know the terrible strain, felt in every muscle of the body, that comes from continually striving against the maximal movement of the ship, trying, sometimes unsuccessfully, to avoid clattering out of a bunk. Nor had he understood that, when the vessel is under full steam in rough deep water, a man must sometimes crawl on hands and knees, gripping the iron battens on a constantly capsizing deck, heading, wet neck first, into a ton of green and white and battering brine, crawl painfully forward every time that he wants to pass from the wheel house to his blankets. Such experiences could be terrifying. And yet, when he had come to know them intimately, Jan found them more exhilarating and less miserable than the trials of warm, smooth water. He could not have anticipated how the depressive confinement forward, with its almost total lack of sanitation, its bullying and its obscenity would have made the drenching and dangerous sea into a healthy relief, almost an escape, from the boredom of his quarters. For though he had understood the physical discomforts of trawling (a single day on the *Caroon* had been enough for that) he had not realised that the same social degradations as are found in Glasgow tenements would operate in the sea slums that sailed from Aberdeen. Compared to this atmosphere even the danger of drowning was revealed as an envigorating experience.

Anyhow, there the ships would lie, twenty, thirty, forty of them, forming a line so close that the propellor of one vessel must have been scraping against the rust on the stem of the one behind. Yet, when the huge baskets of fish had been hoisted to the concrete quay and the lumpers had arranged them in regular lines of hundredweight boxes, there would be a couple of ear-splitting hoots, ropes would slacken and be hauled aboard and then a ship would reverse out of the order, turn itself free in the pool and nose its way out towards the dock gates, hooting occasionally to frighten the herring gulls that clustered around it, but otherwise as sedately and as leisurely as an old lorry might move in an open stretch of road.

NIGHT FISHING

Rothael Kirk *By the North Sea Shore*

As soon as the tide lifted the boats off the ground, they began to move out into the bay. No scene could be more full of stir, movement, and interest than the departure of the herring fleet. The herring-boats drawing out of the harbour in apparently endless numbers; the moving figures of the men as the boats shook clear of each other, and one after another hoisting their brown sails stood away out to sea, added a human interest which it would be hard to surpass.

Towards the harbour mouth the boats moving out formed one solid mass, boat touching boat from one side of the harbour to the other.

The noise, confusion, and bustle were great. The business seemed to be conducted on the principle of a strenuous scramble. Pushing with long poles and boat-hooks; hauling on ropes fixed to pawls at the pier-head; incessant movement and exertion in the process, were the features taken in by the eye; while the accompaniment to the ear was a confusion of sound made up of the rumbling of ropes, the bumping and scraping and creaking of boats pushed against each other by the men or by the movement of the water at the harbour mouth, shouts and commands in stentorian tones rising above the tumult, and the occasional sharp crash of a breaking boat-hook, followed by a swelling chorus of strong words in Gaelic and English.

In the midst of the tumult three men loaded with rugs and artist paraphernalia were seen rushing to the quay-side. When they saw all the boats in motion they seemed to hesitate what to do.

"Can you tell me," said one of them to the Harbour-master, who was superintending the operations, "where is the *Bonnie Mary* of Breidhaven?"

"There she is," was the reply, "right in the middle; you can get her across these boats if you look sharp."

They made their way across the boats like men crossing a moving raft, and were welcomed by Gweebran. They had come to the Laverockbraes coast for artistic purposes, and had made the acquaintance of Gweebran, who, discovering their desire for sketches of the herring fishing, had offered them the opportunity of seeing the whole business on board the *Bonnie Mary*.

It was by this time about one o'clock in the afternoon, the sky bright, and a light breeze blowing. The bay of Inchlargo was studded with boats, some with sails set, standing away to sea; some hoisting sail; some pulling with long oars to get into a convenient position for doing so. The artists were soon busy with their sketching materials, making rapid studies of the varied scene.

The passengers on board the *Bonnie Mary* did not escape observation. On board a Sandend boat about thirty yards off, an old soldier with a stutter—Simon Gow by name—was tugging at an oar. Eyeing the artists, whose advent he had noted from the first, he shouted, "Hullo, G-G-Gweebran! are ye g-g-gaun into the emigration trade?"

"We'll maybe be nearer foreign pairts, Gow, than ye'll be the night," responded Gweebran, "and be back afore ye the morn for a' that."

Gweebran was by this time hoisting the powerful mainsail to the wind, and very soon was sailing away towards the open horizon. The breeze was light, and the progress consequently not very rapid.

Every thread of sail was set. Besides the jib and the mainsail or foresail (which was of the "dipping lug" sort), she carried a smaller sail on a jiggermast near the stern, which sail was called the "bunker". Gweebran's skill was often manifested during the evening. When he was steering, the *Bonnie Mary* crept up, and passed boat after boat, while in the hands of other helmsmen she barely held her own.

The artists were busy and keenly interested.

"What a difference," said one of them, "there is in the boats! Look at that one over there: she's quite different from yours. The bow and stern both slope inwards and downwards towards the keel; yours has both perpendicular, and their mast seems to have rather more rake than yours."

"Oh yes," replied Gweebran, "that's a Moray Firth boat. We ca' them *Scaffies*. They're nae sae deep as our east coast boats. They can run as weel, or maybe better; but they canna reach like ours. We can beat them on the wind, and we think ours is safer in bad weather."

A shout from Kelpie interrupted the discussion. "Look at that whale blawin' awa' to leeward: we're nae far frae herrin', surely."

"I think there's a look o' herrin' here, Kelpie," said Gweebran; "we'll shoot the nets soon."

So in a short while the sail was lowered, all but as much as sufficed to keep drawing the boat away from the nets as they were shot across the tide, and each buoy as it came was heaved over into the sea.

The artists were greatly interested and much surprised.

"Why," said one of them, "it's not what I thought it was at all. I thought they were caught in a bag of net. But there's no bag there. How in the world will these nets catch herring? They must hang in the water like sheets on clothes-ropes."

"Of course they do," said Gweebran. "The lug-stanes keep the lower edge down, and the corks keep the other edge up, and the back-rope's a' the length o' the buoy-ropes below the surface o' the water."

"And how much is that?" said the artist.

"Oh, whiles more, whiles less," said Gweebran. "I gae them a' the length o' the ropes—that's about six fathoms—thi' night, because it's a light night. If it were a dark ane, I would cast a knot on the ropes and mak' them shorter, and that would bring the back-rope nearer the tap o' the water."

"But how in the world are the herrings caught?" said the artist.

"Weel, ye see," said Gweebran, "the lug-stanes pullin' down mak' the mesh hang like a narrow diamond. Ye see we shoot them across the tide. Weel, the herrin' swimmin' wi' the tide come up against the net and put their noses through the mesh. They canna get through, nae even to the gills, so they back water. The stanes pullin' down mak' the thread o' the net follow the sides o' their heads till it gets stuck ahin' the moustache-like thing that comes down by the corner o' their mouth. So they canna get through, and they canna get back, and maun just wait till we haul them up. Ye'll see the process ere mornin'."

The mast was then lowered into a crutch, and the boat rode with the fleet of nets attached to the stern by a rope called the swing. There was little wind, but a heavy swell, causing the boat to roll a good deal, so that the lowering of the mast made her ride much more easily, to the considerable comfort of the landsmen on board.

Night fishing

Now and then in the dim moonlight a boat could be seen close by, and sometimes the buoys of some one else's nets would appear in what to the uninitiated appeared dangerous proximity; while all round, as far as eye could reach, the boats' lights twinkled on the sea like the stars in the sky.

There was now nothing to be done for hours. Some therefore went below, where there was a bunk with sleeping accommodation and a fire, and resigned themselves to sleep. Others, and among them the artists, remained on deck, and bethought themselves of hand-line fishing to occupy the time.

The first net was hauled in for a moment, and enough herring for bait found in it, and shaken out for use. The hand-lines were provided with hooks strong and large as the bend of one's finger, and with leaden sinkers as large as three fingers. The hook was baited with a whole herring, and put over the side. Line having been paid out till the bottom was felt, it was hauled up a little off the ground, and the fisherman waited for a nibble.

As the night advanced, this operation became more unpleasant and difficult, for the wind was freshening up, and the movement of sea and boat very perceptibly increasing. So in the end the hand-lines were stowed away.

About three o'clock all hands were on deck, preparing to haul the nets. The mast was hoisted up again, and the crutch put away, leaving all clear aft. The hatch, or opening into the hold, is not far from the stern of the boat. Gweebran and the rest of the crew had appeared from below in yellow oil-skins and sea-boots. Gweebran took his station at the stern, and Jimmie at the fore-end of the hatch on the starboard side, while two men stood at the port side of the hatch. Gweebran then hauled in the swing, or rope by which the fleet of nets was attached to the stern. When he reached the first net, Jimmie came aft, and catching it where it was bent on to the back-rope, pulled up the edge till he caught the lug-stane in the lower corner, the other two men getting hold of the part between him and Gweebran. They then returned to their places, and began to haul the net. As they did so the net left the water a few feet from the boat' side, sloping upwards towards the hands of Jimmie and Gweebran.

The herring were hanging by the "moustaches" to the threads of the net, but some were so heavy that the "moustaches" gave way, and let them drop into the sea. But they were in no condition to make full use of their freedom. They had been held, possibly for hours, in the net, with the tide flowing past them from tail to head, obstructing the ejection of the water by their gills, and in fact almost suffocating them. So when they fell free into the water, they simply gave a few sleepy and evidently almost insensible movements. No doubt they would very soon have recovered, and swum rapidly away; but Kelpie was there for the purpose of preventing any such result. With a wide-mouthed and long-shafted landing-net, he deftly skimmed them up, and placed them in a basket on deck near the foot of the mast, emptying it when full into the hold, and keeping account of the number of baskets, being paid by results. The net was drawn across the open hatch, and shaken so that the herring should drop into the hold. A large portion of them, however, were taken out by coming over the gunwhale of the boat, so that inside the low bulwark there was soon a heap of herring almost knee deep, squeaking like mice. The artists were by this time again busy with their sketching tools, intensely surprised to see Gweebran and Jimmie, wading among herring on a slippery deck, which was rolling with the movement of the sea, yet never showing the slightest symptom of slipping or falling. All round were the sea-gulls looking out for their share. As the men hauled in the nets, the effect was gradually to draw the boat astern. Any herrings therefore that escaped Kelpie's "scumming-net" were soon floating past the bow of the boat, where the gulls kept watch and picked them up.

By the time that the nets were all on board it was five o'clock, and would have been much later, but that the end half of the fleet of nets had very few herrings, a result occasioned by a fleet of nets belonging to another boat. This boat had been about half a mile astern of the *Bonnie Mary*, and a little towards the quarter from which the tide was flowing. The shoal of herrings therefore, coming with the tide, were intercepted by this fleet for about half a mile, and only the foremost half of Gweebran's nets were full. These, however, were so full as to give him a very good night's fishing.

When all were on board Gweebran bore up for home.

A MAN FROM THE SEA

Catherine Gavin *The Hostile Shore*

It was very quiet in the village—so quiet that the sounds of rising storm, when they began to be heard, struck the ear with an added shock. Neither Kirsten nor Lenny had really noticed the clouding-over of the watery sun, or the louder note of the surf; what brought them to their feet was the bursting open of the cottage door, driven inwards by a gust of wind.

David's cottage, unlike many of the houses in Dundargue, fronted the sea, and the gust proved that the wind had changed to the steady nor'-easter of these parts. A blatter of rain struck hard against the window and a puff of smoke from the chimney suddenly filled the kitchen with soft peat ash. For a few minutes all was confusion, Lenny shutting the door and opening it again to let out the smoke, and Kirsten frantically looking for a duster. The same scene was enacted in a score of cottages, where "yon awesome wind" was spoken of long after as the prelude to the great storm of 1938.

For nearly a quarter of an hour the wind raged over the seaboard. It struck Dundargue with all its force, so that Kirsten was presently edified by the sight of young Mrs. West's washing blowing out to sea ("serves her richt, the lazy lump, leavin' her washin' till Setturday," she shrieked in Lenny's ear) and several mothers came to their doors to call their children to the house. The weather-cock above the inn, the pride of Mrs. Downie's heart, furled round madly for a time and then fell off the roof in sheer despair, and two or three chimney-cans crashed after it to the beach. These were joined by the board on which the Aberdeen *Press and Journal* bills were displayed outside the post office, and the sound of two windows of the little hall being smashed in by the gale was drowned by the first rolling of thunder.

"What a mercy the boats are a' in!" cried Kirsten. "Are ye still feared at thunder an' lichtnin', Lenny?"

"Not a bit," lied Lenny, who was very pale. The sky was now entirely black, with a flickering violet light against the rim of the sea. From the heart of the cloud came a jagged fork of lightning which for a second illuminated the headland and the bay. The frightened crying of children arose from the cottages. . . .

During the first two hours of the storm the greatest damage was done in the farming country. The old boiler-house at Dundargue Mains was struck, and a fire broke out which for a time threatened to spread to the other buildings, and was fought not only by everybody at the Mains but by every available person in the neighbourhood. The minister went to help, thereby doing himself more good than by a year's preaching or an alphabet of honorary degrees, and so did J. Telfer and his stalwart wife, and two passing vanmen. "The three drunken horsemen," as Mrs. Fraser called them, gave valiant service, and splashed about enough water to have kept themselves sober till Hogmanay. Every farm, more or less, was struggling with some dangerous consequence of the storm, while near Pitnaburn, on the outskirts of Johnny Cumin's Woodie, an aged tramp, resting against the paling before going up to the house to ask for bread, was killed outright when the wire was struck by lightning.

Under its protecting cliff, Dundargue was free from these alarms. After a truly magnificent display of thunder and lightning lasting for nearly half an hour, the genius of the storm drew off towards the east, and thereafter the steady beat of the rain almost drowned the rising roar of the sea. The only dramatic moment was supplied by two little girls who had been sent to Rosehearty for messages and who had faithfully kept walking home through the worst of the storm. Drenched to the skin and half-paralysed with fright, their stumbling run down the sea-road was greeted with as much sympathetic solicitude as was possible to that stern community.

By five o'clock there were no fires left alight in Dundargue. The rain, pouring down the wide, old-fashioned chimneys, had put them all out. Kirsten boiled a kettle on one of her oil burners, and Lenny and she had a cup of tea, alternatively watching the mounting waves and the women who now began to creep from their homes and make a bolt for the shop, to buy tinned salmon or sardines for the evening meal, since the usual dish of cooked fish was out of the question.

Little traffic had been observed on the sea-ways since the storm began, except for one or two colliers, wallowing deep in the trough of the waves on the horizon. It was Billy Gatt, who had gone to the extreme point of rock below the headland with his powerful binoculars, who presently came splashing along the cottages crying out that he could see a boat in difficulties off Rosehearty.

Inside the homes of the fishermen white-faced women looked at their husbands and sons and gave thanks that they were safe. No race of men feels the suffering of any of its members so acutely as those who follow the sea. The ocean is the great leveller, and the nationality or creed of its victims means nothing to their rescuers. The sensation of thankfulness, so immediate and so natural to the womenfolk, was quickly followed by a general sense of impotence. All the able-bodied men, pulling on their oilskins, ran out on the rocks after Billy Gatt, some with binoculars, some with their naked eyes straining to catch a glimpse of the labouring vessel, which their leader pronounced to be a steamer and a foreigner.

Kirsten, who had been tramping up and down the kitchen in growing excitement, suddenly turned on Lenny.

"I'm goin' out to see what's doin'," she said. "Put on your uncle's oilskin and come wi' me."

Lenny gave one glance at the streaming rain and turned to obey. Kirsten's tone brooked no refusal. Clumsy in the stiff coat and sou'wester, she watched her mother pull on an old raincoat and wrap her red shawl tightly round her head and throat. They went out, bending before the storm, and to Lenny's surprise her mother, instead of making for the knot of men on the rocks, turned up the sea-road. To Lenny's inquiring pull on her sleeve she screamed above the sea, "I'm goin' up on Quarry Head itsel'—get the best view—" The wind carried away the rest.

At the angle of the cliff Kirsten left the path, and began climbing by a "rabbit's roadie" hidden in the grass. It was a gruelling short cut, and Lenny began to resent her city years as she panted after her mother, whose thin and agile body made the ascent without a symptom of distress. . . .

49

When they gained the cliff top they stood clinging to each other for a moment, demoralized by the weight of the wind against them, and then Kirsten, bending almost double, strode on to the farthest point of the promontory, while Lenny close behind her began to dread that a powerful gust would dash them both to the rocks below. But the rain fell in torrents and the seas beat vehemently upon the shore, and Kirsten Gordon stood with head erect, the ends of the red shawl streaming on the gale.

She had brought David's spy-glass in the pocket of her raincoat; a heavy, brass-bound thing which their father had used, and it was said his father before him. One of their few heirlooms, its antiquity made it all the less manageable, and it was Lenny who finally got it in focus and put it to her eye.

In the wavering circle she saw the disabled steamer, plunging and drifting eastward of Rosehearty. When she shrieked this news, Kirsten took the glass away with little ceremony, and presently cried out:

"Oh me, what a job on the poor chaps! She's come by some mischief, and she's runnin' doon on Pitullie Briggs—whaur Dag Larsen's ship was lost—"

Lenny nodded at her vigorously. The shipwreck on Pitullie Briggs was as familiar to her as her own name.

"—And if she clears Pitullie she has Kinnaird Head afore her. His steerin' gear'll be a' ca'ed to hell," said Kirsten; and then, "Sorra tak' ye, Rosehearty! Ye're comin' between me and the bonny boat—"

It was true. When Lenny took the glass again the vessel had disappeared from sight. From east to west there was nothing more to be seen in the glass than she could see with her eyes: the red roofs of Rosehearty, the cliffs of Dundargue, and the headlands of Pennan and Troup all obscured by the waterfall of the rain.

Kirsten led the way downhill. Billy Gatt was waiting for them at the foot of the path, his brown face set in harsh lines.

"Did ye see her, Mistress Gordon?" he began in the fisher sing-song of excitement. "Woe's me the day that I sud hae to stand and see a pretty ship go down and nae could lift a hand to help her!"

"Eh, Billy ma man," cried Kirsten, "you and a' the lads would ha' saved her if you could, we a' ken that. And wha can tell but her skipper will get his steerin' sortit in time to keep her aff the rocks?"

"If he disna," said Billy, walking with them to their door, "then I hope the lads in the Fraserburgh Lifeboat are standin' by. They'll be sore needed soon, or there'll be wives and mothers in some foreign port will curse the saxteenth o' July. . . ."

When David returned at eight o'clock, after the rain had subsided to a drizzle, he found Kirsten sitting moodily over the revived fire, and Lenny presumably at work. She came through to greet her uncle, and ask if he had any news of the wreck which according to the post office intelligence service had taken place on Kinnaird Head.

But David had passed the hours of storm in the Fraserburgh public houses, and was in that state of recovery which demands strong tea as its first necessity.

"As fou' as the Baltic," said Kirsten aside to Lenny. It was an exaggeration. Tea and a square meal proved highly restorative, and David was able to light his pipe and, with no more than an occasional word slurred or omitted give his women folk the story of the wrecked ship.

She was a Norwegian, the *Oslo*, with a load of timber for Aberdeen, and her steering gear, as Kirsten surmised, had been damaged in the storm which then drove her on the grim rocks of Buchan. She had survived Pitullie Briggs, but bore down helplessly on Kinnaird Head, and the Fraserburgh Lifeboat had been ordered out. In this crisis it was discovered that one of the lifeboatmen had fallen off a shed and broken his arm that very morning, and when the captain called for a volunteer to take his place no one was at first willing to venture. Then a man who had been talking to some of the idlers at the harbour came forward and said he could row.

"He wis some sort o' a foreigner," said David. "A German, or a Dutchman, or a Norwegian himsel' maybe. Big strappin' chiel. And my God, he could row. The lifeboat capsized when they launched her and he come up lauchin' an' shakin' the watter frae his hair like a dog. So they hung in, and when the ship struck they got a' the crew aboard, and the skipper had even managed to bring aff his papers. Na, dam't, he must ha' been a Norwegian, for they say he was able to bleather and speak to the lads in their ain language, and helped the port missionary to gie them hot drinks while he was standin' runnin' wi' watter himsel'. And then when a' was bye, Geordie Shangie tellt me, he jist seemed to disappear. I would ha' liket to shak' him by the hand."

"Od, sae would I!" cried Kirsten, with bright eyes. "What a hero! That's the kind o' lad I like! Where had he come from, I wonder?"

Speculation on the stranger kept them talking over the fire for another hour. But about half-past nine, when the kitchen was almost completely dark, they were startled by a sudden crash.

"Something in the parlour!" said Lenny, and lighting a candle, they hastened through to find that the portrait of David's father-in-law had fallen to the floor.

"Eh, what an ill omen!" cried Kirsten. "Man, Dauvit, I hope it disnae mean ye're taken for death."

"Eh, lass, I dinna like it—I dinna like it!" stammered the old man, while Lenny looked from one to the other in amazement.

"Good heavens, mother!" she said, "you can't attach any significance to this.

The cord was rotten—look at it—it's as old as the hills. It was bound to give way sometime. It doesn't mean a thing."

But the brother and sister refused to be comforted. The strong superstitious streak in the fisher nature had gained the upper hand, and all they had learned of freits and fancies in their childhood came back to torment them.

The death watch, the tap on the pane, the falling picture, all explicable by natural phenomena, to them were intimations from the other world. Even when they were back by the fire again and Kirsten had made some whisky toddy to put heart into them, Lenny perceived that her mother, quite undismayed by the fury of the elements, was unmanned by the fraying of a cord. . . .

Suddenly she lifted her head.

"Hearken!" she said.

In the utter blackness and silence of the night a foot-step was approaching the cottage. A footstep that hesitated as if its owner were uncertain of the way, and then came on again. Kirsten, with chilling heart, stood up and put her chair between her and the door.

Her fear infected David and Lenny. They too looked up in wonder and alarm. A heavy breath was heard snuffing outside the door, which had been left slightly ajar. While they watched, it slowly opened to admit a shaggy head, in which gleamed two red-rimmed eyes.

"God preserve us!" shrieked Kirsten. "it's the Enemy himself!"

"Mother, it's only a dog!" said Lenny. A huge St. Bernard stood in the room before them. Simultaneously a loud knock fell upon the doorstep and against the yawning cavern of the night and the sea they saw a tall man, whose powerful body was clothed in a fisherman's blue serge and guernsey, and whose fair hair rose crisply from a brown and smiling face.

The stranger made a formal bow.

"My name is Larsen," he began, and was interrupted by a gasp, as Kirsten fell back on Lenny's arm in the first and last faint of her life.

CITY, TOWN AND VILLAGE

City, Town and Village

ABERDEEN IN 1661

James Gordon of Rothiemay Description of Both Touns of Aberdeen

Aberdeen exceeds not onlie the rest of the tounes of the north of Scotland but lykeways any citie whatsoever of that same latitude for greatness, bewtie and frequencie of trading. The air is temperat and healthful about it, and it may be that the citizens owe the acuteness of their wits thereunto, and their civil inclinations, the lyke not easie to be fund under so northerlie climats, damped for the most part with air of a grosse consistence. . . .

The buildings of the toune are of stone and lyme, rigged above, covered with slaits, mostly of three or four storeys high, some of them higher. The streets are all neatly paved with flint stone, or a grey kind of hard stone not unlike to flint. The dwelling houses are cleanly and beautiful and neat both within and without, and the syde that looks to the street mostly adorned with galleries of timber, which they call forestairs. Many houses have their gardings and orchards adjoining; every garding has its posterne and these are planted with all sorts of trees which the climat will suffer to grow, so that the quholl toune, to such as draw near it . . . looks as if it stood in a garding in a little wood. . . .

Upon the east syd of the citie and of Futtie there lyes many fair fields, fruitfull of corns, quheat, beir, oats and pot herbs and roots. These are marched by fields near the sea syde callit the Lynks. The Lynks extend themselves almost betwixt the two rivers of Done and Dee. Here the inhabitants recreat themselves with severall kinds of exercises, such as foot ball, golfe, bouling and archerie. Here lykewise they walk for their health. Next to this is the sea shore, plain and sandy, where at low water there is bounds for horse races no less than two mylls of lenthe.

ABERDEEN

Lewis Grassic Gibbon *Scottish Scene*

Bleakness, not meanness or jollity, is the keynote to Aberdonian character, not so much lack of the graces or graciousness of existence as lack of colour in either of these. And this is almost inevitable for anyone passing his nights and days in The Silver City by the Sea. It is comparable to passing one's existence in a refrigerator. Aberdeen is built, largely and incredibly, of one of the most enduring and indestructible and appalling building-materials in use on our planet—grey granite.

It has a flinty shine when new—a grey glimmer like a morning North Sea, a cold steeliness that chills the heart. Even with weathering it acquires no gracious softness, it is merely starkly grim and uncompromising. The architect may plan and build as he will with this material—with its variant, white granite, he may rear the curvetting spires and swooping curlecues and looping whirlimagigs of Marischal College—and not escape that sense of one calamitously in jail. Not only are there no furbelows possible in this architecture, there is amid it, continually, the uneasy sense that you may not rest here, you may not lounge, you cannot stand still and watch the world go by. . . . Else presently the warders will come and move you on.

To know that feeling in its full intensity the investigator must disregard the publicity posters and visit Aberdeen in November. Whatever the weather as his train crossed from Kincardineshire into Aberdeenshire, he will arrive at Aberdeen Station in sleet. Not falling sleet or drifting sleet, but *blown* sleet— blown with an infernal and unescapable persistence from all points of the compass, from the stretches of the harbour, from the Duthie Park, down Market Street. And through this steely pelt he will see the tower and lour and savage grimace of the grey granite all about him, curdling his nerve centres even as the sleet curdles his extremities. If he holds by Guild Street and Market Street up to the pride of Aberdeen, Union Street, he will discover how really vocal this materialization of an Eskimo's vision of hell may become. Aberdeen is, without exception, the most exasperatingly noisy city in the world. Paris is bad—but one accepts Paris, it is free, it is anarchistic, the cabmen are trying to kill each other—a praise-worthy pursuit—and Citröens were made by devils in hell and manned by chauffeurs from purgatory—and it is all very amusing. But Aberdeen is not amusing in its epitome, Union Street. This street is paved with granite blocks, and over these, through the sleeting downpour, trams rattle, buses thud, and (unescapable) four large iron-wheeled drays hauled by Clydesdale horses are being drawn at break-neck speed. There is no amusement in the thought of the drivers being killed: you can see in each gaunt, drawn face that the driver is doing it not for pleasure or the fun of life or because he is joyously and righteously drunk—he is doing it to support a wife, five children, a blind grandmother, and a sister in the Aberdeen Infirmary.

Aberdeen is the cleanest city in Britain: it makes you long for good, wholesome dirt, littered roadways and ramshackle buildings leaning in all directions, projecting warm brown sins and rich smutty reds through an enticing, grimy smile. Union Street has as much warmth in its face as a dowager duchess asked to contribute to the Red International Relief. If you escape the trams and the drays and the inferno where Market Street debouches on Union Street, and hold west up Union Street, you will have the feeling of one caught in a corridor of the hills. To right and left tower the cliffs, scrubbed, immaculate and unforgiving. Where Union Terrace breaks in upon Union Street there is an attempt at a public Garden. But the flowers come up and take one glance at the lour of the solicitors' offices which man Union Terrace, and scramble back into the earth again, seeking the Antipodes.

BUILDING A CITY

Alastair Mackie "My Grandfather's Nieve"
Lallans (no. 5, 1975)

Whit did ye bigg, granda? The sillert mansions o Rubislaw and Mannofield; the twistit crunny* and orra stink o Crooked Lane, the brookit* tenements o Black's Buildings, the Denburn, the Gallowgate, East North Street and West North Street . . . the offices and shops and banks o the toun's steery hert, its mile-lang monument to the grey skinkle* and mica een o the quarry-hole, a pavit river that took the jossle and stour o fowk and traffic aa bent on their ain ploys. . . .

Granite for Edward the Seventh's statue, the fat clort, wi the doos' shite on his brou. Ahint it, auld deen men in ruggity duds* and tint een, and dowie-faced trails o weemin hunched in a half circle like a bourach* o the damned. Granite for Union brig wi its metal lions black and kenspeckle; and aneth them, the

crunny opening   *brookit* shabby   *skinkle* glitter   *ruggity duds* rags
bourach group

steam trains wheezled and shunted or skirled hame to the Jint Station wi the reek rippit aff the funnels. And O ye could staun at the ither side and watch the lift breist back aa the buildins, and see Torry clim up the hill on the shouthers o its tenements. And the croods that hotched ower thon brig. . . .

Or were ye in Canada when the Marishal gaed up, oor Kremlin to college lear, and made aa the weather-cocks jealous? The masons' hemmers dung oot reels and strathspeys on the keys o granite squares and the bumbazed★ steen spieled★ fae the foonds★. Its tormentit diamant bleezed grey in the wink o its million een; and abeen aa, wee gowd-yella pennants were stuck like a stray notion at the hinner-end, never to flame in ony wind that blew. . . .

A year or twa back the quarry stoppit for good. Nae mair the hubber and rattle-stanes o the muckle crusher; nae mair the dirlin birr o the dreels; nae mair the grey smoor o stew; nae mair the blondin's pulley-wheels breel★ on their iled road ower yon howkit hole. . . .

bumbazed astonished   *spiel* climb   *foond* foundation   *breel* move swiftly

THE KING'S BIRTHDAY RIOT

William Robbie *The Heir of Glendornie*

It was on the 4th June, in the year 1802, that Andrew Gilmour, along with his sister, found themselves entering the town by the Gallowgate, which was then the main entrance to the city from that part of the country in which Inverburn was situated. The town did not wear its usual quiet aspect, but seemed to be in an unwonted state of bustle and confusion. The narrow street was littered with articles of furniture, chiefly of an old and dilapidated description. Heaps of chaff lay burning at the head of every close, emitting a most disagreeable odour, and the street round about each of these smoking heaps was generally strewed with old shoes, tin pans, minus their bottoms, broken bottles, and such like useless rubbish. Occasionally the sharp report of some sort of firearm was heard, sometimes close at hand and again more distant, relieved at intervals by the explosion of a squib or the detonating reports of a "cracker".

Until these indications that something unusual was going on were observed, it had not occurred to our friend the merchant that the 4th of June was the anniversary of the birth of His Most Gracious Majesty George III, who then ruled over these realms; and, in addition to this, that the same day was (as indeed it still is) what is locally known as the annual "flitting term".

The stabling at which the merchant usually put up was in the Schoolhill, and, arrived there, Betty descended from the cart and began to discuss with her brother the order of business.

"I micht hae had as muckle rumgumption aboot me," said the merchant, "as mindet 'at this was the King's birthday, an' defarr't comin't the toon till the morn, but I never had a bit mind o' sic a thing till we cam't the Gallowgate heid; I doot this winna be a gweed day for business."

"The toon seems to be in a terrible steer," said Betty, "But I suppose a' the chops 'ill be open as uswal. Nyod, there's nae muckle fear but we'll get plenty o' fouk t' deal wi's when we come wi' the bawbees in oor han', which we ey dee; an' as for the stockin' merchan', I'm sure I've heard ye say yersel' 'at there was fyou fouk stack closer t' the back o'the coonter than auld 'greasy moggins' did."

"Wisht, wisht, 'oman!" said the merchant, "Dinna speak that gate here. Though the auld wives about Inverburn sometimes speak in that disrespectfu menner aboot Maister Moggins, it disna become you nor me t' dee't. Nae doot the man has his waik pints, like the rest o's, but he's a vera uppish man, mind ye, an' ane o' the magistrats o' the ceety forbye. I 'sure ye, Baillie Moggins is a man o' great importance in Aiberdeen, an' nae to be lichtlie spoken o'."

"Far be't fae me t' lichtlifee the man," she said. "Naething was forder fae my min'. A' 'at I meant t' say was, 'at fatever micht be adee, an' fa-ever micht be oot o' the road, ye wad be likely to get him at 's post as uswal."

"Weel, if it had been ony ither day than the ane it is," he replied, "I daursay we micht 'a reckon't on gettin' 'im; but bein', as I said, ane o' the baillies, I doot he'll hae ither things till atten' till—things o' mair importance than takin' in hose an' gi'en oot worsit." The magistrates of these days were loyal "to the backbone", as we say, but on the principle, we suppose, that men are never more liberally disposed than when they can be generous at another man's expense, or dip their hands into the public purse, so, on no occasion was the loyalty of the Aberdeen Magistracy more prominent than when it took the form of consuming large quantities of liquors, and solids as well—the latter in the shape of "partan claws" and such like dainties—the cost of the whole being, as a matter of course, defrayed out of the Guild Wine Fund, a benefaction which the hospitality of a former age has provided for this special purpose. On the King's birthday they kept open table in the Town-Hall from morn to eve, feasting themselves, and as many of their cronies or of the leading citizens as chose to drop in to drink the King's health.

It was the knowledge of this fact that made our friend, Andrew Gilmour, so dubious about being able to see Baillie Moggins, for he knew that, if once the hospitalities of the Town-Hall had fairly commenced, there would be but small chance of his being able to do any business with him on that particular day. Accordingly, he lost no time in making his way to the Baillie's premises, which were situated in what was known as the Narrow Wynd, a street or lane which then existed opposite the foot of the Broadgate. The houses on the south side of the Wynd stood in the centre of what now forms part of Union Street, but instead of the present wide and magnificent street, there was at that part but a mere lane, in which it was almost impossible for two carts to pass, although it was, even at that early period, the busiest part of the town. As our friend had jaloused, the Baillie was not to be seen, and the only representative left on the premises was a raw looking youth, an apprentice, who, if he could have had his own way, would have locked the door and gone with the rest to see the "fairlies", but his master might return at any moment, and, as he was a strict disciplinarian, such a proceeding was not to be thought of.

"Is the maister aboot han'?" inquired Andrew Gilmour, as he entered the shop.

"Na, he's nae in enoo," replied the youth.

"Hae ye ony idea fan I cud see 'im?"

"Cudna say," was the answer. "He may be in in a wee whillie, an' he mayna be in again the day ava."

"Dear me, I dinna ken weel hoo I'm t' dee than. Ken ye faur he is, if it be a fair question?"

"I suppose he's roon aboot the Chaumer some wye. It's nae mony meenits sin' he gaed oot. Geordie Turra, the toon's offisher, cam' for 'im, saying' 'at the Provost an' ithers war a' conveen't i' the Toon-Hall, an' war waitin' for 'im; so he threw a'thing at's heels an' gaed aff withoot sayin' a word aboot fan he was t' be back, or onything."

"It's an awfu' pity 'at I wasna here a whillie earlier," said the other. "Hooever, I hae twa-three ither bits o' gates t' gang an' I'll leuk in again. If he comes in ye'll tell 'im 'at I'm i' the toon wi' ma hose, an' he kens'at I maun see 'im if it's possible ava."

There were great doings in Aberdeen that day. The weather was fine, and it was a gala day for all the community. The bells rung forth a merry peal; flags fluttered in the breeze on every point of vantage; certain of the trades walked in procession, carrying aloft the insignia of their different crafts; the "Sillerton loons" proceeded to the Cross, where they sang "God Save the King"; and the soldiers fired a *feu de joi*, finishing up with such ringing cheers as made the welkin ring again.

The day passed away rapidly, and Andrew Gilmour had called at the Narrow Wynd more than once in the hope of finding his man, before he succeeded in doing so. At length, about four in the afternoon he called again. He had not appeared, but, as good luck would have it, just as our friend was standing at the counter reflecting on the awkwardness of having to stay in town till next day, the Baillie walked into the shop.

In personal appearance Baillie Moggins had a short, dumpy figure, and there was but little character in his features. His nose was large, but of no particular shape, the lips were prominent, and his rubicund complexion led one to conclude that he lived well. His face was clean shaven, but he wore a wig which was slightly powdered, in accordance with the prevailing custom of the time.

The appearance of this wig was somewhat peculiar. There was no "shed", or parting of the hair, but, taking the crown as a centre, the whole hair radiated from it in even lines to cover the head, so that in front it came straight forward to the brow and temples, and the only relief to its uniform smoothness was that, above the forehead, a small tuft was turned up like a drake's tail. On a particular occasion like the present, he was dressed, of course, in black, with a white neck-cloth, and his shirt-front was set off by a carefully-dressed ruffle.

The Baillie was a bachelor, and his character might be broadly stated in two sentences—He gave close personal attention to every department of his business and he had awfully high notions of the dignity and importance of the office which he held as one of the magistrates of the city. But truth compels us to add that he was very illiterate; his education had never been carried further than a decent acquaintance with the three "R's", and he always spoke in the broadest dialect of the city of his habitation. It might be considered an impertinence in humble chroniclers like ourselves to say that the Baillie was "fou" when he entered the shop, but, to put it mildly, he had, as the song says, "a wee drap in his e'e", which had the effect of making his manner a little more cordial than usual, and of bringing out in a very marked degree the sense of importance he entertained of his official dignity.

"Gled t'see ye, Maister Gilmour," he said, as he shook our friend warmly by the hand, "Hoo's a' wi' ye, man?"

"I canna compleen," the merchant responded, "I houp ye're weel?"

"Fine, thank ye, but jist terrible ta'en up wi' public business. A' the big fouk fae far an' near hae been at the Toon's Hoose the day, an'ye see his at's in office maun be there to coontenance them."

"I wid think", said the merchant, "'at the like o' that wid be a terrible fash t' ye, an' an awfu' hinner t' business forbye."

"An' sae it is, but we canna help that. Place an' pooer ey bring duties and responsibilites alang wi' them. On a day o' this kin' we maun be loyal, my dear sir, we maun be loyal subjec's. Hoo can we expec' the commonality t' be that unless their rowlers show them the gweed example?"

The King's birthday riot

"Weel, I wid hardly hae thocht 'at there was sic a close connection atween ae man's loyalty an' anither man's eatin' an' drinkin'. Hooever, what I'm maist concerned aboot enoo is whether ye can spare me an hoor t' pit behan' my little bit o' business, an' lat me awa' hame."

"Impossible, Maister Gilmour. Quite impossible, my dear sir. What wye d'ye think 'at a man in *my* position cud hae convainience t' gang o'er a big bundle o' hose at a time like this? I'm jist gaen awa't'—"

"But if ye wid only begin", said the other interrupting him, "ye wid manage a' it's t' dee i' the time at we're stan'in here speakin' aboot it."

"Hae patience, man. Hae patience, an' hear me oot. I'm jist gaen awa' o'er bye this meenit till an entertainment 'at we're t' gie t' the offishers fae the barricks— fine hearty chiels they are, I's assure you—an' in fac' I only leukit in t'tell the laddie here t' pit on the shutters an' lock up, 'cause, towards evenin', the crood's ill for gettin' some ootstreepolis kin', an' they micht tak' it in t' their heids to brak some o' ma lozens."*

"Hoot fye!" exclaimed the merchant, "nae, an' you a Baillie. That wid be bit a sorry return for the gweed example o' loyalty 'at ye've been showin' them the day."

"Baillie or no Baillie," said the other, "feint a hair wid they care, I suppose, if they got the chance. But we've sworn in a lot o' special constables, an' depen' upon't we'll see 'at the peace is keepit. I'se wauger we'll lat them a' ken at the Magistrats o' Aiberdeen dinna beir the swoord in vain."

"Weel, but it'll pit me terrible aboot if I canna win awa' the nicht", said the merchant, "an' what mak's't mair awkward still is 'at ma sister's i' the toon wi'ma, so that things are leeft in a gey heedless kin o' a wye at hame. Only, if it maun be, it maun be—that's a' 'at can be said aboot it."

"Toots, never think on't man," said the Baillie, "it's only ae nicht, an' as seen's ye like after brakfast time the morn I'll be ready for ye. Man, when ye're here at onyrate, it wid be a pity to loss the opportunity o' seein' what's t' be seen. Forbye the shottin' an' the squeebs, and the crackers, an' the Roman caunles, the on-gaens aboot the Plainstanes i' the evenin' are aften rael amusin'. Ye'll jist bide an' see the fun."

"Though we dee bide," said the merchant, "I think we'll be as wise t' keep gey weel oot o' the road. It sometimes happens 'at a crood o' thochtless haivrells* are nae ower ceevil t' quintra bodies at a time like this."

"Weel, leuk here noo," said the Baillie, "I can tak'ye oot o' that diffikweltie tee. I'll gie orders t' John Home till accommodate ye baith wi' seats at ane o' the Toon Hoose windows, faur ye'll see a' 'at gangs on withoot the possibility o' ony

lozen window   *haivrell* idiot

62

annoyance fae the crood. Noo, noo, I maun rin", he continued, "gweed-bye t' ye, enoo. Ye see what it is t' hae dealin's wi' a magistrat—t' hae a frien' at coort, as we say." So saying, Baillie Moggins hurried off to the magisterial symposium, and Andrew Gilmour went to find his sister, and to inform her that they could not leave the town that night.

★   ★   ★

When Andrew Gilmour told his sister that Baillie Moggins had kindly offered to get them seated at one of the windows of the Town Hall that evening, in order that they might see the fairlies, she said it was "rael kind o' the carle t' think o' t", and she urged her brother to avail himself of the offer, which he agreed to do, though with some reluctance, and chiefly on his sister's account, for he himself felt quite indifferent in the matter. About seven o'clock, therefore, they made their way to the place indicated. On enquiring for John Home, they found that the Baillie had been as good as his word, and had paved the way for them, so that they were at once accommodated with seats at the eastmost window on the first floor, immediately adjoining the old Tolbooth. Although John was somewhat taciturn in his disposition, especially towards strangers, yet under the stimulating influence of the good cheer of which he had freely partaken in common with his betters, even he was disposed to be talkative. Having accompanied them into the room, he remarked, "Baillie Moggins said ye wid likely be along aboot this time, an' he tell't me t' pit ye in here. . . . "

A large crowd of young and thoughtless lads had assembled in Castle Street, who were indulging in the noisy demonstrations usual on such occasions. A temporary guard-house for the accommodation of a party of soldiers stood at the east end of the Plainstones, the regiment then stationed in Aberdeen being a Highland Militia corps, known as the Ross and Cromarty Rangers. The Magistrates were carousing with the officers in the Town-Hall, the windows of which were open, and, as the different toasts were honoured with the cheers of the revellers within, a volley of musketry was fired by a detachment of the military without.

This was all very well, and our friends were rather enjoying the fun, till some young blackguard had actually the hardihood to throw a burning squib in at the open window at which they were seated. The missile struck Betty Gilmour on the side of the head and fell hissing on the floor, where it exploded with a loud crack.

She started up in the utmost alarm, exclaiming—"Mercy me! I'm shot."

"Faur about?" cried her brother in some trepidation.

"Richt throw the heid, I do believe," she answered.

"I doot if that was the case", he replied, feeling much relieved, "ye widna be able t' tell's sae weel aboot it! An' yet, what div I see?" he continued, "reek risin' fae the side o' yer heid. Turn aboot 'oman, till I see what's the maitter."

A hasty examination showed that Betty's mutch had been set on fire, and that already a big hole had been burned in it. Other than the fright, this was all the harm the worthy woman had received, but, though it was a small matter, she was very angry about it, and described the act as a "piece o' daurin' impidence". "The mair sae", she added, "at sic a thing sud be deen jist at the vera lug o' the law, an ' as ye micht say, ooner the vera noses o' the magistrats assembled i' their nain Toon-Ha'."

"Weel, weel", said her brother soothingly, "say naething mair aboot it, 'oman, say naething mair aboot it—it micht hae been a hantle waur."

At an earlier period of the evening a large party of roughs made a rush down Marischal Street to the Shore, with cries of "A boat, a boat"—their intention being to seize the first boat they could lay their hands on and drag it up to the Castlegate, there to make a bonfire of it. At that time there was no Quay wall but a flat sandy bank on which a number of boats were usually drawn up, but as such an attack had been expected as quite a usual occurrence, the owners of the boats had mustered in considerable strength for the purpose of protecting their property, and after a sharp encounter they succeeded in beating back their assailants.

Foiled in their attempt to bring up a boat, the crowd returned to Castle Street in a still more mischievous mood. A good deal of glass was broken, and every respectable person who had occasion to pass was pelted with whatever of the nature of filthy garbage the mob could lay their hands on. Any attempt at remonstrance only made matters worse, and the only hope of escape was to disappear as quickly as possible.

The soldiers in the guard-house came in for a large share of these polite attentions, which had the effect of producing an exceedingly hostile feeling on their part towards the rabble, a feeling which was destined to find fatal expression before the close of the day's proceedings. About eight o'clock the officers descended from the Town Hall to the street, and it was evident that some of them were very drunk, the Colonel of the regiment in particular being so far gone as to be unable to keep his feet, so that before he was taken in charge by some of the others, who were more sober, he fell several times amid the shouts and laughter of the mob. It was only what might have been expected, that this state of matters should attract the almost undivided attention of the crowd, who at once began to level their jibes and insults at the gentlemen in uniform, who, by their too free circulation of the bottle, were making ridiculous fools of themselves in the public street.

Accordingly, the mob began to bespatter the officers with mud—the poor Colonel was bullied by a man-of-war sailor, who shook his fist in his face, and, with a profane oath, told him that he had served his king and country, and done a great deal more for them than the Colonel had done. At the same moment, as if to bring this insulting procedure to a climax, some scoundrel threw a dead cat at the Colonel's head, which to say the least, did not improve his personal appearance.

As a riot was now imminent, a junior officer suggested to the Colonel that the guard should be reinforced. "Yes, yes", he hiccupped in reply; "bring down the regiment."

The order was given—the drum beat to arms—the regiment was turned out, and drawn up in line near the east end of the Plainstones, facing the mob.

By this time the Colonel had been conveyed to his quarters, and matters had assumed a most dangerous aspect, when some of the leading citizens interposed and insisted that the soldiers should be drawn off, which, after some parleying, was agreed to by the officer who had taken the command. The order, "right-about-face", was given, and the march towards the barracks was commenced, the mob hooting and howling at their heels. The soldiers were just leaving Castle Street, and passing into the lane leading to the barracks, when a shout of derision was raised by the crowd, and some very insulting epithets made use of, which raised their Highland blood to such a pitch that they could stand it no longer. A voice (it was never known exactly whose it was) was heard to give the order, "Halt—front—charge!" on which they wheeled round and charged the mob along Castle Street with fixed bayonets, and ultimately fired on them. One man was shot dead on the spot, while three others were mortally wounded and died next day. It was a wonder that many more lives were not sacrificed, for the bullets came hurtling along Castle Street, striking the ends of the houses in the Narrow Wynd and Exchequer Row; but it is believed that many of the soldiers intentionally fired over the heads of the people. In all probability there would have been a repetition of this bloody work, had not Provost Hadden, at considerable personal risk, sought out those in command, and, by using both threats and entreaty, induced them to retire to their quarters.

For a few moments after they were fired upon the crowd was paralysed with terror, but recovering from their surprise they surrounded the barracks, hooting and howling like infuriated demons. The gates were closed, however, and nothing more was seen of the gallant Ross and Cromarty Rangers in the "braif toon", for it is currently stated that they took their departure from the city at midnight by unfrequented routes and it is certain that very soon after this they were disbanded. . . .

Between nine and ten o'clock next morning Andrew Gilmour repaired again to Baillie Moggin's shop, for he was now anxious to be off as soon as possible. As if to make up for the loss of the previous day, he found the Baillie already at work.

"Come awa', Maister Gilmour," he said, as our friend entered. "I'm sorry 'at I sud hae deteen't ye i' the toon, but public men canna at a' times suit their ain convainience. I suppose ye saw a' yon serious wark the street,* did ye?"

"Weel, I cudna say," he replied, "at we saw a' thing, but we saw plenty—mair than we expecket t' see, an' things 'at we wid hae far raither nae seen."

"Aye, I believe ye there, frien'. Terrible wark yon, man, terrible wark as ever was heard tell o'. T' think that daicent law-abidin' fowk sud be shot deid i' the public street; the like never happen't afore, an' I canna oonerstan' for the life o' me what wye it happen't the streen."

"Beggin' yer pardon, Baillie," said the merchant. "I canna help thinkin' 'at the magistrats were a gweed bit t'blame for 't themsells."

"Foo man? What wye d'ye mak that oot?"

"O, just 'at ye war o'er free wi' the drink. Sen'in' fouk oot t' the street hardly able t' haud a fit, an' the vera men tee 'at sud hae had a' their wits aboot them, an' been ready t'pit doon ony mischief 'at wis likely t' happen."

"Weel, I believe there was some o' the offishers gey far gone, but *we* didna force the drink on them. Nae doot there was plenty a-gaen, as there behoved t' be when the Lord Provost an' magistrats o' a Ceety like this war the enterteeners, but there was nae compulsion on ony man t' tak mair than was gweed for 'im."

"Bit still, ye see," insisted the merchant, "that a sort o'brings the blame hame t' your door."

"Weel, weel, the less 'at's said aboot that the better, maybe, bit didna the Provost behave nobly noo? Man, if it hadna been for what he did immedently aifter the firin' yon wid hae been bit the beginnin' o' the mischeef."

"Fatever he did," said the merchant, "it wid hae been mair t' the purpose surely if it had been deen afore the firin'. It was gey like steikin' the stable door aifter the steed was stown. But what was't 'at he did?"

"Man, he jist gaed richt in afore the baignets, an' teuk haud o' the muckle Heilan' sergean' 'at was leadin' them on, an' order't 'im t' call aff the sodgers direckly, as he wid be ammenable till his superiors."

"An' wha the teevil are ye?" said the sergeant.

"I'm the Lord Provost o' the City," was the answer, "an' ye must obey my orders."

"Och, her nain sell kens naething apoot Provosts," said the fellow. "Faur's her commission?"

the streen yesterday night

"Syne the Provost teuk oot his goold chyne an' badge o' office, an', Hielan' cataran though he was, the man kent at ance 'at *that* representit a pooer 'at daurna be triflet wi', so he turned his men t' the richt aboot, an' made aff as quickly's possible. A' his 'at's magistrates," continued the Baillie, "have a chyne an' badge o' the same kind. Did ever I happen t' lat ye see the ane 'at I hae, Maister Gilmour?"

"No, I dinna think ye ever did."

"'Od, that's a won'er noo,' he said, "but ye sanna hae that t' say again, for here it is see; I ey cairry 't upo' me," and, with a feeling of gratified vanity, he undid the strings of his apron, took off the gold chain and appendage, and placed it in Andrew Gilmour's hand. "Jist fin' ye the waucht o' *that* noo," he said, very proudly, "there's a gey vailue o' gowd there. The Provost's is just the same, but a wee bitty bigger, an' some mair variorums upon 't. Weel," he continued, "ilka man 'at's made a baillie, is investit wi' a chyne like that, an' it's a symbol o' the pooer o' the ceevil magistrate, t' which Holy Writ assigns a vera high place, as nane kens better than yersell, Maister Gilmour, for he sud be a terror t' evil doers, an a' praise an' protection t' such as do weel."

"Aye, *should* be"—said the merchant, "only there's a gey difference atween what sud be, an' what is. But we needna be takin' up time discussin' *that*."

PEACOCK'S CLOSE

John R. Allan *Northeast Lowlands of Scotland*

Nothing remains of the medieval Aberdeen except the ground plan of the older streets. That is not for surprise, because houses were built of wood and clay, with thatched roofs: and what fire did not destroy, weather decayed. Temporary houses are no new thing in Scottish towns. None of the public buildings remain. The Kirk of St Nicholas had to be rebuilt, the Greyfriars and the Blackfriars were removed, and the remote past has gone as if it had never been. There is not now much left from the sixteenth and seventeenth centuries, except empty spaces along the Shiprow, the Guestrow and the Gallowgate, and to the north of Castlehill whence in my own time the houses of the old merchants were swept away as slums. And what slums they were. Shuttle Lane and Peacock's Close were tremendous places forty years ago. Their names were names to conjure with, and conjure is the word, for some of the women who lived in them were as near like witches as latter-day mortals could be.

I remember well those fearful citizens. When I was five or six and thereabout my grandfather grew perhaps ten or fifteen acres of potatoes every year. Then, as now, potatoes were lifted by casual labour—and our casual workers were the dragons of Peacock's Close and Shuttle Lane. A dozen of them came out every morning in two taxis, driven furiously by men in fear of their honour, and even of their lives. They got, as I remember, danger money for the job. The women were of all ages, but they had some things in common—high, tearing voices; a vocabulary limited in everything except scolding, swearing and obscenity, but in these it would have been a lexicographer's manna from heaven; their clothes were old and various and stank, and there were very, very natural after their fashion. Every morning there was a tremendous row before they started work; a great screaming from them, a great swearing in a rude baritone from my uncle Charles; the whole thing working up to a climax in the rudest gestures of final contempt. Then some older and wiser woman said, "It's time I had ma mornin'," and produced a bottle of whisky from out of her petticoats, and others did the same and passed them round till everybody had had their mornin' and the work proceeded, and proceeded happily all day, with much conversation of the directer kind. As a little boy of five or six or seven I loved them all very much. Now and then at the break time, some woman would cry "Daena dae that" or "Daena say that in front o the bairn", but I couldn't see what the fuss was about, for everything they said and did was exciting, just as the burns were exciting when they were in spate. Sometimes an old harridan with whisky on her breath and the smell of immemorial filth on her clothes took me into her bosie and kissed me and told me about the chamber pots they emptied on the policemen's heads in Shuttle Lane, and that was as good as a fairy-tale from the shores of a resounding sea. One day the foreman, a gallus chield I hated, took some liberty with one of the women at the dinner hour and got his face harrowed with bloody weals.

Great ladies: they were my friends. I had in them confidence, and for them love. Perhaps love of human kind was the only decency left to them. They had that in plenty. And they had a something else that was perhaps truly of Aberdeen. Their week at the potatoes was more than a way of getting some extra money for whisky. They enjoyed it, even when the days were wet and the fields were glaury. They enjoyed being in the country. There was an elderly woman called Meggie, the one who was always first to bring out the cutter, a grey-haired creature, soaked and sodden in whisky, who used on fine, dry days to rub the mealy earth between her hands and say to me, "It's like new meal from the mill." I remember those hands yet, feeling the texture, the sap and the coolness

Alastair Mackie

of the earth. As I discovered a long time after, she came from a farm, had been
seduced and left, had taken her shame to town where it throve and, as they would
have said in those days, completely ruined her. When she could not get whisky
she drank methylated spirit, which makes a dead furnace in the wame, but every
autumn, drawn by a homing instinct, she came out from Shuttle Lane for a short
contact with the sane and fruitful fields. I think that some others came for that
reason, because the heart beat an echo of a country heritage, and the circling
blood hungered for the country air, and the senses for the country sounds and
smells. And perhaps even in Peacock's Close they remembered the harvest, and
in their hearts remembered its ancient wonder, and, even in a time when the
poor were nothing, knew their right in it. The potato-gatherers were well paid
according to the ideas of the time, for my grandfather was always generous with
what he never had; but over and above their pay the women demanded potatoes.
Every night they took home bags and baskets with a stone or two. I would not say
that the potatoes were more to them than the money, and no one would have
dared to pay them entirely in kind, but it seems to me now that the potatoes had
an occult value. To some at least the potato-gathering had an emotional value for
the slum dwellers, reminding them of the country slums from which their people
had come, and giving them for a little while that contact with nature without
which the spirit must wholly die.

TENEMENTS

Alastair Mackie, "My Grandfather's Nieve"
Lallans (no. 5, 1975)

Doun the close and up the stane ootside stairs and intil the unforgettable foosty
stink o the room wi the lie-ins that made the space crubbit,* whaur the furniture
could streek its linth but ye were fair pit till't to get a seat in comfort. O the
nippit livin-rooms o the workin class afore the war! The side-boord and table, the
shewin machine and the ingleside cheers, and the sink aye a sotter of pottit plants
and the leavins o denner-time; the press ablow the sink whaur the pots and pans
were kept in the mirk and the craal o spiders. O aye, and the swan craig* o the

crubbit cramped   *craig* neck

tap. And the sense o a human steer ye couldna redd up. There was the keekin-gless whaur my uncles shaved, twistin sideways to look at their faces as they scythed awa the sapples* fae their chin. Ootby in the simmer aifterneen the trees dandled their greenery on a level wi the sink tap and ye heard the chirr and flaff o the birds, and ever and aye the gaitherin thunder o the trams as they shoogled back and fore fae the toun.

sapples stubble

THE LANE

Jessie Kesson *The White Bird Passes*

Our Lady's Lane; that was what the Monks had called this thoroughfare eight hundred years ago. The name may have fitted it in their time; perhaps it had been a green and cloistered place in those distant days. But, in this Year of Grace 1926, it was no longer green, although it still remained cloistered.

Lady's Lane was a tributary of High Street, one of many such tributaries of long, narrow wynds that slunk backwards from the main street, gathering themselves into themselves, like a group of women assuring each other proudly, "We keep ourselves to ourselves", and, at the same time, usually knowing more than most people of what is going on around.

If you rushed down High Street in a hurry, you wouldn't notice Lady's Lane at all, so narrowly and darkly does it skulk itself away, but Lady's Lane would most certainly see you. At all hours of the day a voluntary look-out lounges against the entrance to the Lane. It may be Poll Pyke, Battleaxe, or the Duchess. For those ladies of the Lane are in some mysterious way self-appointed guardians of the Lane. The Duchess is the supreme guardian of course. Poll Pyke and Battleaxe are merely her faithful henchwomen, competent enough to take over temporary command on those not infrequent occasions when the Duchess is forcibly removed to Barclamp Jail for ten days without the option, and wary enough to step down from office the moment the Duchess's "time" is up.

The less ambitious occupants of the Lane were quite content with this order of things. It meant that they could swipe the bugs from the walls of their sub-lets in peace, in the sure and certain knowledge that, if anything exciting and untoward was taking place in another part of the Lane, they wouldn't miss it; they would receive a clarion call from the Duchess to come and bear witness to such goings on.

Jessie Kesson

Only the children of the Lane were irked by such vigilance. To get up through the Lane unnoticed took on the face of an adventure, and became triumph indeed, if they could reach their own doors without the Duchess confronting them with a pillow-slip, threepence, and a threat: "Run up to Riley's back-door for a stale loaf, tuppence of broken biscuits. And see you that the loaf isna' too stale." Or Annie Frigg trapping them with her tin plate, her persuasive voice, and a promise: "My fine queanie take a runnie down to Lossie Will's for a tanner of herrings. Your legs are younger nor mine. And I've got something for you. A great big ball. All the colours of the rainbow it is. Blue, red, green, and yellow. And there's something else about this ball that I've got. It will never burst. Run on now, for my herrings. That's a queanie!"

And though the Lane's children knew from experience that Annie's promises never came true, they grew up and they grew old before they finally lost their hope that one day Annie Frigg might really give them a ball of all colours that would never burst. . . .

It was Janie's day to be "caught".

"That you, Janie?" Mysie Walsh's voice called to her from across the landing. "Run a message for me, luv?"

Janie needed no second bidding. Doing something for Mysie Walsh brought its own reward, and it wasn't the threepenny bit she always gave you either. She was big and bright and safe. And next to Janie's own Mother, Janie thought her the loveliest woman in the Lane, with a smile that sucked you right into the core of its warmness, and plump arms that caught you and squeezed you when she was excited, and left your small body trembling with something of her own sudden excitement. Sometimes, with a sudden impulse to please the women grouped round the entrance to the Lane, Mysie Walsh would dance to the music coming from the chip shop's gramophone, her petticoats whirling, her garters showing, real and silk, her voice rising above the gramophone; and, like her smile, her voice gathered you right into it, so that her song seemed to come from you, too:

> Yes, I'm goin',
> Yes, I'm goin',
> And soon I'll be hullo-in
> That coal black Mammy of Mine!

In moments like those the Lane became so alive and full of colour to Janie that she felt suddenly and intensely glad for just being alive in a world of song, and colour, and whirling petticoats and warm, dark women like Mysie Walsh.

"What message do you want me to get?" Janie sniffed the room. It smelt, as

71

always, different from all the other rooms in the Lane, of powder and cream and scent, all mixed up together and coming out in one great sweet smell, which Janie thought of as the smell of a woman that's lovely.

"Cheese. A quarter will do, luv."

The request, as much as the tone in which it was requested, aroused Janie from her contemplation of the room. Mysie Walsh lay on top of her bed, her face hidden in the pillow. Janie had never seen Mysie Walsh without her face, dark and laughing. She sensed there was something wrong.

"Have you been taken ill?" she asked the head on the pillow.

"No. Not ill. You'll find money for the cheese on the mantelpiece, or on the table somewhere."

"You're awfully sad, then?"

"Real sad. Hurry, Janie, or you won't catch McKenzie's open."

"Just cheese? Nothing else?"

"Just cheese. Just a quarter. Shut the door behind you."

Cheese. Not like Mysie Walsh's usual messages, Janie thought to herself, as she ran up High Street. Mysie Walsh's messages were usually as delightful as herself. Phulnana from the chemists, a smell of it, a little on your own cheeks, rubbed well in by Mysie Walsh herself, and the promise of the jar to yourself forever and ever when the cream was done. Or a comb from Woolworth's, the brightest one you could find, with gold stars on it, that shone through Mysie Walsh's hair, even when it was tucked away, and her old comb with only some of the teeth out for yourself. Or cream buns, not stale ones either. "And we'll have one with a cup of tea together when you come back, luvie." All the other people in the Lane bought a quarter of cheese, or polony, or a tin of condensed milk. "And tell McKenzie to mark it on the book." But not Mysie Walsh. You never had to get it marked on the book for her, because amongst all her other enchantments, Mysie Walsh also always had money.

Twenty minutes later Janie stood in the Lane debating what to do with the money in her hand. Two shillings. The biggest amount she had ever had. More than Mysie Walsh had ever given her before. "Keep the change, Janie," Mysie Walsh had said, when she delivered the cheese.

"But there's two shillings change," Janie pointed out. "The cheese only cost sixpence, and I took half a crown."

"Keep it," Mysie Walsh had insisted. "Run off now, Janie, and bang the door behind you."

There were so many ways to dispose of two shillings, that Janie couldn't decide on one of them. Hide it away till my Mam's broke and give her a real surprise. Or just give her a shilling and me a shilling. Or don't say a word to anybody at all, and spend it myself. . . .

Up the Lane at 285, Janie contemplated the results of her "luck".

"Mysie Walsh must be doing all right to give you two bob all in a once," her Mother said, through the hairpins in her teeth. "Did you see my side combs anywhere, Janie? Was Mysie Walsh getting ready to go out, did you notice?"

"I don't know." Janie was absorbed in clearing the table to find room for her book. "She hadn't got her curlers in. She was just lying on top of her bed. She looked fed up. There's a new word for meadow, Mam. A Red Indian word. Muskoday. On the muskoday. The meadow. Muskoday. Musk-o-day. It's in this book. It sounds right fine, doesn't it?"

"Was that what you bought with your two bob?" Liza sounded amused.

"And your tobacco!" Janie protested against this forgetfulness. "You are glad about the tobacco, aren't you, Mam?"

"Yes, of course I am. Get a lace out of one of my other shoes, Janie, this damned lace has snapped!"

"You'd hardly any tobacco left, had you, Mam?"

"No, hardly any. Not out of that shoe, Janie! Use your eyes, that's a brown one."

"Your black shoe must be under the bed then. If you'd had one wish, it would have been for tobacco, wouldn't it?"

"Yes, Janie." Liza's voice came slow and quiet and clear. "I'm glad you bought tobacco. I had hardly any left. And if I'd had one wish, it would have been for tobacco. Now. Have you found my shoe?"

The surprise of Mysie Walsh's two bob was over. Dimly Janie realised that her Mother's gladness at getting, just didn't equal her own gladness in giving. . . .

It was Betsy's young Alan, who started the whisper:

"Mysie Walsh's done herself in. Hanged herself. The bobbies are up at 284 now."

"Making a right barney about her being cut down before they got the chance to do it themselves," Betsy added to the information.

"Who cut her down, Son?" Battleaxe demanded like a furious general who had been overlooked, but still had a right to know. "Who was it that cut her down?"

"Chae did. Chae Tastard, with his sharp cobbler's knife."

"Liars!" Janie screamed in a small panic. "She isn't dead. I took cheese to her."

"Yeah?" Betsy's young Alan shot his tongue out at Janie and passed on, anxious to spread all the news to the more important grown-ups. "And do you know what? A bit of cheese was stuck in her mouth when they took the rope off."

Ted Howe, only drunkenly comprehending the news, forced his way through the crowd. "Take my boots off when I die. When I die." And beneath the lamp the Salvationists sang for their own edification:

> Dare to do right.
> Dare to be true.
> God who created you
> Cares for you, too.

For the crowd had deserted them and were following Ted towards the door of Mysie Walsh who was.

MISCHIEF IN GLAMERTON

George MacDonald *Alec Forbes of Howglen*

The spirit of mischief had never been so thoroughly aroused in the youth of Glamerton as it was this winter. The snow lay very deep, while almost every day a fresh fall added to its depth, and this rendered some of their winter-amusements impossible. At the same time the cold increased and strengthened their impulses to muscular exertion.

"Thae loons are jist growin' perfect deevils," said Charlie Chapman, the wool-carder, as he bolted into his own shop, with the remains of a snowball melting down the back of his neck. "We maun hae anither constable to haud them in order."

The existing force was composed of one long-legged, short-bodied, middle-aged man, who was so slow in his motions, apparently from the weight of his feet, which were always dragging behind him, that the boys called him Stumpin' Steenie, and stood in no more awe of him than they did of his old cow—which, her owner being a widower, they called Mrs Stephen—when she went up the street, hardly able to waddle along for the weight of her udder. So there was some little ground for the wool-carder's remark. How much a second constable would have availed, however, is doubtful.

"I never saw sic widdiefows!"* chimed in a farmer's wife who was standing in the shop. "They had a tow across the Wast Wynd i' the snaw, an' doon I cam o'

widdiefow vandal, i.e. one who deserves to be hanged

my niz, as sure's your name's Charlie Chapman—and mair o' my legs oot o' my coats, I doobt, than was a'thegither to my credit."

"I'm sure ye can hae no rizzon to tak' shame o' your legs, gude wife," was the gallant rejoinder; to which their owner replied, with a laugh:

"They warna made for public inspection, ony gait."

"Hoot! hoot! Naebody saw them. I's warran' ye didna lie lang! But thae loons—they're jist past a'! Heard ye hoo they saired Rob Bruce?"

"Fegs! they tell me they a' but buried him alive."

"Ow! ay. But it's a later story, the last."

"It's a pity there's no a dizzen or twa o' them in Awbrahawm's boasom. —What did they till him neist?"

Here Andrew Constable dropped in, and Chapman turned towards him with the question:

"Did *ye* hear, Mr Constable, what the loons did to Robert Bruce the nicht afore last?"

"No. What was that? They hae a spite at puir Rob, I believe."

"Weel, it didna look a'thegither like respeck, I maun alloo.—I was stannin' at the coonter o' his shop waitin' for an unce o' sneeshin'*; and Robert he was servin' a bit bairnie ower the coonter wi' a pennyworth o' triacle, when, in a jiffey, there cam' sic a blast, an' a reek fit to smore ye, oot o' the bit fire, an' the shop was fu' o' reek, afore ye could hae pitten the pint o' ae thoom upo' the pint o' the ither. 'Preserve's a'!' cried Rob; but or he could say anither word, butt the house, scushlin in her bauchles, comes Nancy, rinnin', an' opens the door wi' a scraich: 'Preserve's a'!' quo' she, 'Robert, the lum's in a low!' An' fegs! atween the twa reeks, to sunder them, there was nothing but Nancy hersel. The hoose was as fu' as it cud haud, frae cellar to garret, o' the blackest reek 'at ever crap oot o' coal. Oot we ran, an' it was a sicht to see the crater wi' his lang neck luikin' up at the chimleys. But deil a spark cam' oot o' them—or reek either, for that maitter. It was easy to see what was amiss. The loons had been o' the riggin, and flung a han'fu' o' blastin' powther down ilka smokin' chimley, and syne clappit a divot or a turf upo' the mou' o't. Deil ane o' them was in sicht, but I doobt gin ony o' them was far awa'. There was naething for't but get a ladder, and jist gang up an' tak aff the pot-lids. But eh! puir Robert was jist rampin' wi' rage! No'at he said muckle, for he daur hardly open his mou' for sweerin', and Robert wadna sweer, ye ken; but he was neither to haud nor bin'."

"What laddies war they, Charles, do ye ken?" asked Andrew.

"There's a heap o' them up to tricks. Gin I haena the rheumateese screwin' awa' atween my shoothers the nicht it wonna be their fau'ts; for as I cam' ower

sneeshin' snuff

75

frae the ironmonger's there, I jist got a ba' i' the how o' my neck, 'at amaist sent me howkin' wi' my snoot i' the snaw. And there it stack, and at this preceese moment it's rinnin' doon the sma' o' my back as gin't war a burnie doon a hillside. We maun hae mair constables!''

"Hoot! toot! Charles. Ye dinna want a constable to dry yer back. Gang to the gudewife wi't," said Andrew, "she'll gie ye a dry sark. Na, na. Lat the laddies work it aff. As lang's they haud their han's frae what doesna belang to them, I dinna min' a bit ploy noo and than. They'll no turn oot the waur men for a pliskie* or twa.''

pliskie prank

COUNCILLOR ETTERSHANK

David Grant *Scotch Stories*

The Crimean War had happily come to an end, an' it had done very weel for me, as a general merchant, on the Market Square i' the toon o'Keckleton.

An' here I wud tak' the leeberty to remark that, in a general waye, war does weel for tradesmen like mysel' inasmuch as it enables us to lay on an extra bawbee, or penny, on articles o' sale, arisin' to twenty-five, fifty, or sometimes even a hunner per cent.

For example, a customer wud come in to me, an' something like the followin' conversation wud tak' place in the coorse o'transac':

Customer.—"Gie's a bawbee's worth o' tackets, Mr Ettershank" (Ettershank bein' my name).

Mr E.—"Wi' pleesure" (serving customer).

C. (coontin' tackets).—"Hoo's this, Mr Ettershank? Ye used to gie a dizzen for the bawbee, but there's only nine here!''

Mr E.—"That's quite true; but dae ye no' ken that tackets are up in consequence o' the war?"

C.—"Dear me! is that really the case?"

Mr E.—"Deed is't. There's sic mairchin' an' coonter-mairchin' upon roch roads, an' aften upon nae roads ava, that the airmy cobblers can hardly keep the sodgers' soles frae the grun', an' the tackit mackers, workin' nicht an' day, can barely supply the deman' for tackits."

C.—"Dear me! Weel, I wud never hae thocht o' that" (an' gangs awa weel pleased).

Second Customer.—"A penny can'le, Mr Ettershank."

Mr E.—"Dae ye no'ken that the penny can'les are noo three bawbees, in consequence o' the war?"

C.—"Nonsense! The sodgers are nae fechtin' wi' can'le licht!"

Mr E.—"But they hae to keep watch an' ward through mony a dark an' dismal nicht, an' that canna be dune withoot can'le licht, I'm thinkin'. A fine look oot a camp wud keep for an enemy in the lang nichts o'Crimean darkness, which is sae great that it's aften taen by Milton in *Paradise Lost* to represent the darkness o' the bottomless pit."

C.—"I had nae idea o' that, Mr Ettershank; but ye're just a wonnerfu' man for learnin'" (an' gangs awa' as weel pleased as Customer No. 1).

Third Customer.—"A pun o' yer fourpence saip, Mr Ettershank."

Mr E.—"Wi a' the pleesure in life, mem, I'll gie ye a pun' o' saip; but I hinna an ounce i' the shop at fourpence. The fourpenny saip is up to saxpence in consequence o' the war, mem."

C.—"Hoo's that, noo, Mr Ettershank? I wadna hae thocht that the sodgers wud hae had muckle time for mackin' use o' saip, wi' a' the sair fechtin' that's gaen on at Sawbastapol."

Mr E.—"Saip, mem! There's tons upon tons o' saip used ilka day. The very dragoons, ay, an' their Generals, are at wark like washer-women, keepin' the neebourhood o' Sawbastapol clean, it seems. But here's the paper read for yersel', mem."

C.—"I hinna my glasses upon me, Mr Ettershank. What does it say?"

Mr E. (takin' up the news paper an' glancin' at it).—"Lord Cardigan and his dragoons are daily engaged scouring the suburbs and country for miles around Sebastopol to keep them clear"—stoppin' at—"of the enemy."

C.—"Weel, that beats a'! Mr Ettershank; whatever gars them set the puir lads o' dragoons to sic unusual wark as scourin' the neebourhood o' a toon?"

Mr E.—"O, dootless, to keep doon disease, colera, an' sic like, mem."

C.—"Nae doot, Mr Ettershank, nae doot. I've heerd that colera was something fearfu' in the Eastern countries."

Mr E.—"It is that, mem, an' sae they hae to exercise great care in the maitter o' cleanliness, for there is nae greater breeder o' disease than dirt; an' oor Government, kennin' that colera in the British or French camp wud be waur than the Czar an' a' his Rooshians, are sendin' oot ship-loads o' saip ilka ither day, an' the very dragoons are kept eident* at the scoorin'."

C.—"Weel, it just dings a'" (an' gangs awa' in a maze o' astonishment).

eident busy

An' similar wud be the case gin a customer ca'd for a penny pirn. It wud be up to three bawbees in consequence o' the vast quantities o' thread required for stitchin' up sodgers' sarks, torn in the battles, tyin' up their woon's an' sic like ither necessities connected wi' the war. Or lat the demand be a red herrin'—the fishers were a' oot wi' the fleets, keepin' the Rooshians in their ain seas, an' herrin' were hardly to be got at ony price; or a box o' spunks—lucifer matches were bein' sent to the Crimea to licht the sodgers' pipes, an' so the twa boxes had to be raised frae three bawbees to tippence; or even a horn spoon—the story wud be that the French, Sardinians, an' Turks engaged wi' oorsel's in the war had taen to suppin' their parridge, brose, an' kail wi' Scotch horn spoons, an' wud use naething ither.

For my ain pairt, weel kennin' the vailue o' the adage aboot makin' hay while the sun shines, I didna aye confine my transactions to the sale or purchase o' the articles within the legitimate limits o' my ain trade, but sometimes made a bit hit ootside them. An' ae example, an' only ane, I'll tak' time to gie afore proceeding wi' the story which I hae undertaen to relate.

Ae mornin' Birdie Briggs, frae the Gutter Wynd, comes hulking into my shop wi' a very pretty canary in a sma' wicker cage o' his ain makin' an' wanted me to buy the bird, offerin' to tak' half the price in tobacco.

Noo, I was nae bird fancier at the time, at least o' cage birds, though I wasna averse to a transaction in eggs an' pootry, when the same was likely to prove profitable; an' so I was very short an' dry wi' Birdie, an' gae him a pretty broad hint that my time was my money, for I didna want him hangin' aboot the coonter, lest onything sud stick till his fingers, kennin', as I did, the character o' the man.

But as he was gaen oot at the door mutterin' till himsel' something aboot the "vailue o' a tippeny merchan's time", for he's an impudent blackguard, a thocht struck me, an' I cried aifter him, "I say, Birdie!"

Birdie halted, an' slewed roon', and luikit at me wi' ane o' his impudent glowers, dootless thinkin' that I was to ca' him to account for his muttered remarks.

But sic was far frae my purpose, seein' I had the makin' o' a bargain wi' him in view. An' so I said, wi'a gude-natured smile upon my face,—"What micht ye be seekin' for the bit creatur', gin a bodie were inclined to trade wi' ye, man?"

Birdie made answer, assumin' my ain tone an' mainner when servin' a customer, as nearly as he cud,—"O, birds like that *were* seven-an-sax, but they're up to fifteen 'bob' in consequence o' the war."

"I canna afoord tae buy canaries at war prices," quo' I; "an' even seven-an-sax is twice the worth o' the creatur' an' mair; but I'll tell ye what I'll dae wi' ye, I'll gie ye twa shillin's an' twa ounces o' rael Irish twist, first quality."

"Twa shillin's and twa ounces o' rael Irish twist, your grandmither!" sneered the vulgar scum, an' he made as gin he had been to mak' aff, but as I made nae motion o' recal, he slewed roon' an' hulkin' up tae the coonter, ahint which I was stanin, set doon the bit cage afore me, an' began praisin' the canary to the nines, concloodin' wi' these words—

"An' noo merchan', this is my last an' lowest offer: tak' the bird or want it. The bird an' cage is yours for half-a-croon in cash, an' half-a-croon's worth o' tobacco o' my ain selection."

I haggled lang wi' him owre this price, but a' that I cud mak oot o' him was a wee bit better a cage, an' the canary becam' my property, and was hung up at the back o' the shop for I daurna tak' it in to the hoose, else the wife wud soon hae become sae fond o' it that she wudna hae alloo'd me to pairt wi't for love or siller.

Everybodie that cam' into the shop admired the canary, an' haen risen in the scale o' ownership, as I may surely weel venture to say, it rose in vailue accordingly, so that afore nicht I cud hae sold it three times owre for twice my ain siller.

But there is aye this feelin' in an up-gaen market. Ye're inclined to hang on an' on till ye're sometimes taen in the turn o' the tide an' carried back till your buying price, or even lower.

In this case, however, I made up my min' either to get a guinea for the bird or to mak' a present o' it to the wife; an' the langer I keepit the creatur' the firmer I becam' in this resolution, because it was a gran' singer, an' I was becomin' quite charm'd wi' it mysel'.

But as I kent that the fairmers were gettin' guid sale for a' their commodities as weel as mysel', I believed gin I keepit the bird oot o' the wife's sicht till the Friday's market, I was sure to get my price for't, an' sae it cam' to pass. On the Friday I had offers o' twal shillin's, fifteen shillin's, an' auchteen shillin's for the bird an' cage, but I never budged frae the guinea.

In the coorse o' the aifternoon, Mrs Robbie o' Greenslack cam' in for some things, an ane o' her servan' lasses along wi' her, to carry the goods hame.

"Ye've come doon wi' ae load, an' ye'll hae to gang hame wi' anither, lassie," quo' the gudewife to the servan'; then turnin' to me, she says, "We cam' doon wi' oor butter to the market, ye ken, and noo we've come to leave the muckle half o' the price o' it wi' you."

"I'm muckle obliged to you, but ye micht hae come to me wi' the butter at ance," quo' I, "an' that wud hae saved you the fash o' stan'in' in the market."

"But I thocht ye werna buyin' just noo, Mr Ettershank," quo' she.

"Weel," quo' I, "I dinna generally buy for curin' purposes till the weather's a bit caulder, but I hae bits o' orders for fresh butter, and I widna hae been ill pleased to execute some o' them wi' Greenslack butter," for I kent the gudewife was prood o' her butter, and nae athegither without reason.

A' this time the gudewife had been e'ein' the canary, an quo' she, "Weel, I wud gie ye a guid mony punds for the bonnie birdie o' yours, for oor ane deet in the winter, an' the cage's stanin' empty, for I wis sae fond o' my canary that I never cud think o' buyin' anither aifter't; but I think that ane o' yours beats it for beauty."

Weel, I took doon the cage aff the hook, and brocht the bird for her to examine at leisure, while I was servin' anither customer. She was in perfect raptures wi' the creatur'; but she sent awa' her servan' lass afore sayin' a word to me aboot the purchase o' it. Then she spiert what I was seekin' for the bird without the cage, but I never altered frae the guinea.

"It's a hantle o' siller for't, bonnie as it is," quo' she; "Oor last ane only cost ten shillin', an' it was said to be a pure canary."

"That micht weel be," quo' I, "but then canaries are a ransom at present on account o' the war."

"Gae awa' wi' ye!" quo' she, laughin'. "What can the war hae to dae wi' the price o' a canary?"

"Just this, Mrs Robbie, that nae British tradin' ship daur venture to the Canary Islands, in the teeth o' the Rooshian fleet, to fetch ony mair birds in the meantime, an' the stock in the market at hame here is sold oot," quo' I, wi' the air o' a man o' superior knowledge.

"I dinna see hoo Rooshia cud keep oor ships frae the Canary Islands," quo' she. "Isna Britain Queen o' the Seas?"

"In a mainner she is, an' in a mainner she's nae," quo I, rather evasively, for I saw that I was gettin' upon ticklish grun'.

Mrs Robbie's neist question increast the difficulty o' my position, for she asked me point blank—"Whaur are the Canary Islands, Mr Ettershank?"

This was really a poser, for I had nae mair notion o' the whereabouts o' those islands than gin I had been a Hottentot. Hooever, it was necessary either to confess ignorance or gie the islands a site somewhere, so I made a plunge for't, and answered,—

"Whaur sud the Canary Islands be but i' the Caspian Sea, Mrs Robbie?" an' I added wi' the view o' puttin' an extinguisher upon her zeal for geographical knowledge—"But it's a' very weel for bairns at schule to thresh their brains aboot the situations o' foreign places; your bairn-time an' mine are baith past, I fear, Mrs Robbie."

"But ye surely dinna think that it's a faut to seek usefu'—or at least hairm-less—knowledge at ony age, Mr Ettershank?" quo' she, wi' feminine persistency.

I felt it necessary to assert my superiority, for I somehoo considered my dignity at stake in the contest, an' so, wi' a severely credulous air, I replied, "I dinna say it's a faut to seek usefu' knowledge, Mrs Robbie, but ye've got the information ye asked for; that is to say, we've agreed to locate the Canary Islands in the Caspian Sea; an' I think ye'll no pretend that even Sir Charles Napier, wi' a' the Horse Marines at his back, wud undertak' to sail the British fleet into the Caspian, as maitters stand at this critical juncture o' international an' Continental affairs?"

Mrs Robbie was for a moment, but only for a moment, flabergasted by the terrible facer I had just dealt her, but she rallied immediately an' came up to the scratch wi'—"I see nae reason hoo oor ships sudna sail into ony waters that ither ships sail into sae lang as Britain remains Queen o' the Seas. But to return to the bird, Mr Ettershank."

"Was ye wantin' to buy't?" quo' I, weel pleased to withdraw frae the Canary Islands, which I was beginnin' to doot that I had raither misplaced.

"A guinea's a big price for't," said she musingly, "an' yet I'm delighted wi' the creatur'. Wud ye tak' nae less, merchan'?"

"Nae ae single bawbee less," quo' I firmly; "an' mair than that, I really dinna want to pairt wi't at a' in the meantime, Mrs Robbie," for I saw the gudewife had set her min' upon the creatur', an' I kent weel that, the mair I seemed disinclined to sell, the mair she wud wiss to buy.

"But I maun hae the birdie at ony rate," quo' she, wi' a sudden spurt o' resolution.

"Mrs Robbie," quo' I, "ye're a woman o' will, an' what ye say ye *maun* hae, ye *will* hae."

"I canna weel spare the siller jist noo, Mr Ettershank, for I paid a big bill to the dressmaker this very day," quo' she.

"Dinna lat that stan' in your waye, Mrs Robbie," quo' I. "The bird's yours at a guinea gin ye like to tak' it hame wi' ye, an' sen' me back the cage. I cud trust the gudewife o' Greenslack wi' a bigger debt than ane-an'-twenty shillin's ony day."

"Ye're very kind," quo' she, no ill-pleased wi' the flattery; "but I'm no willin' to be in your buiks for a birdie, which is nae athegither a necessary ye ken."

"I'll tak' barter—butter, eggs, or pootry," said I, fearin' that the sale micht miscairry aifter a', an' at the same time seein' my waye to a fair addition even to the guinea in a case o' barter.

"Sae be't," quo' the gudewife, eagerly; "I'll gie twenty-ane punds o' butter—for butter's a shillin' the day in the market—but ye maun tak' the rate o' seven punds a week, commencin' neist week, because I canna spare mair, aifter servin' the hoose an' supplyin' several customers wi' fresh butter."

"Say aucht pund per week for the neist three weeks, an' the bird's yours; for ye ken I wud require some sma' allooance for the chance o' a fa' in the merket, Mrs Robbie," quo' I.

"Ye're a hard, hard man, Mr Ettershank, but we'll say it's a bargain," quo' the gudewife, wi' ane o' her winsomest smiles, an' she was at that time a rael bonnie woman.

An' so the canary gaed to Greenslack, an' I served a few customers, wha were regardless o' price, wi' fresh Greenslack butter at fourteen an' saxteenpence the pund for the remainder o' the season.

I wisna athegither hard-hairted wi' my winnin's either, for Birdie Briggs' wife—a puir, trauchlt bodie—ca'd, an' wantit aboot a croon's worth o' things on credit.

"I daurna begin giein' credit except whaun I'm sure o' my siller, else I wud soon be ruined oot at the door," quo' I; "but I'll tell you what I'll dae wi' you, Mrs Briggs" (puir bodie, she had seen better days afore she mairrit her scum o' a man, an' was aye ca'd "Mrs" through a' Keckleton), "I'll gie the bits o' things ye want free, gratis, for naething—for I've been daen gey weel in trade sin' this war began,—but ye maun say naething aboot it, an' ye maunna come back seekin' goods withoot siller."

Weel, the puir bodie was that gratefu' for the bits o' things that, haen observed the empty cage hangin' at the back o' the shop, she gaed hame an' brocht me a young canary in a present, which I gae to my ain wife on her birthday, which luckily happened to fa' that week. The bird grew up to be a fine singer, an' nae muckle ahint the gudewife o' Greenslack's bird in point o' guid looks; an' sae proved to me, gin I had been needin' ony proof, that a kindly act till a fellow creatur' may be rewarded even in this warld.

MOUNTAIN AND MOORLAND

Mountain and Moorland

MAN AND MOUNTAIN

Nan Shepherd *The Living Mountain*

Up on the plateau nothing has moved for a long time. I have walked all day, and seen no one. I have heard no living sound. Once, in a solitary corrie, the rattle of a falling stone betrayed the passage of a line of stags. But up here no movement, no voice. Man might be a thousand years away.

Yet, as I look round me, I am touched at many points by his presence. His presence is in the cairns, marking the summits, marking the paths, marking the spot where a man has died, or where a river is born. It is in the paths themselves; even over boulder and rock man's persistent passage can be seen, as at the head of the Lairig Ghru, where the path, over brown-grey weathered and lichened stones, shines as red as new-made rock. It is in the stepping-stones over the burns, and lower in the glens, the bridges. It is in the indicator on Ben MacDhui, planned with patient skill, that gathers the congregation of the hills into the hollow of one's hand; and some few feet below, in the remains of the hut where the men who made the Ordnance Survey of the eighteen-sixties lived for the whole of a season—an old man has told me how down in the valley they used to watch a light glow now from one summit, now another, as measurements were made and checked. Man's presence too is in the map and the compass that I carry, and in the names recorded in the map, ancient Gaelic names that show how old is man's association with scaur and corrie: the Loch of the Thin Man's Son, the Coire of the Cobbler, the Dairy-maid's Meadow, the Lurcher's Crag. It is in the hiding-holes of hunted men, Argyll's Stone on Creag Dhubh above Glen Einich, and the Cat's Den, deep narrow chasm among the Kennapol rocks; and in the Thieves' Road that runs south from Nethy through prehistoric glacial overflow gaps—and somewhere on its way the kent tree (felled now) to which the prudent landlord tied a couple of his beasts as clearance money. It is in the sluices at the outflow of the lochs, the remnants of lime kilns by the burns, and the shepherds' huts, roofless now, and the bothies of which nothing remains but a chimney-gable; and in the Shelter Stone above Loch Avon, reputed once to have been the den of a gang some thirty strong, before the foundation stones that hold the immense perched rock shifted and the space beneath was narrowed to its present dimensions: wide enough still to hold a half-dozen sleepers, whose names, like the names of hundreds of others, are recorded in a book wrapped in waterproof and left within the shelter of the cave.

Man's presence too is disturbingly evident, in these latter days, in the wrecked aeroplanes that lie scattered over the mountains. During the Second World War more planes (mostly training planes) crashed here than one cares to remember. Like the unwary of older days who were drowned while fording swollen streams, or dashed from the precipices they attempted to climb, these new travellers under-estimated the mountain's power. Its long flat plateau top has a deceptive air of lowness; and its mists shut down too swiftly, its tops are too often swathed in cloud, pelting rain or driving snow, while beneath the world is in clear sunlight, for liberties to be taken with its cruel rock. I stood one day on the Lurcher's Crag and heard the engine of a plane, and looked naturally upwards; but in a moment I realised that the sound was below me. A plane was edging its way steadily through the great gash that separates the two halves of the plateau, the Lairig Ghru. From where I stood, high above it, its wing-tips seemed to reach from rock to rock. I knew that this was an illusion and that the wings had ample room; that the boys who shoot their planes under the arch of a bridge, or through the Yangtze gorges, had the same exuberant glee as the boys below me were doubtless experiencing; yet if mist had suddenly swept down, that passage between the crags would have been most perilous. And even in the brief time needed to negotiate a plane through the Lairig, mist might well descend in this region of swift and unpredictable change. I have experienced this. Out of a blue sky cloud has rushed on the mountain, obliterating the world. The second time I climbed Ben MacDhui I saw this happen.

I had driven to Derry Lodge one perfect morning in June with two gentlemen who, having arrived there, were bent on returning at once to Braemar, when a car came up with four others, obviously setting out for Ben Macdhui. In a flash I had accosted them to ask if I might share their car back to Braemar in the evening: my intention was to go up, the rag-tag and bob-tail of their company, keeping them in sight but not joining myself on to them. The request was granted and I turned back to say farewell to my former companions. When I turned again, the climbers had disappeared. I hastened after them, threading my way through the scattered pines that lie along the stream, but failing to overtake them and hurrying a little more. At last I got beyond the trees, and in all the bare glen ahead, I could see no human being. I could not believe that four people could have walked so fast as to be completely out of sight, for my own pace had been very fair. Prudence—I had only once before been on a Cairngorm—told me to wait; I had begun to suspect I had out-distanced my company. But I couldn't wait. The morning was cloudless and blue, it was June, I was young. Nothing could have held me back. Like a spurt of fire licking the hill, up I ran. The Etchachan tumbled out from under snow, the summit was like wine. I saw a thousand summits at once, clear and sparkling. Then far off to the south I saw a wall of cloud like a foaming breaker. It rolled on swiftly, blotting out a hundred summits a minute—very soon it would blot out mine. I threw a hasty glance around, to fix my bearings, and pelted down towards the ruined surveyors' hut, from which the path downwards by Coire Etchachan is clearly marked by cairns; but before I reached it I was swallowed up. The whole business, from my first glimpse of the cloud to the moment it washed over me, occupied less than four minutes. Half a mile down, drinking tea in the driving mist by the side of the path, I found my lost company still ascending. On another occasion, seated by a summit cairn, gazing through a cloudless sky at peaks and lochs, I found myself unable to name some of the features I was looking at, and bent close over the map to find them out. When I raised my head, I was alone in the universe with a few blocks of red granite. This swiftness of the mist is one of its deadliest features, and the wreckage of aeroplanes, left to rust in lonely corners of the mountains, bears witness to its dreadful power.

Man's touch is on the beast creation too. He has driven the snow bunting from its nesting-sites, banished the capercailzie and reintroduced it from abroad. He has protected the grouse and all but destroyed the peregrine. He tends the red deer and exterminates the wild cat. He maintains, in fact, the economy of the red deer's life, and the red deer is at the heart of a human economy that covers this mountain mass and its surrounding glens. There are signs that this economy is cracking, and though the economy of the shooting estate is one for which I have little sympathy, I am aware that a turn of the wrist does not end it. The deer himself might perish from our mountains if man ceased to kill him; or degenerate if left to his wild; and on the crofts and small hill-farms wrested from the heather and kept productive by unremitting labour, the margin between a living and a sub-living may be decided by the extra wage of ghillie or under-keeper. Without that wage, or its equivalent in some other guise, the hill croft might well revert to heather.

CAIRNGORM COMMENTARY

Tom Patey *One Man's Mountains*

The Three Fifteen from Bon-Accord Square was a special bus tactfully set aside for climbers by Messrs. Strachans Ltd., following incidents in which old ladies had been isolated at the back of the bus by a mountain of rucksacks, only effecting an escape, several miles beyond their destinations, by a desperate hand traverse.

These were the real mountaineers—not mere "hill bashers" like ourselves who had that day tramped many an endless mile in search of a minor 3,009-foot Munro top away out in the middle of the Great Moss. We had built a little cairn on what appeared the most elevated undulation and been well satisfied with our day's achievement. These men spoke of icy vigils and gigantic ice-falls; routes that finished long after dark; remote bivouacs in faraway corries, riotous nights in bothies, late-night dances in Braemar and brimming tankards in the Fife Arms. Adventure, unconventionality, exuberance—these were the very elements missing from our scholarly conception of mountaineering which had led us with mathematical precision up and down the weary lists of Munro's Tables.

The northeast climbers of the early 'fifties were all individualists but never rock fanatics. There are no crags in the Cairngorms within easy reach of a motorable road and a typical climbing week-end savoured more of an expedition than of acrobatics. If the weather turned unfavourable, then a long hill walk took the place of the planned climb. All the bothies were well patronised—Luibeg, Lochend, Gelder Shiel, Bynack, the Geldie Bothies, Altanour, Corrour and of course the Shelter Stone. At one and all you would be assured of friendly company round the fire in the evening. Everybody knew everybody and formal introductions were unnecessary. . . .

An occasion followed, on which Gordon Lillie, dislocated a shoulder while seconding Kenneth (Grassick) on another Lochnagar climb. They made their way down to the nearest roadhead and were rescued by none other than Princess Margaret. Lillie sat miserably beside the chauffeur; while Grassick in the back seat made intelligent conversation with Royalty. Next morning the press reported the rescue on the front page and Grassick, never slow to seize his share of the limelight, was quoted as saying—"She was radiant. . . . I never knew anyone could look so beautiful. . . . Her pictures just don't do her justice"—a graceful tribute from a commoner of Grassick's lowly station. We looked in vain for his name in the New Year's Honours List.

The Kincorth Club under the joint leadership of Freddy Malcolm and Alex "Sticker" Thom were formidable rivals. The majority of their new routes were located in the Coire na Ciche of Beinn a' Bhuird, which came to be regarded as club property. The Club headquarters was sited at the Howff, the exact location of which is still a secret for the excellent reason that the head gamekeeper turns a blind eye to its occupants. The construction is partly subterranean and is the eighth wonder of the Cairngorms, with a stove, floor boards, genuine glass window and seating space for six. The building materials were brought from Aberdeen to the assembly line by the herculean labours of countless torchlit safaris which trod stealthily past the Laird's very door, shouldering mighty beams of timber, sections of stove piping and sheets of corrugated iron. The Howff records the inaugural ceremony—"This howff was constructed In the Year of Our Lord 1954, by the Kincorth Club, for the Kincorth Club. All climbers please leave names, and location of intended climbs: female climbers please names, addresses, and telephone numbers."

BLOODSPORTS ON DEESIDE

John R. Allan *Northeast Lowlands of Scotland*

Clear skies and bright colours—Deeside in autumn is just a little incredible. Nature should not be as pretty as a picture, as bravely coloured as a romance. Deeside has everything. Castles—yes, like a fanfare of trumpets: Crathes in the cleft of the woods; Aboyne, a stronghold of the Gordons; Birse, a perfect little thing from a fairy tale in the empty Forest; Braemar, fantastically turreted, where the standard was raised in 1715 for the Old Pretender's rebellion; Balmoral—ah, Balmoral, how the willing heart can be stirred by the old loyalties. So many other fine things—mansions and shooting lodges where parties go out in the morning to shoot birds, accompanied by women whose tweeds are nearly as loud as their voices. I can't go on—this heart is not willing, except to be stirred the wrong way round by romantic and social Deeside.

I do not understand blood sports very well; and in so far as I do understand I deplore them. Not that I can take up a high moral attitude in the matter. As a farmer I breed cattle that eventually go to the butcher. As one who likes a good diet of meat I will wring the neck of a duck. Indeed, all who like a steak or a cut off the breast should have to kill and disembowel occasionally in case they become over-refined. I have killed birds and beasts, but always with a sense of regret, or even guilt. When you take a trout from the water and that most exquisite agility dies between your hands, you have destroyed something you can never replace. There is no essential difference between taking the life of a bird or a fish and the life of a man or a woman; the difference is only in degree. In our defence we can quote only the necessity that knows no law greater than itself. It is part of the human predicament that there is so often a conflict among our instincts and impulses. I destroy the lovely caterpillars that strip the leaves from my young poplar trees because I am in great need of trees for shelter, but as I destroy them I feel a slight chill, an intimate desolation, at the ruin of those innocent and lovely creatures. I doubt if there is any escape from the predicament. We live only by the death of others. Of course the vegetarians have an answer; but how valid is it? Who knows what agonies the cabbage suffers as the reticulations of its heart are shredded down to recreate a classical economist? We must accept the fact that we are beasts of prey and live by murder. . . .

Perhaps it would be good if slaughterhouse service were like jury service—if ten citizens of each town received an order from the Sheriff to attend at the slaughterhouse next morning and kill the day's intake. Not to cut up the meat—that's nothing once the life has gone; but to deliver the bolt at the broad forehead and strike with the agony of death and see the fading of the bright eyes. What a sauce it would be at dinner that day; the high sharp sauce of realising that all our pleasures are taken precariously on the lip of the grave, that the hunters at any moment become the prey.

The slaughterer kills because it is his living. What can we make of the people who kill wholesale in the name of sport? When a gentleman goes to the moor with several friends and they shoot two hundred grouse and various other birds and creatures, they can hardly plead necessity. On the contrary, the fact that the killers are neither hungry, nor forced to kill for a living, is a mark of very high social position. To enjoy a successful day with the guns must require a great atrophy of feeling, an advanced state of decadence. As for the idea that there is something manly about shooting game, it is a little comic. What fortitude is required to hit a bird with shot scientifically prepared to be propelled out of an expensive gun? Fortitude—there was a lot more shown by that fine old sportswoman the farmer's wife when she cut off the tails of the three blind mice.

The great grouse shoots were one of those forms of vulgarity that sometimes become marks of social distinction. They were marks of conspicuous waste and very expensive at that. The grouse shooters were often rather pathetic people, going through a ritual imposed on them because they could afford it. They came north to live in draughty castles and damp, dark shooting lodges. They dressed themselves in tweeds and trudged through the heather, drenched by mists or tortured by horseflies. They were stung, by everything and everybody. From the laird who let his moor for £3,000 and the grocer who charged quite as fantastically, down to the youngest beater with an eye for a shilling, the countryside knew the sporting tenants were their game. That is not an honest way for a countryside to live. And how pathetic that for fifty years only the rents from the moors kept many estates from total bankruptcy. In days when it did not pay to feed a bullock for the professional slaughterer there was good money in raising a grouse for the amateur one.

The days of the big house parties and the organised shoots would seem to be over. When cattle and sheep are more important than grouse on the hills again, Deeside will be a sweeter and a saner place to live in.

ROYAL DOMAIN

Cuthbert Graham *Portrait of Aberdeen and Deeside*

This may be the place to explain the sporting aspect of the royal domain. It would be wrong to think that Royal Deeside's fame as a hunting, fishing and shooting playground dates from Queen Victoria's arrival on the scene in 1848. A few statistics may help to clear up misconceptions. Balmoral lies within the parish of Crathie and Braemar, by far the largest in Aberdeenshire. It extends to 286 square miles and includes several lochs. If the water area is deducted it has 182,219 acres of which 165,647 acres consist of well-stocked deer forests. The rest of the land is made up of woodlands (11,500 acres), grouse moors, and arable land (2,400 acres).

This enormous wilderness, with a tiny fringe of farming country in the river valley, has been a hunting paradise from the earliest times. It is only the nature of the hunting that has changed. In the eleventh century Malcolm Canmore built a castle at Braemar as a hunting seat. He and his successors regarded the deer forests as royal hunting grounds specially and eternally reserved for their own enjoyment. The position had not very much altered by the early seventeenth century when the Earl of Mar, as the King's representative, enjoyed the prerogative of organising deer hunts on a huge and spectacular scale. There are many references to such hunts, but the most vivid and detailed comes down to us in the book called *The Penniless Pilgrimage* by John Taylor, the Water Poet, dated 1618. He told how five hundred to six hundred men were dispatched "early in the morning" to scour an area "seven, eight or ten miles in circumference" to bring down herds of deer in enormous numbers to an appointed rendezvous where the "lords and gentlemen" awaited them. At one hunt he attended "in the space of two hours four score fat deer were slain".

Such massacres, which involved the use of deer hounds, appear to have continued into the eighteenth century, but after the Jacobite Rebellions attempts were made to introduce hill sheep which did not meet with much success. In 1778 Glen Lui in the upper valley was cleared of sheep and reverted to deer forest. It is claimed that the present era of Highland sport really dates from 1800, when Sir John Maxwell took a ten-year lease of Abergeldie. In 1826 the Forest of Mar was advertised as "the finest shooting district in Scotland" and Mar Lodge was let at £1,800 per annum.

In the early part of the century the great game drive, the *battue en masse* did continue. At Breadalbane in 1842, as Queen Victoria records in her journal, the Earl himself with 300 Highlanders went out beating for the royal guests. The organised hunt must have been a spectacular occasion, but the bag as the Queen records it was a modest affair of "nineteen roedeer, several hares and pheasants and three brace of grouse".

But very soon the real sportsman preferred the individual ardours of the deer-stalk to the mass slaughter of game. This demanded a far higher degree of skill and for the Prince Consort at Balmoral normally involved a walk with a gun or rifle and a couple of ghillies.

The Prince Consort's successors as lairds of Balmoral have all been good shots. Edward VII learned shooting as a boy and before he was 18 boasted of killing two stags to his father's one. George V had superb skill with a rifle and in grouse drives his inerrable aim was famous. Eric Linklater, who watched him in a day's shooting at Geallaig Hill, to the north of Balmoral, has testified that "every bird that fell to the King's gun was dead in the air before it dropped. When a large covey came, and another closely followed, there were two, three, four dead birds in the air before the first had fallen. . . . It was the very summit of markmanship".

Edward VIII was not so deeply interested in Balmoral, but George VI had inherited his father's passion for a day on the moors and in his later years, when leg trouble was a certain handicap, he took advantage of cross-country motoring to get to the less accessible grouse-butts. The Duke of Edinburgh continues the tradition of high skill on the moors.

FIRST ASCENT OF LOCH-NA-GAR

Queen Victoria *Victoria in the Highlands* (ed. David Duff)

Saturday, September 16, 1848

At half-past nine o'clock Albert and I set off in a postchaise, and drove to the bridge in the wood of Balloch Buie, about five miles from Balmoral, where our ponies and people were. Here we mounted, and were attended by a keeper of Mr. Farquharson's as guide, Macdonald—who, with his shooting-jacket, and in his kilt, looked a picture—Grant on a pony, with our luncheon in two baskets, and Batterbury on another pony. We went through that beautiful wood for about a mile, and then turned and began to ascend gradually, the view getting finer and finer; no road, but not bad ground—moss, heather, and stones. Albert saw some deer when we had been out about three-quarters of an hour, and ran off to stalk them, while I rested; but he arrived just a minute too late. He waited for me on the other side of a stony little burn, which I crossed on my pony, after our faithful Highlanders had moved some stones and made it easier. We then went on a little way, and I got off and walked a bit, and afterwards remounted; Macdonald leading my pony. The view of Ben-na-Bhourd, and indeed of all around, was very beautiful but as we rose higher we saw mist over Loch-na-Gar. Albert left me to go after ptarmigan, and went on with Grant, while the others remained with me, taking the greatest care of me. Macdonald is a good honest man, and was indefatigable, and poor Batterbury was very anxious also.

I saw ptarmigan get up, and Albert fire—he then disappeared from my sight, and I rode on. It became cold and misty when we were on Loch-na-Gar. In half an hour, or rather less, Albert rejoined me with two ptarmigan, having come up by a shorter way. Here it was quite soft, easy walking, and we looked down on two small lochs called Na Nian, which were very striking, being so high up in the hills. Albert was tired, and remounted his pony; I had also been walking a little way. The ascent commenced, and with it a very thick fog, and when we had nearly reached the top of Loch-na-Gar, the mist drifted in thick clouds so as to hide everything not within one hundred yards of us. Near the peak (the fine point of the mountain which is seen so well from above Grant's house) we got off and walked, and climbed up some steep stones, to a place where we found a seat in a little nook, and had some luncheon. It was just two o'clock, so we had taken four hours going up.

But, alas! nothing whatever to be seen; and it was cold, and wet, and cheerless. At about twenty minutes after two we set off on our way downwards, the wind blowing a hurricane, and the mist being like rain, and everything quite dark with it. Bowman (Mr. Farquharson's keeper) and Macdonald, who preceded us, looked like ghosts. We walked some way till I was quite breathless, and remounted my pony, well wrapped up in plaids; and we came down by the same path that Albert had come up, which is shorter, but steeper; the pony went delightfully; but the mist made me feel cheerless.

Albert kept ahead a little while for ptarmigan, but he gave it up again. When we had gone on about an hour and a quarter, or an hour and a half, the fog disappeared like magic, and all was sunshine below, about one thousand feet from the top I should say. Most provoking!—and yet one felt happy to see sunshine and daylight again.

The view, as one descends, overlooking Invercauld and the wood which is called Balloch Buie, is most lovely. We saw some deer in the wood below. We rode on till after we passed the burn, and had nearly got to the wood. We came another way down, by a much rougher path; and then, from the road in the wood, we walked up to the Falls of the Garbhalt, which are beautiful. The rocks are very grand, and the view from the little bridge, and also from a seat a little lower down, is extremely pretty. We found our carriages in the road, and drove home by six o'clock.

TO MEET THE QUEEN

Ian Macpherson *Pride in the Valley*

Ewen Cattanach, chief shepherd of Garvamore on the Upper Spey, is summoned to Cluny Castle by his clan chief, Cluny Macpherson. The year is 1847.

"You came, Ewen," Cluny enunciated.

"I came at once, Cluny."

"The Queen will be here in April, Ewen. She has expressed a wish that two of my people, representing my clan, should have their portraits painted wearing Highland costume, and their portraits will hang in Windsor Castle. You are not a Macpherson, Ewen, but nevertheless you are of my clan. I am aware that some of my own name will say that they alone should be taken, for they are my people, my blood and my house. But I feel it is my duty to bind our confederate clans together, now as they were in the past when they fought like one—when they fought like one for a thing that was dear and is now no longer to be remembered. We are not so many as we were, Ewen, Cattanachs, and Macphersons, and all our people, make a small company. There's the more need to keep together what remains."

"Will Cluny not represent his own clan?" Ewen asked in a low voice.

"No, Ewen, it is the Queen's wish—I have chosen Ranald Macpherson at Crathie to take the right hand side. He will carry the Green Banner and the Prince's sword."

"He will carry them well, Cluny."

"And you to stand with him."

"I am only a herd, Cluny."

"You are one of my people, Ewen."

"You're putting such honour on me that I'm shamed, Cluny."

Cluny's voice rang with pride. "Honour can never make shame" he cried, "though it weighs our backs to the ground."

"Will you be able to come here at least once a week?" he inquired. "A great artist will stay with me until the work is done."

"It'll need to be Sunday, Cluny, or else at night" Ewen remembered his sheep.

"He must have light. Sunday will serve. Ewen, many will see you that you never dreamed of."

Cluny sent word that Ewen was to take no thought of his dress. It would be provided.

The weeks hastened on towards the Queen's coming, and nothing else but her visit was talked about in Badenoch, unless the painting of Ranald Macpherson's and Ewen Cattanach's portraits. "For to hang in the Queen's Palace," diverted men's minds for a time from the subject of their Chief and the Queen.

The portrait was completed in the last week of March. Mrs. Cattanach deeved her husband with entreaties until he asked Cluny if she might be allowed to view it.

"Most certainly, Ewen," Cluny said in a gracious voice. "I expect a great many people will wish to see it."

The entire family . . . was gathered to travel to Cluny. . . . Ewen ushered them diffidently into the room where the painting stood on its easel. Mrs. Cattanach gazed and gazed upon her man's image. "It's like you," was all she would say.

Cluny met them, asking, "Did you see your husband, Mrs. Cattanach?"

"It was lovely! lovely!" she breathed and smiled. "I'm taking a fresh notion of him, Cluny."

"You can be proud of him."

"I was ever that, Cluny."

"Ewen—" Cluny called the shepherd aside, "the Queen is arriving in three weeks."

"Three weeks! The time goes like the wind, Cluny."

"Too fast for all there must be done. I shall send you word when I want you."

"Will you be wanting me more, Cluny? I thought the painting was finished. The lambing—"

"To present you to the Queen."

"Cluny! I can't! I'm not fit! It's beyond me! If I was to send my excuses—"

"The Queen's wish admits no excuses, Ewen."

"She will have grand folk round her! Surely she'd let me off if you were to explain—what would I be doing amongst them, me!—a shepherd!"

"You will wear these clothes, Ewen." He indicated the picture.

"Sword and shield and all!"

"No Ewen, the time for them is past. Our swords and shields are laid down at her feet."

*   *   *

The greatest occasion comes at length and time dispatches it even as the daily routine of men's lives; great and small, there is no difference but they must pass, save that the small are ever renewed with each young day; men's memories hold the great event.

The Queen had come and gone. . . . Ewen had supped on glory and now it made him content to live by common things; he had seen his Queen, and the sheep would come to the shearing; his portrait hung in a royal palace; ah, he looked down the Glen, along the river, the birches were green; he would not change to live in palaces.

One evening in June, when the strath was beginning to close in upon itself with night, he sat down at the door of his house on the boulder he had laid there when he first came to Garva. His wife came to the door of their house to watch his pensive face. She came to stand by his side.

"It was good of Cluny to send us the little copy of your picture," she said. "Ewen—"

"Yes, Nan?"

"Tell me about the Queen."

"But I told you!"

"Not right. Oh, you men!—you think when you've seen a thing, everybody must know all about it without you telling them. Now if it was me that went, I'd come back and give you everything so plain you'd think you were seeing her. Was she wearing her crown, Ewen?"

"No," he smiled.

"What was she like? Go on Ewen, it's not fair to tease me."

"She wasn't very big—" He hesitated.

"And she wasn't very small," she mocked. "Was she about my height, Ewen? I'm sure she was tall and stately."

"No."

"Oh, she'd be a stout little body like me."

"But not so bonny."

"Ach, away with you! Now start at the very beginning, Ewen."

"But, where would that be?"

"When you came to the door of Cluny Castle—I can see you so far as that myself,—"

"Well—" he plunged desperately into his memory—"well, Cluny came out and he said, 'Ewen, when it comes time for you to go in you will walk straight through the room, and there will be ladies there, and many, many folk, but you will not heed them. Ewen you will not take off your bonnet, Ewen, or heed them, till you see my lady, and then you will take off your bonnet—'"

"Oh!" she cried: "Oh! you never told me that bit of it, Ewen."

"Yes, I did," he expostulated.

"You never did—to think of it!—the rudeness of him! He was putting bad manners on you for the sake of his stinking pride! Oh! him and his lady! What on earth did you do, Ewen?"

"Well—" he smiled diffidently—"well, you see, Nan—it was very stupid of me —just by accident I happened to take off my bonnet while I was standing there and I laid it on a seat and when I went to look for it—"

"What?"

"—it was lost."

"Ewen Mhor, darling that you are! Oh, aren't you like yourself! What did Cluny say?"

"I never saw him."

"Man, man, I'm proud of you, silly that I am to tell you."

She put her hand on his shoulder and bent down to kiss him. The sheep were bleating farther and farther away as they climbed to the new herbage of the corries. The river sounded loud beneath the pale sky.

LIFE IN GLENGAIRN

Amy Stewart Fraser *The Hills of Home*

In the Glen, life assumed a rhythm dominated by the seasons which were clearly marked by the lengthening and shortening of the days; summer went out with the first autumn gales; winter was one long snowstorm after another. Each season brought its own work and its own way of life.

Sunrise being late in December, not till about ten o'clock were the hills flushed with a rosy glow but, long before that hour, beasts had to be fed and byres mucked out. Men stumbled round in the dark by the wavering light of stable-lanterns, using hessian sacks to protect them from the weather . . . one worn as an apron, another slung round the shoulders, and a third draped over the head.

There was a considerable period during the winter when little could be done on the farms. The darkest mornings were round about Christmas-time and winter clamped down on farm life for a couple of months.

It was a fine sight to see from the Manse windows a herd of red deer trek across the white waste of Geallaig, with a noble stag in the rear. At the slightest sound of danger he appeared to move forward and lead the herd, with the hinds following, strung out in a long line. Only when desperate for food were they to be seen on the lower reaches in daytime. It was generally at night that they, and the mountain hares in their winter garb, came down from the corries where they normally grazed, driven by hunger to raid parks and turnip-fields.

*   *   *

Apart from the small farms, most of the acreage of the Glen consisted of hill-pasture for the hardy blackface sheep. There were families, like the Andersons, Macdonalds, and Murisons, who provided successive shepherds for flocks pastured on hills rented to owners who lived in other districts, but most of the flocks belonged to the farmers who had grazing rights on the hills adjoining their land. Shepherds went south with their flocks before winter came, and returned in spring for the lambing; but small farmers could not afford to do this, so the care of sheep was often associated with hazardous winter work. When storms came they had to go out in blizzards when they could hardly see a hand in front of their face; many times in a night they would go out with a lantern to inspect the huddled yowes and see that all was well.

Came the spring, and in a single day they might be dazzled with sunshine and half-blinded by stinging rain and hail. The old men called them lamb-storms.

They swept across the hills when the early lambs were taking their first weak strides, making the pathetic creatures wish they had never been born. Lambing-time called for constant vigilance and attention, and often a feeble, motherless lamb shared the warmth of the kitchen, bottle-fed, wrapped in an old shawl in the ingle-neuk. The sheep were rounded up . . . "gaithered" was the word used . . . at lambing, clipping and dipping, and the familiar call could be heard, "Come in ahint, min!" to an over-eager young dog, one of the friendly collies that stood on their hind-legs at any farmhouse door, and put front paws on our shoulders, with tails wagging furiously. Older dogs were watchful and aloof to all but their master and the job in hand.

Clipping in summer was done by hand, a laborious undertaking requiring great skill so that the surface was left in even ridges. Experienced clippers with their shears twinkling in and out of the wool could clip a docile sheep in a matter of minutes, but a few awkward yowes could slow down the number clipped in a day.

The yowes were then driven back to the hills where they remained till the severe weather arrived; but, prior to this was the dipping which was supposed to free them from parasites. They awaited their turn in a primitive pen of planks and hurdles adjacent to a burn which had been diverted to fill a concrete tank. A benevolent policeman looked on as the law demanded, and neighbours turned out to give a hand, restraining a struggling sheep while it was dipped in the solution of sheep-dip and encouraging it to flounder out at the other end of the four-foot tank, when it ran off, shaking itself and loudly protesting at the indignity it had suffered. . . .

A year with the sheep ended with the autumn lamb sales. We used to see on an early morning the shepherd from Daldownie travelling slowly down the road across the water behind his flock, with a couple of collies frisking round to keep them on the road. There were no double-decker motor-lorries in those days to transport them swiftly to their destination. They had to be walked, but not over-tired, every mile of the way.

Shepherds are silent folk not much given to talking about their job. Instead of speaking they would, in passing, merely give one a friendly nod with an upwards sidelong twist, a typical gesture very difficult to describe. With country folk, to pass a fellow-traveller on the road on foot or bicycle without recognition would be thought the height of bad manners; always there must be a civil word of greeting, even a nod, or that peculiar twist of the head.

*   *   *

For the tweed-hatted, knickerbockered gamekeeper, life was strenuous all the year round. In spring his face was clouded with anxiety when heavy rain and spreading floods threatened to ruin the breeding-season of game-birds. Later in the year he had to keep a sharp look-out for poachers.

Every keeper I ever knew had a wonderful constitution and a vigorous nature, exulting in the bracing hill air, revelling in his chosen occupation; trudging knee-deep in heather, allowing for the wind, noting the light, keeping down vermin, in daily observation of all branches of wild life. Muir-burning in spring to get rid of old rank heather was done in systematic patches for the sake of the young grouse who cannot struggle through dense growth. It was heavy work for the keeper and his helpers, straining to keep the fire within the selected stretch for, once out of control, it might spread for miles, and beating it out was an exhausting business. From a distance the burned patches gave a curious chessboard appearance, and in the following spring the mass of bloom on the young shoots was vivid in colour.

The first heather to bloom was the crimson bell-heather, but when autumn came, the moors were richly purple with ling, and the sound of shots echoed over the landscape, sending grouse toppling out of a blue sky, to be retrieved by the gun-dogs from the keeper's kennels and brought to the feet of the marksmen.

The latter were known as the guns and those at Gairnshiel, as I remember them, had a decided look of a gathering of variously-built editions of Sherlock Holmes, enveloped in immense ulsters of a style and material familiar to all readers of early illustrated productions of Conan Doyle's masterpiece, and since copied, more or less accurately, on television. Breeches and Norfolk jackets, and thick-knit stockings were weightier than anything worn nowadays, and must have felt like chain-mail when rain-soaked; peaty soil clung to the hand-made, well-oiled boots built like battleships, with soles encrusted with enormous tackets. At a grouse-drive the guns stayed in the butts with loaders, and beaters drove the birds in the approved direction. Because of the way the butts were sited, the hill was no place for the foolhardy; only by continual alertness and strict adherence to discipline were shooting accidents avoided. Any gun who followed a bird beyond the line of safety was a source of constant worry to the keeper. It was every gun's ambition and expectation to bring grouse down right and left when they swerved in hundred-miles-an-hour pace over a wind-swept ridge. The joys were not confined to those who carried a gun; ladies who were not "out with the guns" joined them for lunch, and stayed to watch the well-trained labradors at work on the sun-dappled moors. At Gairnshiel the game-larder was outside the kitchen door. It was made of metal gauze. In it the game-birds were left hanging by their necks for perhaps a week, and were then considered fit to prepare for the table. In that primitive larder, long before deep-freeze methods were practised, the game actually kept for months.

In the grouse-driving season, men who could be spared from farm work were glad to earn money as loaders, gillies and beaters. All the boys were engaged as beaters at five shillings a day (and bring your own flag), their mothers depending on their earning enough to get new suits and winter boots. They took a "piece" to the hill and were "gey hungert and trauchled" when they got home at the end of the day. When it was a royal shoot, lunch was provided, men getting in addition a bottle of beer apiece.

The small farmer, also, took his sheltie to the hill to bring down the game in panniers, which were covered baskets shaped to lie on the pony's sides, but I remember, long before Land Rovers were designed, a car with caterpillar wheels, built for Alexander Keillor of Morven, crawled over the hills on that estate, bringing down the day's bag, thus outmoding the panniered-pony.

In his youth King Edward VII had been tireless on the hills, but when he came to the throne he was close on sixty and had become stout. In spite of this, he liked to be out on the hills and moors, seated on a pony with his Inverness cape wrapped about him. When he used to shoot over Geallaig a sturdy pony was provided to carry him up the quarry road to the Royal Butt above Delnabo. On the Gairnside moors he had the reputation of being the cheeriest of the party, and his geniality made the day enjoyable for all who served him. It amused him to use the speech of the locality, which he did with a faultless accent. On one occasion he noticed among the gillies, Peter Robertson, who for years had been his personal servant at Abergeldie Castle and had long retired. Delighted, he at once approached him and shaking his hand vigorously he exclaimed, "Man, Peter, foo are ye?"

I TO THE HILLS

Ian Macpherson *Shepherd's Calendar*

The second day of January was a day of storm. John ran about the steading, trying to close chinks which let in the drift. There were heaps of snow here and there in the court. John and Callum and Mrs. Grant worked together, nailing up bags in the corn loft where the snow drifted under the eaves, closing holes which let snow into the hen-house. They emptied the chaff-house and put the chaff into the hen-house. Snow filtered in here and there in spite of their efforts. A man could not stand against the fury of the storm outside. When the Grants had to go between the house and the steading they were buffeted by the wind, flung about by the wind, half blinded by the drift.

Allan did not help with the work which kept his son's mind from the fury of the storm. He rose before daylight. He put on his boots for the hill, huge tacketed things with upturned toes, curved like a crescent moon. He put on short puttees about his ankles. He laid his cloak ready, and took the dogs into the kitchen. He got his wife to make a sandwich for him. He sat all day in the kitchen, staring at the fire, and listening to the storm. He did not rouse himself to put wood on the fire when it burnt low. He would not look at food. His sheep were on the hill. No one knew how long this might last. He had intended to move them from their shelter on New Year's Day. On fine days the sheep moved to a place sheltered from the wind. When storm promised they made for shelter. Then when the storm came they were drifted over in the shelter which destroyed them. He had meant to see to them on New Year's Day. His Hogmanay folly left him sick, and his sheep in danger. The wind in the chimney was in his ears all day.

Sandy came over at night. It was a silent household. Allan still had his boots on, ready to be off to save his sheep. The dogs had crept beneath the kitchen bed. They whimpered in their sleep. Sandy had shifted his sheep into the fir wood beside his house on New Year's Day. They were out of immediate danger there, but not out of all danger. They were amongst fir trees, which withstand most storms. This was a storm worse than any of the valley people remembered. The young plantation in front of the Grant's house was flat. First the spruces fell. They were crashing amongst the slower growing larches all day. The gaps they left let in the storm. By night on the second of January the plantation was like a field of laid corn. Here and there a tangle of trees, flung together by veering winds, stood out from the ruin. By morning the fallen trees were hid in wreaths of snow, and still the wind skelloched.

Sandy had known how Allan would be. Sandy did not wish to lose his sheep, because sheep were his means of living. But otherwise he did not care much what happened to them. With Allan it was otherwise. He was a sheep man. It was in his blood to follow the sheep. He had risked his life before now to protect his sheep. He was ready to risk his life again. Sheep meant more to him, though he did not know it, than wife or child. He knew every sheep on the place, knew its history, could pick out a stranger from the flock at a glance. He loved his sheep. He gave to them a wealth of affection. He had been amongst sheep since he could walk; he had herded sheep: borne heat and cold, the beating of the elements, with them; when he found that John looked at sheep as Sandy looked at them, he knew that his son was an alien, and almost hated him for his lack.

He had with his sheep infinite patience. One would scarcely believe, when one saw him dour and cantankerous at home, that this man could nurse a sick sheep with as much care as a mother nurses her child.

Sandy tried to rouse him after supper. Allan knew that he had failed. He should have gone out on New Year's Day. There was but one remedy; he must go out in the morning, good weather or bad.

"They'll be all right," said Sandy. "Wise brutes, sheep. Bally's were buried a month once an' come oot alive."

Allan did not reply. He knew Sandy offered him a sop.

"It can't last like this," said Mrs. Grant.

"It'll maybe last weeks," Allan answered dourly.

"No fear," put in John.

"If it does it'll no' be only sheep that's lost," said Sandy.

Mrs. Grant took the Bible from the top of the sewing machine.

"I think we'll have worship and go to bed," she said.

When they had read they sat a few seconds by the dying fire. Sandy himself was silent, listening to the uproar of the night.

"Hearken to that!" he cried at last. He repeated a verse they had read.

"'Raging waves of the sea, foaming out their own shame; wandering stars for whom is reserved the blackness of darkness.' God, sister, man's a poor thing wi' that screeching aboot him. God pity all poor folks at sea this night."

"Amen," said his sister.

Had the sorrow of humanity a voice, it might cry Amen in such a fashion, girt round by darkness and ravening terrors.

Allan sat and thought of his sheep. The cold of the night began to invade the house. When they had all gone to bed and the lights were out, they lay silent in the dark and knew how frail are the fences man has built against the onset of storm.

Not against them, but against the house, symbol of man's endeavour to be secure, the storm's fury broke, and beat again.

The storm had not subsided in the morning. Nothing could hold Allan now. He was for the hill, though they told him that he could do nothing, and that it was suicide.

"Ye'll no' go alone. Better two than one, even if they are mad!" said Sandy at last, when he saw that his arguments did not touch Allan. The two men got ready. Mrs. Grant laid a gill bottle of whisky on the table.

"Put this in your pocket, Sandy," she said. "I'm thankful it's in the house."

"Your uncle's right," she told her son. "Two will do as well as three. It's best to have a man at home in case—It's best to be safe. Sandy'll look after him."

"I'm glad Sandy's here. I'm glad you've stayed," she said to John when Allan and Sandy were swallowed up by the storm ten yards from the door.

"Listen to that." Snow beat on the windows. "We'll have to keep the light on all day."

The afternoon wore on and there was no sign of the men. John began to grow uneasy. He tried to sit quiet that his mother might not see his fear. The storm raged unabated. Night was not far away. He could endure the waiting no longer. "Mother," he said, "I'll have to go. I can't wait longer. It's a wonder they're not coming."

"Yes, druaghan, you'd better. Oh, laochan, be careful. It's a wild, wild night."

"No fear for me," he said.

She closed the door when he had gone from sight.

"Come and speak to me, Sally," she said. "Come and take your knitting and speak to me. Listen to that, Sally. Lassie, we may be thankful we've a roof over our heads. Sally, I think we'll say a prayer. God send them safe. God help us and protect us. God bring them safe, for Jesus Christ's sake, Amen."

They knelt on the hearth-rug and prayed, pitting the puny might of their faith against the tumult of the world and the falling darkness.

Mrs. Grant began to set the tea. Sally laid her knitting aside.

"Sit you down, Sally," said her mistress. "Be you going on with your knitting, lassie. I'll see to the tea-things." She was glad to have something to do.

"I think I'll mask the tea," she said. "Sandy had aye a good nose for tea."

She took a tablecloth from the table drawer and put it on the table. "It's the New Year and Sandy's here. We must be decent, " she told Sally.

The outside door banged.

"That's them," cried Sally. She jumped up and laid her knitting on the bed.

"Draw in the chairs, Sally," said Mrs. Grant. "It's a good thing we didn't infuse the tea earlier or it would have been wild."

She opened the kitchen door.

"Come in," she cried, "tea's ready."

There was no answer but the banging of the front door, and the sound of the wind in the porch. She stepped into the lobby.

"Sally," she called. They went together out into the porch. The outside door was open. A little heap of snow had drifted in.

"Oh, Sally," said Mrs. Grant, "I shut the door. Sally, I shut the door."

They went back to the kitchen, closing the doors behind them and rattling them to be sure they were shut. They stood beside each other close to the fire. There was companionship in the fire.

The door banged again. They stood quite still. Sally was trembling. Mrs. Grant laid her arm across Sally's shoulder.

"Don't, maital," she said. "Don't be afraid. There's nothing to fear. We have a Helper, Sally."

She walked to the outer door and pushed it to. She prayed silently against her dread. As she shut the door, and tried it, she felt the knob of the door turn in her hand. There was no sound from outside but the sound of the storm. Fear trailed a cold leisurely way across her heart. She prayed aloud and did not know it.

"Oh God, protect me from harm, for the sake of our dear Lord Jesus Christ." She pulled the door open. There was nothing there but the stormy night. She pushed the door shut and stood close behind it, listening. Her courage could not endure much further trial. As the catch fell into place she heard her son's voice:

"Mother!"

She opened the door. She was ready now to brave terror. The men came staggering out of the storm, knee-deep at every stride. They came all in a bunch. Allan hung limp between Sandy and John. John came first into the dark porch, sideways, with his father's arm over his shoulder.

"Oh, Johnny," she said, touching his clothes with her hands.

"I saw the door open and close so I cried out," he explained. "But hurry, mother; get the bed ready, and a bottle in, and something hot."

"Is it your father? Is there something wrong?" she said.

"Yes," he said. "He wasn't fit to stand it. But he'll be all right."

"Haste ye, sister," put in Sandy; "he'll soon come to. Here, loon, help me ben wi' him."

They carried Allan to the kitchen. His beard was hung with dribbles of ice. His beard hid his face but his lips were blue.

"I'm all right," he muttered after they had taken off his clothes and poured whisky down his throat. "Mind the dogs," he said. "Poor Glen." And he fell asleep.

Sandy flung off his cloak and let it fall on the floor. "Sally, see to the dogs or they'll be dead. May, gie me a dram," he said. He slumped into the rocking-chair.

"I thought it was a' up. If John hadna come it might ha' been." The stiff dram roused him.

"Ho, we're no' done yet," he cried to the wind outside. "John! ye canna sit there shivering. Take a dram, loon. May, gie him a droppie toddy!"

"No, give me some hot tea," said the boy.

"Well, I'll be eternally bitched and bewildered! it's him that's the drouth. Tea, begod, tea! Gie him a dram, May. It's you he's feared o'."

Between them they forced John to drink. The raw stuff burned him. He spluttered and coughed.

"Goamichty," said Sandy, "I've seen an infant tak' his noggin wi' more o' an air. May, your poor wee chicken's got the gapes."

"I'm glad you're all safe home," she said. "Come and have tea. Sandy, ask the blessing."

Next day the storm had gone. The sun shone as if such a thing as storm had never been. Sandy and John went to the hill. Snow lay knee-deep everywhere. The hollows were drifted full. Frost had made a crust on the snow, too weak to bear a man's weight. They sank to their knees at every spang.

"We can't do much," said Sandy. "This muck'll tire us oot in no time. The dogs won't stand it. I think there's a good puckle beasts up on the shoulder o' Cor-an-iolair. Them doon close to the burn would ha' got across to the wood. It's the beasts high up I'm afraid for. I think the rest's safe enough. Meall Mhor seems to be blown clean."

The wind had risen since morning, and the crust the two men broke was blown along the top of the snow. In places where the snow was too finely powdered and too dry to freeze the wind raised little puffs of dust. Rabbits and hares, searching for food, sank almost out of sight in the snow. They were quite helpless and the dogs ran about killing them until Sandy scolded them to heel. "I canna abide killing for no end, and we canna take them wi' us," he explained to John.

The sheep had come off better than they expected. Indeed there seemed to have been less snow up on the hills than down below, unless the high land had been blown clean. The sheep were gathered into three lots.

"Wise brutes," said Sandy. "They ken fine when it's to come an onding o' snow. They get thegither jist like what the Free Presbyterians hope to do at the Day of Judgement, wi' their bottoms to the draught."

SHOD AGAIN FOR SCHOOL

Shod Again for School

ANNIE'S FIRST DAY AT SCHOOL

George MacDonald *Alec Forbes of Howglen*

A good many boys and a few girls were assembled, waiting for the master, and filling the lane, at the end of which the school stood, with the sound of voices fluctuating through a very comprehensive scale. In general the school-door was opened a few minutes before the master's arrival, but on this occasion no one happened to have gone to his house to fetch the key, and the scholars had therefore to wait in the street. None of them took any notice of Annie; so she was left to study the outside of the school. It was a long, low, thatched building, of one storey and a garret, with five windows to the lane, and some behind, for she could see light through. It had been a weaving-shop originally, full of hand-looms, when the trade in linen was more prosperous than it was now. From the thatch some of the night's frost was already dripping in slow clear drops.

Suddenly a boy cried out: "The maister's comin'!" and instantly the noise sunk to a low murmur. Looking up the lane, which rose considerably towards the other end, Annie saw the figure of the descending dominie. He was dressed in what seemed to be black, but was in reality grey, almost as good as black, and much more thrifty. He came down the hill swinging his arms, like opposing pendulums, in a manner that made the rapid pace at which he approached like a long slow trot. With the door-key in his hand, already pointed towards the key-hole, he went right through the little crowd, which cleared a wide path for him, without word or gesture of greeting on either side. I might almost say he swooped upon the door, for with one hand on the key, and the other on the latch, he seemed to wrench it open the moment he touched it. In he strode, followed at the heels by the troop of boys, big and little, and lastly by the girls—last of all, at a short distance, by Annie, like a motherless lamb that followed the flock, because she did not know what else to do. She found she had to go down a step into a sunk passage or lobby, and then up another step, through a door on the left, into the school. There she saw a double row of desks, with a clear space down the middle between the rows. Each scholar was hurrying to his place at one of the desks, where, as he arrived, he stood. The master already stood in solemn posture at the nearer end of the room on a platform behind his desk, prepared to commence the extempore prayer, which was printed in a kind of blotted stereotype upon every one of their brains. Annie had hardly succeeded in reaching a vacant place among the girls when he began. The boys were as still as death while the master prayed; but a spectator might easily have discovered that the chief good some of them got from the ceremony was a perfect command of the organs of sound; for the restraint was limited to those organs; and projected tongues, deprived of their natural exercise, turned themselves, along with winking eyes, contorted features, and a wild use of hands and arms, into the means of telegraphic despatches to all parts of the room, throughout the ceremony. The master, afraid of being himself detected in the attempt to combine prayer and vision, kept his "eyelids screwed together tight", and played the spy with his ears alone. The boys and girls, understanding the source of their security perfectly, believed that the eyelids of the master would keep faith with them, and so disported themselves without fear in the delights of dumb show.

As soon as the prayer was over they dropped, with no little noise and bustle, into their seats. But presently Annie was rudely pushed out of her seat by a hoydenish girl, who, arriving late, had stood outside the door till the prayer was over, and then entered unperceived during the subsequent confusion. Some little ones on the opposite form, however, liking the look of her, and so wishing to have her for a companion, made room for her beside them. The desks were double, so that the two rows at each desk faced each other.

"Bible-class come up," were the first words of the master, ringing through the room, and resounding awfully in Annie's ears.

A moment of chaos followed, during which all the boys and girls, considered capable of reading the Bible, were arranging themselves in one great crescent across the room in front of the master's desk. Each read a verse—neither more nor less—often leaving the half of a sentence to be taken up as a new subject in a new key; thus perverting what was intended as an assistance to find the truth into a means of hiding it—a process constantly repeated, and with far more serious results, when the words of truth fall, not into the hands of the incapable, but under the protection of the ambitious.

Not knowing the will of the master, Annie had not dared to stand up with the class, although she could read very fairly. A few moments after it was dismissed she felt herself overshadowed by an awful presence, and, looking up, saw, as she had expected, the face of the master bending down over her. He proceeded to question her, but for some time she was too frightened to give a rational account of her acquirements, the best of which were certainly not of a kind to be appreciated by the master, even if she had understood them herself sufficiently to set them out before him. Still, it was a great mortification to her to be put into the spelling-book, which excluded her from the Bible-class. She was also condemned to follow with an uncut quill, over and over again, a single straight stroke, set her by the master. Dreadfully dreary she found it, and over it she fell fast asleep. Her head dropped on her outstretched arm, and the quill dropped from her sleeping fingers—for when Annie slept she all slept. But she was soon roused by the voice of the master. "Ann Anderson!" it called in a burst of thunder to her ear; and she awoke to shame and confusion, amidst the titters of those around her.

Before the morning was over she was called up, along with some children considerably younger than herself, to read and spell. The master stood before them, armed with a long, thick strap of horse-hide, prepared by steeping in brine, black and supple with constant use, and cut into fingers at one end, which had been hardened in the fire.

Now there was a little pale-faced, delicate-looking boy in the class, who blundered a good deal. Every time he did so the cruel serpent of leather went at him, coiling round his legs with a sudden, hissing swash. This made him cry, and his tears blinded him so that he could not even see the words which he had been unable to read before. But he still attempted to go on, and still the instrument of torture went swish-swash round his little thin legs, raising upon them, no doubt, plentiful blue weals, to be revealed, when he was undressed for the night, to the indignant eyes of pitying mother or aunt, who would yet send him back to the school the next morning without fail.

At length either the heart of the master was touched by the sight of his suffering and repressed weeping, or he saw that he was compelling the impossible; for he stayed execution, and passed on to the next, who was Annie.

It was no wonder that the trembling child, who could read very fairly, should yet, after such an introduction to the ways of school, fail utterly in making anything like coherence of the sentence before her. What she would have done, had she been left to herself, would have been to take the little boy in her arms and cry too. As it was, she struggled mightily with her tears, and yet she did not read to much better purpose than the poor boy, who was still busy wiping his eyes with his sleeves, alternately, for he never had had a handkerchief. But being a new-comer, and a girl to boot, and her long frock affording no facilities for this kind of incentive to learning, she escaped for the time.

It was a dreadful experience of life, though, that first day at school. Well might the children have prayed with David—"Let us fall now into the hand of the Lord, for his mercies are great; and let us not fall into the hand of man." And well might the children at many another school respond with a loud *Amen*! . . .

CHANGED DAYS?

R. F. Mackenzie *The Unbowed Head*

You could say without too much exaggeration that the Scottish educational system is based on the tawse. Take it away and part of the system crumbles. What do you put in its place? many teachers ask. It is an admission that the educational system is based on punishment, depends on punishment. Dark shadows from a pre-Christian world linger in the classrooms of the twentieth century, shadows of fear. Life is a jungle and we are explorers securing our camp for the night. The natural instincts are jungle beasts and must be guarded against, like tigers or savage tribes. The idea that love casteth out fear has no currency in these circumstances.

COUNTRY SCHOOLS

Alexander Gordon *The Folks o' Carglen*

The rising generation are now sent to school in obedience to the requirements of the Education Code, at the latest, at the age of five; but, in the olden times many of the children of the agricultural toilers did not appear in the schoolroom till the age of seven, eight or nine. They were, in addition, most irregular in their attendances, and the cases of young men and women of sixteen, seventeen, and eighteen who were unable to read a difficult sentence, to write legibly, or to spell with any degree of accuracy, were numerous, and as a consequence there were always—especially in the winter time—several big, burly young men and buxom young women to be found in attendance at the country schools. The services of these persons were of course in great demand during the summer and autumn for turnip hoeing, peat cutting, harvesting, potato ingathering, and such like, and the poor struggling parents were compelled to send their sons and daughters into service, in order to eke out the means of a scanty livelihood. When, however, the bitter winter set in with its cold, and frost, and snow, there was less need for the assistance of such people on the various farms, and as a consequence the young men and women (the former in greater numbers) returned to the family roof and renewed their attendance at the parochial school. I can recollect one such establishment where even bearded men were to be seen puzzling their brains through the dreary winter time in improving their acquaintance with reading, writing, arithmetic, grammar, and geography.

THE MUCKLE SCHOLAR

William Alexander *Johnny Gibb of Gushetneuk*

The occasion of a "muckle scholar" coming to the Smiddyward school was an event of some importance. And, therefore, when the embryo mole-catcher presented himself on a Monday morning to meet the scrutiny of the thirty odd urchins under Sandy Peterkin's charge, there was a good deal of commotion and whispering. He wore a pair of moleskin leggings, which extended up to the very thigh tops, and were there suspended by a little tag of the same cloth to the side button of his trousers. When he took off his bonnet his head was seen to be "huddry"*; that is, noticeably huddry for such a civilised place as the inside of a school. He had been to Andrew Langchafts' shop at the Kirktown, and had there furnished himself with a "sclate" and "skallie", a pennyworth of "lang sheet" paper, unruled and two quills for pens. These with an old copy of "the Gray"* were the furnishings for the ensuing scholastic campaign that was to fit him for entering on the practical study of mole-catching.

"Weel," said the new scholar, laying down his equipments on the side of the maister's desk, "aw'm jist gaun to *be* the raith*; an' wud like to win as far throu's aw cud."

"Coontin' ye mean?"

"Oh ay; in fack a body canna weel hae ower muckle o' it at ony rate."

"Fat progress hae ye made in arithmetic?" asked Sandy Peterkin.

The gudge* scratched his head for a little; and then, wetting his thumb, proceeded to turn over the dog-eared leaves of his "Gray". "Fack, I dinna jist min' richt. It's half-a-dizzen o' year sin' I was at the skweel. That was wi' Maister Tawse; an' I daursay your wye winna be the same's his wi' the coontin', mair nor ither things; so it winna maiter muckle."

"Ye've been through the simple rules at ony rate," suggested Sandy.

huddry tousled   *the Gray* Gray's Arithmetic   *raith* term   *gudge* thick-set person

"Hoot ay; aw'm seer aw was that. Nyod, I think it was hereaboot," and the aspirant mole-catcher pointed to the place on the book.

"Compound Division?" said the "maister", looking at the page.

"Ay", said the scholar, with a sort of chuckle; "but aw'm nae sayin't aw cud work it noo—aw wud better begin nearer the beginnin'".

"Weel—maybe Reduction?"

"That wud dee fine. It's an ill-to-work rowle, an' I never oon'ersteed it richt wi' Maister Tawse. Aw won'er gin aw cud win as far throu's wud mak oot to mizzour aff an awcre or twa o' grun, or cast up the wecht o' a hay-soo?"*

"That'll depen' o' your ain diligence," said Sandy Peterkin, with a smile.

"Weel, I ance was neepours wi' a chap't cud a' deen that, as exact's ye like; an' he not nae leems* till't, nedderin, but jist a mason's tape line't he hed i' the locker o's kist."

"It's quite possible to dee that wi' a marked line," answered the dominie.

"It's richt eesefu' the like o' that," said the gudge; "an' fan a body's gyaun aboot like, they wud aye be gettin't adee noo an' than, and cudna hardly foryet the wye. Noo, Maister Tawse wud never lat's try naething o' that kin', 'cep we hed first gane throu' a great heap o' muckle rowles; an' that disna dee wi' the like o' huz't hisna lang time at a skweel."

"An' fat ither lessons wud you like to tak?" asked the maister.

"Ye ken best; only it was for the coontin't I cam; an' leernin to mak oot accoonts maybe."

"We hae a grammar class noo—wud ye try it?"

"Na, na; aw winna fash wi't," said the gudge, with a decisive shake of the head. "It's nae for common fowk ava that gremmar".

"Maybe geography than? I've a gweed chart on the wa' here't ye cud get a skance o' the principal countries upon vera shortly."

"Weel, but is't o' ony eese to the like o' me, that geography? I wunna lickly be gyaun to forrin pairts."

If there was one branch more than another on which Sandy Peterkin set a high value, and on which, as a travelled man, he loved to descant, it was geography. So he pressed its importance, and a dubious consent was given to trying an hour at it once a week, it being understood that the future mole-catcher would not be subject to the "catechis" lesson on Saturdays. Then, as he had a suspicion that his new pupil was not too well up in his general literature, Sandy suggested the propriety of his taking a reading lesson.

"Na; aw hardly think't I'll fash wi' that edder," was the reply. "I was never that deen ill at the readin', an' I was i' the muckle Bible class afore aw leeft the skweel."

hay-soo hay stack   *leems* apparatus

"But ye maybe hinna read muckle sinsyne! an' ye wud get a lot o' usefu' information i' the Collection* lesson."

"But the like o' me's nae needin' to read like the minaister," said the muckle scholar, with a laugh, "an' it wud gar's loss a hantle o' time fae the coontin. An' oor at that, an' syne the vreetin—the day wud be deen in a han'-clap, afore a body cud get oot mair nor a question or twa."

However, Sandy succeeded in persuading him to take the "Collection" lesson. When the lesson came, he did not like to bid him stand up among a dozen urchins so much smaller than himself. The muckle scholar sat with his sturdy legs crowded in below the incommodious desk. He floundered through his turn at reading in a style at which his junior class-fellows did not always conceal their mirth. But he was too self-centred to be particularly thin-skinned, and Sandy Peterkin was indulgent, even to the extent of taking care that the graceless young rapscallions should spell every hard word in the muckle scholar's hearing, while Sandy spared him such trials; albeit he improved the time when the gudge's turn came by a short homily on the importance of attention to correct spelling. Then would our mature class-fellow seize his "sclate", and gravely set onto the piecemeal solution of "the Gray", from which occupation it was found that none of the ordinary devices would distract him. And at writing time, when the dominie sat in his desk, knife in hand, with a *chevaux de frise* of quill feathers, held in idle or mischief-loving hands, surrounding his nose as he diligently mended, or new-made, pens for a score of writers, the muckle scholar spread himself to his task, and grimly performed his writing exercise. He would also at times stay after the school was dismissed, and get the benefit of Sandy Peterkin's private instruction for an hour or so.

In short, there could be no doubt that the gudge would pass into the world again accomplished beyond many of his contemporaries; and thereafter he could hardly fail of attaining something of distinction in his destined walk, and with that distinction the attendant emoluments.

Mason's Collection a reading book

PLAYING TRUANT

David Toulmin *Hard Shining Corn*

I sneezed in spite of myself and it almost proved my undoing. I sat very quiet in the drying loft over the kitchen where my father was at his dinner.

"Is that loon at the school the day?" I heard the old man ask.

"Of coorse he's at the school," mother lied, "what sorra made ye think that he wasna?"

"Och, I thocht I heard a soone!"

"Ach," mother scorned, "Ye're a muckle gipe, it's only the cat sneezin'. Sup yer broth man, and if ye are as hungry as ye usually are ye winna listen for ferlies."

So I sat very quiet, hoping that Flora, my little sister, wouldn't betray me. She was just at the stage when she might blurt out anything, and to warn her against it was like tempting her the more.

The skylight was a fixture, rusted with age and damp and curtained with cobwebs. Dry rot was crumbling the rafters and the floor-boards were porous with woodworm activity. There was dust and grime in every seam of the place, but also an atmosphere of romanticism and adventure which lent an air of bravado to my truancy.

It was in this loft that all my trophies were stored out of Flora's reach: my Hotspurs and Rovers, Sexton Blakes, Buffalo Bills, Nelson Lees, Comic Cuts and Comic Chips; cinema advertisements cut week by week from the newspapers, stacked high and neatly by the hatch where the ladder came up, and all my cardboard cut-outs, soldiers, ships and motor cars; it just wouldn't do to let Flora get her hands on these. And most precious of all was my shoe-box theatre, with its aproned stage and tiny chairs, the props and characters all set for a performance of "Mill O' Tifty's Annie". I had just seen the play performed in the local hall and I was burning to have it done in puppetry.

My old man fell asleep after his heavy meal and my behind grew numb sitting on the hard floor boards. I felt like a Jack on the Bean Stalk awaiting the Giant to awake from his snooze. The old man was a heavy eater and to-day he had brose after his usual dinner and it had sent him nearly into a coma.

When confronted with a normal meal the old man would storm at mother about its lack of stamina. What would have satisfied the appetite of most working men was no use to the old man. "Some licht woman," he would screech, "some licht; I canna work a yokin's wark on that—I'll need brose!"

So mother would set out the oat-meal bowl, salt and pepper, and a jug of milk, and when the kettle came to the boil he made brose. To-day had been no exception and I heard him stirring his brose with the handle of his spoon. He always sat bolt upright on the edge of his chair at meal times, and I could picture it all quite plainly while I listened and waited.

And if it wasn't brose for dessert it was "melk and breid", oat-cakes warmed at the fire and crumbled into a bowl of milk, sometimes with a dash of cream, sprinkled with pepper and supped with a spoon, a tasty and invigorating diet, which I sometimes shared with the old man.

I heard Flora come and rattle the door at the foot of the loft stair. She had remembered for a moment where I was and I held my breath in fear. But she went away again and all was quiet.

Mother got the tea ready. I heard the tinkle of teaspoons going into the cups. The old man had come to life again. I heard the scrape of his chair on the cement floor as he dragged it back to the table. He was preparing to face another hard yokin' at the neep park and the coo byre and I knew he did more than he was bargained for.

"Woman," says he, "see that the loon comes tae the byre the nicht: he could hash the neeps or cairry a pucklie strae—maybe gie the calves a sook, it's aye a help ye ken."

Mother was washing the dinner plates in a basin at the other end of the table.

"Oh aye," says she, "but ye maun gie the laddie time tae tak' his denner. He has tae travel a lang road frae the school. And never a copper does the fairmer gie 'im for his wark."

"But it's me he's helpin' woman, ye canna expect the fairmer tae pey him for that!"

"No, no, but sometimes the fairmer trails the laddie awa' tae something else and he gets naething for that. He tak's the sap oot o' you but he's nae gaun tae tak' it oot o' the loon as weel. He'll hae tae work for a livin' when his day comes and surely that's time aneuch!"

"A' richt woman, but I'll be lookin' for 'im onywye. It's better than throwin' steens on the sklates or fleein' aboot wi' a gird. The laddie maun learn, woman!"

I heard the old man pushing his chair back from the table. I knew he would be putting on his sweaty cap and stroking mother's crow-black hair: "Ye're a bonnie crater though," he would purr, "aye are ye though."

"G'wa tae yer wark ye gock," I heard her say.

Then I heard the old man say a few silly childish words to Flora as he stepped over her dolls at the door.

I lifted the latch and descended the ladder into the lobby and the kitchen. The baker's van had been in the forenoon and I glanced at the table to see if there were any fancy pastries on the breadplate. Snatching a pancake, the only thing available, I sneaked to the door to see how far the old man had gone on the road.

I had to do this because the water cistern blocked my view from the window. I couldn't see the old man from the door so I crept outside and peeped round the corner of the cistern.

Ah ha! too soon! The old man was just entering the farm loanin' when he looked round and saw me. He shook his fist at me while I stood there like a fool with my mouth full of pancake.

He hadn't time to come back because it was too near yokin' time at the farm. Shaking his fist was all the malice he had resource to at the moment, but it was enough for me until nightfall when I could expect heavier punishment.

I ran back into the house and told mother.

"Weel weel," said she, as she wrung out her dishcloth, "Ye'll catch it when he comes home, and ye're supposed tae gyang tae the byre tae hash the neeps and feed the calfies. Ye should hae kept oot o' sicht a whilie langer."

"I wunna gyang tae the byre. He'll stab me wi' a fork like he tried the last time he was angered, the time he chased the foreman oot o' the byre."

I should have gone to the byre and softened the old man's wrath. But I cowered behind mother's skirts and hoped that she would stick up for me. And there was always the risk in the byre that the old man would take a fork over my back if he was thoroughly roused. Just the other day I had seen him chase the foreman out of the byre with a graip. Some tittle-tattle of evil gossip the foreman had spread around and it brought the old man into conflict with the other men.

"Spit it out!" I heard the foreman say, but he didn't wait for the old man to spit out anything, but ran like a schoolgirl when the old man charged him with the fork and well he may, for it was like a Highlander's charge at Prestonpans.

So I was in for it, and as the afternoon wore on my feeling of guilt grew stronger. From behind the window curtains I watched some of my classmates trudging home from school, boys and girls from outlying crofts, and the sight of them made me feel ashamed. It made me realise that I shouldn't play truant; that I should go to school like other respectable kids, and that I shouldn't deceive the old man, though mother let me off with it.

Mother lit the paraffin lamp and pulled down the blinds. She laid the supper plates on the table and took a bowl of meal out of the oak barrel to make the porridge.

I went up to the loft for my shoe-box theatre and arranged it on the dresser. "Mill O' Tifty's Annie" must go on at all costs. Flora was already seating her dolls around the stage to witness the performance. I had already done "Jamie Fleeman", and although the old man had snored through it all mother and Flora thought it was first class.

The old man had never thrashed me although I suppose I deserved it often enough. Once he had smacked my backside in a playful manner, under the bedclothes, and I had buried my face in the pillow with embarrassment because he could do this to me.

But now I could hear his footsteps outside on the gravel as he approached the door. Then he lifted the sneck and burst in upon us like a hungry bear. . . .

"Fut wye was ye nae at the skweel?" His eyes were like hot pin-heads that burned into mine as I retreated before him to the meal-barrel in the corner.

He never even glanced at the table, which he usually did, whenever he opened the door, to see what was there for his ravenous belly. He fixed his searing eyes on my miniature theatre, stanced on the dresser, and with one swipe of his King-Kong arm he scattered the lot on the floor; stage, scenery, puppets, props and tiny chairs for my imaginary audience went flying under the table and over the fireplace.

That single action was symbolic of what he meant to do with my whole life. He seemed determined I should earn my bread the hard way, as he himself had done, and he had no respect whatsoever for any other inclinations I might have.

"D'ye ken I'm on my last warnin' for nae sendin' ye tae school? D'ye hear?" he roared, while I squeezed myself in behind the meal-barrel.

Frustration brought his anger to fever heat. He danced round the barrel in a frenzy, while little Flora hung on the tail of his jacket, trying to pull him away. He wrenched her off and sent her spinning into a corner, where she sat on her doup, howling, with hot tears on her cheeks.

"D'ye want me tae stand in jile for ye? Ye damned rascal!" And he lashed out at me with his open hand.

The blow toppled me out from behind the meal barrel and sent me rolling over the floor. He was on me in a moment and I crawled under the table to escape his groping hands.

Now he was thoroughly roused and began chasing me round the table, first one side and then the other, and all the time I dodged him, while he stretched out his arm to prevent me reaching the door.

The table began to rock, rattling the cups in their saucers and spilling the milk from the porridge bowls. This nettled mother and she flew at the old man like a tigress, dragging him away from me by the jacket.

"Ye senseless fool," she screamed, "What sort o' wye is that tae carry on in the hoose? Folk wad think ye was mad!" And when the old man turned on her I bolted for the door.

He raised his arm to strike her but she grabbed the poker from the fender and dared him to try it. Her eyes gleamed with defiance and her lips quivered on set teeth.

The old man lowered his fist. "Oh aye," he yelled, "Ye'll tak' his bludy pairt will ye, and hae me stand the jile? Ye're spoilin 'im as it is. He'll never do a stroke o' wark when his day comes. But mind I'm tellin' ye he's nae gyan tae lie aboot here in idleness. He'll hae tae work for a livin' the same as I did afore his day. I'll see that he does it. You wait and see!"

Mother shook the poker in his face and his eyes wavered confronting her.

"Gyang tae yer supper man and lat the loon alane. You keep yer hands tae yersel and I'll see that he goes tae school."

"But woman, it wunna dee at a'! Can't ye see I'm on my last warnin? And what wad become o' ye a' if I gaed tae jile?"

"Ach, awa' man, ye're saft; they'll never send ye tae prison. They juist say that tae scare ye!"

So the old man cooled off and sat down to his porridge, now getting cold with a skin on top, so he didn't have to blow on the spoon, and it humoured him a little.

I sneaked inside from the cold to gather up my theatre. Flora gave me a hand, her great soft eyes swimming in tears and her golden curls glistening on her shoulders. The stage had been buckled in the scuffle and the scenery squashed and scattered, but we managed to arrange it somehow.

After supper Flora re-arranged her dolls on a chair in front of the stage. I had painted a fine back-drop in watercolour of the old Mill of Tifty, with a model of the waterwheel in front, and when I brought Bonnie Annie and Andrew Lammie on to the stage Flora gave a little gasp of delight.

And then I began my soliloquy:

> At Mill o' Tifty lived a man
> In the neighbourhood of Fyvie,
> Who had a lovely daughter fair—
> Her name was Bonnie Annie. . . .

But the old man was asleep, bolt upright on a hard chair, his head hanging over the back, his mouth agape, snoring.

He never did really understand me.

THE TWO CHRISSES

Lewis Grassic Gibbon *Sunset Song*

For she'd met with books, she went into them to a magic land far from Echt, out and away and south. And at school they wrote she was the clever one and John Guthrie said she might have the education she needed if she stuck to her lessons. In time she might come out as a teacher then, and do him credit, that was fine of father the Guthrie whispered in her, but the Murdoch laughed with a blithe, sweet face. But more and more she turned from that laughter, resolute, loving to hear of the things in the histories and geographies, seldom thinking them funny, strange names and words like Too-long and Too-loose that convulsed the classes. And at arithmetic also she was more than good, doing great sums in her head so that always she was first in the class, they made her the dux and they gave her prizes, four prizes in four years she had.

And one book she'd thought fair daft, *Alice in Wonderland* it was, and there was no sense in it. And the second, it was *What Katy did at School*, and she loved Katy and envied her and wished like Katy she lived at a school, not tramping back in the spleiter of a winter night to help muck the byre, with the smell of the sharn rising feuch! in her face. And the third book was *Rienzi, the Last of the Roman Tribunes*, and some bits were good and some fair wearying. He had a right bonny wife, Rienzi had, and he was sleeping with her, her white arms round his neck, when the Romans came to kill him at last. And the fourth book, new given her before the twins came to Cairndhu, was *The Humours of Scottish Life* and God! if that stite was fun she must have been born dull.

And these had been all her books that weren't lesson-books, they were all the books in Cairndhu but for the Bibles grandmother had left to them, one to Chris and one to Will, and in Chris's one were set the words *To my dawtie Chris: Trust in God and do the right.* For grandmother, she'd been father's mother, not mother's mother, had been fell religious and every Sunday, rain or shine, had tramped to the kirk at Echt, sitting below some four-five ministers there in all. And one minister she'd never forgiven, for he'd said not GAWD, as a decent man would, but GOHD, and it had been a mercy when he caught a bit cold, laid up he was, and quickly passed away; and maybe it had been a judgement on him.

So that was Chris and her reading and schooling, two Chrisses there were that fought for her heart and tormented her. You hated the land and the coarse speak of the folk and learning was brave and fine one day and the next you'd waken with the peewits crying across the hills, deep and deep, crying in the heart of you and the smell of the earth in your face, almost you'd cry for that, the beauty of it and the sweetness of the Scottish land and skies. You saw their faces in firelight, father's and mother's and the neighbours', before the lamps lit up, tired and kind, faces dear and close to you, you wanted the words they'd known and used, forgotten in the far-off youngness of their lives, Scots words to tell to your heart, how they wrung it and held it, the toil of their days and unendingly their fight. And the next minute that passed from you, you were English, back to the English words so sharp and clean and true—for a while, for a while, till they slid so smooth from your throat you knew they could never say anything that was worth the saying at all.

ACCEPTABLE SPEECH

R. F. Mackenzie *The Unbowed Head*

In no part of Scotland has the traditional Scottish speech survived so strongly as in Aberdeenshire and the north-east. Some pupils find little difficulty in being bi-lingual; others are obviously translating the home speech into the standard Scottish-English insisted on in most schools. Humorous stories are told about literal translations of Scottish idioms. In Aberdeenshire, enquiring about our neighbour's health we ask "Fit like are ye the day?" Well-brought-up people translate this literally into "What like are you today?" unaware that the idiom is not standard English. Some of the more independent-minded Aberdonians, and especially younger Aberdonians, make fun of this unsuccessful effort at translation.

People may say, "What's the relevance of all this about local speech?" I think it is central to the Summerhill story, which is the story of pupils who refuse to be steamrollered into an acceptable middle-class, London-dictated mould. It is one of the facets in the story of a society in transition. Political and educational overtones are rarely absent from this theme of speech patterns.

If the Summerhill pupils spoke in the historic accents of their homes, it was regarded as outlandish and uncouth and impolite. If they modified their speech too much to the required English pattern, they were regarded as letting their own side down. Sometimes when I asked them a question they would give the answer "aye", which was immediately translated into what teachers regard as the "proper" word, "yes". A growing number of working-class children in

Aberdeen see standard English as the imposed, required speech, the use of which, like the use of "sir", will be a sign that they accept the rules and regulations, the deference due and the obedience expected. It is a sign of submission to the imposed culture. I was brought up in this attitude of deference to the required speech. The local words were "vulgar", not as bad as swearing but nevertheless to be avoided by all well brought-up children. You could play tennis for a whole, long, summer afternoon and evening at our village tennis club and never hear this standard Scottish-English departed from. Later, studying German, I was surprised to find that many German words were pronounced in the Scottish way (for example, *finger*), and it was strange to find this pronunciation, not respectable in Scotland, regarded as respectable and acceptable in Germany. It was like finding a local farmworker at a seat of honour at an embassy banquet. I felt like asking, "How did *you* get in here?" Thus the teachers who didn't find the speech of many of their pupils acceptable were unaware alike of the long history of the local speech and of the pressures brought upon young people by the collision of two cultures.

TWO TONGUES

Eugen Dieth *A Grammar of the Buchan Dialect*

The chief enemies of the dialect are, without a doubt, the press, the pulpit and above all the public school, that systematic suppression of any thing with a local flavour. Time and again I was told: "We're no longer allowed to say that." The result is most deplorable; not because Standard English takes the place of good old *braid Scots*—from a utilitarian point of view that would be an excellent thing, well worth the price—but because the effort almost invariably ends in a compromise. The young folk have no sooner escaped the *dominie's* rod, than they slip back unconsciously, to their natural way of talking. The return, however, is not complete; the effect of the teaching lingers on in their speech. Utilitarians might argue that thereby the extreme, dialectal form had been mitigated and made at least universally intelligible. True, but the dialect henceforward is dead. It is a commonplace to speak of the dying doric and to accept this disintegration as bound to run its full course. It most certainly will, unless the schools step in, not killing but saving. . . .

Two tongues

A man's native speech is part of himself; his articulation part of his physiological system. No logical reasoning, therefore, will induce a Buchan speaker to reform his way of pronouncing the plosives or diphthongs &c. It is different with syntax, whose standard can be taught and explained and, what is more, learnt by the side of the dialectal usage. In their fight against the use of multiple adverbs and prepositions, against the Scottish use of *to mind, seek, learn, want, a doot* &c. schoolteachers are all too apt to discard the local form as bad or inferior. They should try to create a feeling for its special value and thus preserve it.

Already it is late in the day. . . .

A MAN AND A MAID

A Man and a Maid

RUSTIC COURTSHIP

William Alexander *Johnny Gibb of Gushetneuk*

Tam Meerison had been servant to Johnny Gibb only from the term of Whitsunday, that is to say, for about three weeks previous to the date of which I have been writing. He was a stout fellow of six or seven and twenty, with a broad, good-natured face, and straggling, but very promising whiskers of light complexion fringing his cheeks. On his head he wore a sort of nondescript blue bonnet, and going downwards on his person you found a remarkably substantial sleeved vest of moleskin and a pair of cord trousers, narrow at the knees, and spreading somewhat about the ankles, with about half-a-dozen buttons at bottom overhanging the heavy "beetikin" on either foot. The servant lass, Jinse Deans, a sedate-looking, red-haired damsel of fully Tam's age, had been a resident at Gushetneuk for a couple of twelvemonths by-gone; and when Johnny had set out for the Wells the two were master and mistress of the place for the time being. Tam pursued his work industriously afield through the day, along with the "orra man", Willie M'Aul, a youth of sixteen or seventeen, and son of the souter of Smiddyward. When six o'clock p.m. had come, Tam incontinently "lows't". Then came supper of kail and kail brose, of which the three partook in company, amid no little badinage, consisting mainly of equivocal compliments to Jinse on her housekeeping capabilities, from Willie M'Aul, or as he was more commonly designated, "the loon", who was of that particular character fitly described as "a roy't nickum".* Tam next lighted his pipe and blew clouds of smoke to the kitchen roof, as he watched Jinse "washing up" her dishes, an operation which Jinse invariably performed with an amount of clattering and noise that made the beholder marvel how it happened that she did not break at least one half of the crockery as it passed through her hands. Whether Tam was admiring Jinse's dexterity and vigour in going through her work or not I cannot say; I rather think, at any rate, that Jinse was not altogether unconscious that she was making a considerable display of these qualities before the new ploughman. At last she

roy't nickum wild young rascal

127

had finished, when, addressing "the loon", she said—

"Gae 'wa', ye haveril, an' fesh hame the kye, till I get them milket."

"An' fat'll aw get for that, Jinse?"

"Gin ye get fat ye deserve, ye winna braig aboot it."

"Wud ye gi'e's a kiss gin aw war to dee't?"

"Ye're a bonny ablich* to seek a kiss. I'se rug yer lugs t' ye gin ye dinna gae this minit."

"Hoot man, ye've nae pluck ava", exclaimed Tam, as "the loon" retreated towards the door to escape from Jinse, who had shown a distinct intention of suiting the action to the word. "Canna ye tak' a grip o' 'er?"

"I wudna advise you to dee that, Tam, or ye'll maybe fin' 't she's a sauter"*, replied Willie, as he marched off for the cows.

Later in the evening, when the cows had been milked, the calves properly attended to, and the work of the day fully concluded, Johnny Gibb's three servants were to be seen loitering about the kitchen door, and talking over the "countra clatter". Tam, who was seated on the big "beetlin" stone by the door cheek, had spoken once and again of going to bed, and had given "the loon" emphatic warning of the expediency of his immediately seeking repose, as he might depend on it that he, Tam, would pull him out of the blankets by the heels if he were not up by five o'clock next morning. Notwithstanding his urgency with "the loon", Tam himself did not give any distinct indication of hurrying to bed. But as "the loon" failed to "obtemper" his repeated hints, he at last started to his feet, and went clanking across the causeway and up the trap stair to the "chaumer" over the stable. And, while "the loon" proceeded to undress, Tam yawned once and again portentously. He then, very deliberately, wound up his watch, and, seating himself on his "kist", began, by-and-by, to "sowff"* over "My love she's but a lassie yet". When he had got Willie fairly into bed, Tam next rose, and, under pretence of going to the stable, slipped down the trap and out by the door, which he quietly locked to make sure that Willie M'Aul would not follow him. In somewhat less than two minutes thereafter, Tam Meerison and Jinse Deans were seated side by side on the "deece"* in Johnny Gibb's kitchen.

I don't know all what Tam Meerison said to Jinse Deans that summer "gloamin". How should I? The whispers of lovers are hard to catch. Nor am I able to say how far Johnny Gibb would have approved of the sort of sederunt that took place on this occasion, in his absence, between his servant maid and his servant man. But certain it is that this was not the first time that Jinse had been wooed in a similar manner, and in that same place. Not by the same wooer,

ablich scamp   *sauter* salty or sharp person   *sowff* whistle
deece a long wooden seat in the form of a sofa

William Alexander

certainly, for until three weeks ago she had been utterly unaware that such a man as Tam Meerison existed.

At any rate, if Jinse saw no harm in receiving a little attention from an additional sweetheart, Tam, evidently, found her company the reverse of disagreeable. The time fled swiftly past, as it is wont to do in such circumstances. It had worn on to twelve o'clock, to one o'clock, and the lonely corncraik, which had so long kept up its rasping, yet cheery note, to break the stillness of the summer twilight, had at last ceased its cry, and gone to sleep. It was still and quiet as quiet could be, when footsteps were surely heard approaching the house of Gushetneuk.

"Wheest!" exclaimed Jinse, in a low whisper. "Fat's that?—I hear a fit."

"Nonsense," said Tam, "It's some o' the horse i' the park at the back o' the hoose."

"It's naething o' the kin'. Here, I say—there's somebody comin' up the close! In aneth the deece wi' ye this minit!" whispered Jinse, in great excitement.

Tam felt there was nothing for it but to do as he was bid; not that he liked the idea of doing it, or that his judgment was fully convinced of the propriety of the course prescribed, but he failed in getting up any valid negative to oppose to Jinse's urgency; and so, giving way to the force of her exhortation, Tam proceeded to squeeze his inconveniently-bulky person under the deece, among a horde of old shoes, dilapidated brooms, and "sic like", with all the celerity he could achieve. And he was not a moment too soon, for the head and shoulders of some person were already dimly discernible at the front window. The deece stood opposite to this window, at the back wall. A tap or two on the pane were immediately heard, followed by a loudly-whispered "Jinse!"

Now, Jinse's position at the moment *was* a little awkward. With womanly tact she had remained by the deece, to cover Tam's retreat, which had been accomplished with tolerable success; but here there were one, if not two pairs of eyes staring through the uncurtained window, and there was yet light enough to enable the owners of those eyes to follow the movements of any one inside, and even to discover their whereabouts, if they happened to be fully in view of the window, which the occupant of the deece unluckily was. She hesitated, yet remained still; but the call was persistently kept up, "Jinse, I'm sayin, Jinse!" Jinse's wits could scarcely have been calmed to the point of keeping continued silence under the increasingly-violent demand of the assailants of the window to have audience of her; to pretend that she was in bed was hopeless, and so, starting up in a fashion to knock over one or two chairs and stools—not a bad feint either—Jinse advanced to the window, and indignantly demanded what the midnight brawlers wanted.

129

"Ou, Jinsie, 'oman, dinna tak' the huff—nae fear o' the aul' cock the nicht. We ken brawly that Gushets an' 's wife tee's awa' fae hame."

"Futher they be awa' fae hame or no, ye hae nae bizness comin' here at this time o' nicht disturbin' fowk."

"Wus ye sleepin' terrible soun', Jinse?"

"Sleepin'!" exclaimed the second voice; "the fowk o' Gushetneuk sleeps noo oot o' their beds, an' wi' a' their claes on!" And at this sally of wit the two men laughed loudly.

"Gae'wa' this minit, I tell ye", exclaimed Jinse, with increased vehemence.

"I wauger she has a man wi' 'er, the jaud", was the only reply that proceeded from the first speaker.

Jinse, who either did not hear, or pretended not to hear, this remark, then in a rather less indignant tone, asked, "Fat are ye wuntin here, I'm saying?"

"Fat are we wuntin! Wuntin in tae see ye, Jinse; fat ither", said the voice that had spoken most.

"Gae awa' hame, I tell ye."

But, at this juncture, Jinse, to her great horror, heard the latch of the door softly lifted, and the door itself, which of course had never been locked, evidently opening—a doubtful illustration, I daresay, of the saying that "love laughs at locksmiths". Before she could hinder it the two men were inside, and advancing towards the kitchen. They were quite well known to Jinse to be two of the servants at the farm of Mains of Yawal—one of them, indeed, averred that he had been "here afore"—but, for all this, it was decidely inconvenient to have them in the house with the avowed intention of searching out the man who, as they asserted, was there before them, and all to see "fat like" he was.

"Faur hae ye pitten 'im noo, Jinsie?" exclaimed the more demonstrative of the two; "jist tell's, 'oman—we winna hurt 'im."

"I say!" cried Jinse, excitedly, endeavouring to push him back.

"Jock, min", continued the man, addressing his friend, who had not yet emerged from the "trance"*; Jock, canna ye come ben an' gi'e Jinse the fawwour o' yer company. Oh-ho! he'll be i' the bed, I wauger", and the fellow darted across, and opened the doors of the "bun"* bed in which Johnny Gibb's servant maid slept. Partly through vexation and excitement, partly perhaps as a stroke of policy, Jinse had now resort to a woman's last defence—her tears. Her tormentor, failing to find the man he had groped for in the bed, and with his compunctions slightly stirred, perhaps, seized her round the neck.

"Weel-a-wuns, than, Jinsie", exclaimed the equivocal comforter, "we'se lat 'im rest 's banes in peace an' quateness"; saying which he swung Jinse round, and they both together came down on the deece with ponderous force. Now,

trance lobby   *bun bed* closed-in bed

Johnny Gibb's deece, though a substantial piece of furniture on the whole, did yield slightly, perhaps, under severe pressure; and, moreover, in the process of pushing himself under it, Tam had unsettled the deece from the two fragments of thin slate on which its front legs stood. The result of this was that, inasmuch as Tam Meerison was bulky enough to require in any case all the accommodation he could find between the deece seat and the floor, the "doosht" of the two persons falling on it had the effect of bringing his person into such violent contact with a three-cornered ironing "heater", which happened to be under him, that Tam uttered an involuntary "Go-ch!" with considerable emphasis. The general noise going on fortunately prevented this exclamation being heard; but, as Tam lay there a very close prisoner indeed, without the power of stirring a hair's-breadth, the sweat gathered on his brow plentifully, and he began seriously to reflect what was to be the end of it, for the second man had now also taken his seat on the deece, and horrible pictures of being squeezed as flat as a skate rose in his mind; still he hoped the deece would hold out, and so long as it did so, he might hold out too, seeing he certainly had not more than half the super-imposed burden to sustain.

No doubt it was a weary lie for Tam, for a full hour and a half had elapsed before Jinse managed to get rid of the two intruders. In the course of the conversation overhead of him, Tam had the pleasure of hearing his sweetheart questioned in a very direct and unceremonious fashion about himself, under the title of "Gushets' new man", the interrogator adding, as his own private opinion, "He's a queer-leukin' hurb,* at ony rate." It need hardly be said that Jinse answered discreetly in the circumstances.

When the unsought visitors had left, I daresay she and her companion exchanged some words of mutual congratulation and comfort; but day-light was already showing itself, and the feelings of both Tam and Jinse had been too rudely disturbed to admit of their settling down again at that time to a quiet and loving conference. Tam hung about for a little after he had risen from below the deece, and spoke widely of giving the two disturbers of his enjoyment their "kail throu' the reek some day", and then he slipped out to the stable, and crept cannily up the "chaumer" stair. Tam had hoped to get quietly to bed, at any rate; but, just as he had deposited the last article of his removable garments on his "kist" lid, and stood in nocturnal attire, ready to creep in amongst "the plaids", his bed-fellow, Willie M'Aul, turned himself with a drowsy "grane", and muttered, "Ay, ay! ye're a gey boy, comin' to yer bed at three o'clock i' the mornin'."

"Haud yer jaw, min!" was Tam's abrupt response.

hurb large, clumsy fellow

SANDY'S WOOING

Gavin Greig *Logie o' Buchan*

Meanwhile Sandy was coming more frequently than ever to Millbog. At length he summoned up courage to broach the subject of marriage to old John and his wife, asking the hand of their daughter Bell. Both gave their most cordial consent. With this Clyacks* seemed to be satisfied; but Marget who, having interrogated Bell, knew that he had never spoken to her on the subject, gently hinted that he would "Maybe need to speak to the lassie hersel'".

This was a new ordeal for poor Sandy to face, and it took him about a week to get his courage screwed up to the required tension. He was such a diffident wooer that he stood sorely in need of help to come to the point; but Bell, so far from giving him any assistance in his courtship, made it as difficult as possible, being at one time shy, at another mischievous, and meeting all his hints with an innocence or a density that was most disheartening to the poor man.

One night he came determined to bring the matter to an issue.

"Weel, Bell, fu' auld wid ye be?" he began.

"O, auld eneuch for a' the guid I've deen", said Bell with a laugh.

This disconcerted him a bit. He sat smoking a while and looking in the fire. The two had the place to themselves, Marget having, as usual, found a job for every other body that would keep them out of the way a while. This Bell always noted, and silently contrasted the facilities afforded Sandy with the obstacles thrown in Jamie's way.

After a while Clyacks took the pipe from his mouth, looked half round, and spoke again.—

"Isn't it time ye were marriet?"

"O fie, I'm but a lassie yet."

"But ye're aye growin' aulder."

Sandy, who thought the reflection embodied in this last remark of his quite impressive and almost solemnising, was so distressed to find it greeted with merry laughter, that he didn't say another word that night.

The next time he came back he began where he had left off.—"Ye wid like to be marriet sometime, widna ye, Bell?"

"O ay, but I'll be in guid time, Sandy."

Again, as before, there came a smoking interlude.—

"And fu wid I dee for a man, Bell?" he said at last, but without looking up.

"O guidsakes, Sandy, nae ava jist!—Ye're ower auld for me."

"Fu auld wid ye think I wis noo?"

Clyacks Sandy of Clyacksneuk

"O, maybe fifty."

"Na, I'm only forty-sax. I cam' in wi' the century."

"That's awfu' handy. Ye'll hae nae diffeeculty in mindin' your age."

Poor Sandy was bound to reflect on the advantage to which Bell had referred, which carried him so far away from the point he had been making for that he couldn't get his mind into position again for renewing the attack.

And so he did no more courting that night.

But Bell's mother had overheard this little bit of conversation, and, when Sandy went away, she took her daughter to task about it.—

"Fat wye did ye say yon to Sandy, ye stupid limmer?"* she demanded, in unusually sharp tones. "Dinna ye ken a guid offer when ye get it?"

But Bell was silent. She had learned the efficacy of this weapon of silence.

"My certies", her mother went on, "mony a lass wid jump at Clyacks".

There was no reply.

"Gin ye lat an offer like that by ye, ye deserve to want a' your days.—Sic anither coo 'll never low at your door again, I tell ye."

Bell's continued silence so irritated her mother that she went close up to her, patted her foot, and almost shrieked,—

"Fat d'ye mean, lassie?—Lat's hear ye!"

Bell had to speak. Her answer was sullen and short,—

"Weel, I'm nae for Clyacks."

"Fa are ye for than?"

"Naebody."

And Bell walked away, leaving her mother looking after her in anger, pity, and amazement. . . .

A night or two after Clyacks called again, and once more returned to the subject of marriage. Bell felt there was little use hedging any longer. She had better face the crisis at once and have done with it.

"Sandy", she said, "I canna be your wife. I like ye—rale weel; but—but I've anither lad."

"Yea?" said Sandy. And he sat silent a while, till he should get hold of the import of the words.

Afraid that he wasn't quite understanding the situation, she added,—

"An' I like him best."

"Vera likely," was the quiet response. Clyacks spoke in his slow sententious way; but feeling the thing very much more than one would have thought from his outward deameanour, which was stolid enough.

"And fa micht this ither lad be?" he asked at length.

"Och!—never min'."

limmer bad or mischievous girl

But Sandy wouldn't be put off. He must know.

"Weel than, it's—it's—Jamie Robertson."

How difficult it was to say the name.

"Yea?" said Clyacks, and relapsed into silence. But he wasn't done with the subject. Somehow, when the conversation got off and away from himself, he felt more freedom.

"An' ye like him best?" he said, after a little.

"Ay," was Bell's brief answer, but blushing and simpering spun it out.

"And has he socht ye?"

"Ay,—a kin' o't."

There followed another and a longer pause. There wasn't much sign that Clyacks was exercising himself over the matter to any particular extent; but inwardly a struggle was going on,—and, for a man of his phlegmatic nature, a deep one. Bell suspected that he was feeling more than he showed, and she was sorry for him.

At length he sat up, and Bell instinctively felt that he had made up his mind in some way or other.

"Weel than, Bell", he began, speaking with great deliberation, "I winna seek ye again. . . . Jamie's a guid lad. . . . He ance did me a guid turn, and I hinna forgotten't till 'im."

"O thank ye, Sandy", Bell broke in, "ye're awfu' guid!"

He took no notice of the interruption, but went on.—

"Noo, gin Jamie take ye, it's a' richt. But gin he *dinna* tak' ye, or gin ye dinna want to tak' *him*, ye'll maybe min' that I'm aye willin'."

Clyacks flourished in other times and circumstances from Barkis, but in their way of putting proposals matrimonial the two men seem to have approximated somewhat.

SILK BOTH SIDES

Lorna Moon *Doorways in Drumorty*

"And two and a half yards o' four-inch black satin ribbon."

Jessie MacLean added this last fatal item with an upward jerk of her head lest Mistress MacKenty, at the other side of the counter, should think she was ashamed of her purchase. But Mistress MacKenty had a nose for news rather than an instinct for tragedy, and by the suppressed eagerness in her voice as she asked, "And ye'll want it silk on both sides I'll warrant?" you could see that she was already half-way down the road to the smithy to spread the news that: "Jessie MacLean had lost heart and would be out in a bonnet in the morn, so help her Davey."

"Aye, silk both sides," Jessie answered, letting her eyes range the shelves carelessly to prove that there was nothing momentous in her buying bonnet strings.

Silk both sides proved it! A satin-faced ribbon might have many uses, but silk both sides was a bonnet string by all the laws of millinery known to Drumorty.

Telling about it five minutes later, Mistress MacKenty said, "I might hae been wrang when she bought the silk geraniums, and I may hae been over-hasty when she said 'half a yard o' black lace'—but silk both sides is as good as swearing it on the Bible".

In Drumorty, a bonnet with strings tied below the chin means that youth is over. About the time the second baby is born, the good wife abandons her hat—forever—and appears in a bonnet with ties. She may be any age from eighteen to twenty-five; for matrimony, and motherhood, and age, come early in Drumorty. The spinster clings longer to her hat, for while she wears it, any bachelor may take heart and "speer" her; and if she be "keeping company" she may cling to her hat until she be thirty "and a bittock"; but after that—if she would hold the respect of her community, she must cease to "gallivant" about "wi' a hat" and dress like a decent woman, in a bonnet with ties.

And Jessie MacLean was six and thirty as Baldie Tocher could tell you, for did he no' have the pleasure of burying the exciseman the very morning that Jessie first saw the light of day, and was it no' the very next year that Nancy MacFarland's cow got mired in the moss?

Drumorty had been very lenient with her. Many a good wife thought it was high time that Jessie laid aside her hat, but always she held her peace, remembering her bridal gown and the care with which Jessie had made it, for Jessie was the village seamstress, and it was a secret, whispered, that she charged only half price for making wedding gowns, because she liked to make them so much.

Another reason for their lenience was Jock Sclessor. For fifteen years Jock had "kept company" with her; not one Sunday morning had he missed "crying by" for Jessie to go to morning service. He would come round the bend of the road from Skilly's farm just as the sexton gave the bell that first introductory ring which meant "bide a wee till I get her goin' full swing and then bide at hame frae the kirk if ye dare"; and Jessie would come out of her door and mince down the sanded walk between the rows of boxwood to the gate, and affect surprise at seeing Jock just as if she had not been watching for him behind her window curtain this past five minutes.

Jock was the cotter on Skilly's farm. Every year he intended to "speer" Jessie when thrashing was over. Tammas, his dog, will tell you how many times he had been on the very point of asking her the very next day, but—always the question of adding another room came up and not for the life of him could he decide whether to level the rowan tree and build it on the east—or to move the peats and build it on the west; and by the time he had made up his mind to cart the peats down behind the byre and build it on the west, lambing was round again and he let it go by for another year.

And every year Jessie was in a flutter as thrashing was nearing the finish. One year she had been so sure that he would "speer" her that she bought a new scraper; for Jock could make your very heart stand still, he was that careless about scraping the mud off his boots. Often when she was alone, she would practise ways of telling Jock that he must clean his boots before he came in: "Good man, hae ye forgotten the scraper?" was abandoned because it wasn't strictly honest, for Jessie knew full well that he always forgot the scraper. "Gang back and clean your feet," was set aside also, because it was too commanding and "Dinna forget the scraper" was also discarded because it isn't good to nag a man before he has set foot in the door. But none of the expressions had been tried out yet—for when Jock dropped in with her, after service, Jessie hurried him by the scraper as if it might shout at him, "She expects you to speer her!" and so put her to shame.

But now thrashing had been over for weeks, and every Sunday since then, she had looked for the white gowan in Jock's coat, for what swain "worth his ears full of cold water" ever asked the question without that emblem of courage in his buttonhole? It is a signal to the world that he means to propose, that he is going in cold blood to do it—and forever after his good wife can remind him of that, should he suggest that he was inveigled into it by some female wile.

Last Sunday, on their way to church, Jessie cleared her throat nervously and grasped her new testament, bracing herself as she asked in a thin voice that was much too offhand: "Would your peats no' be better sheltered in the lea o' the byre?" and Jock replied: "Na, they are better where they are."

And so a hope, nourished fifteen years, died, and through the service she sat gazing straight ahead, with her eyes wide open, for the wider eyes are open, the more tears they can hold without spilling over. And next Saturday she bought black satin ribbon "silk both sides" and the world, meaning Drumorty, knew that Jessie's tombstone would not read "Beloved wife of—"

In Jessie's cottage the blinds were drawn on Saturday evening, and you who have suffered will not ask me to pull them aside and show you how a faded spinster looks when she weeps; nor how her fingers tremble when she sews upon bonnet strings; but let me tell you how bravely she stepped out next morning wearing her bonnet, with never a look through the curtain to see if Jock was on his way, nor a glance to see if the neighbours were watching. Her step was just as firm upon the sanded path, and her head just as high; perhaps she grasped her testament more tightly than usual, but what soul on the rack would not do that?

Jock came round the bend as she reached the gate. She clung to the latch to keep herself from tearing the bonnet from her head. Oh, Fate, that sits high and laughs, have you the heart to laugh now? Jock was wearing a white gowan. It was just a dozen steps or so back to the house, and a hat, and happiness; but the world knew that she had bought bonnet strings and was that not Mistress MacKenty watching from behind her curtain? Go forward, Jessie—there is no turning back, and go proudly! Open the latch and answer his "guid morning" and smile—and don't, don't, let your hands tremble so, or he will surely guess!

Look your fill from behind the curtain, Mistress MacKenty! You can not see a heartache when it is hidden by a black alpaca gown and when the heart belongs to Jessie MacLean!

Jock Sclessor, your one chance of happiness is now! Lead her back into the house and take the bonnet from her head! No, laggard and fool that you are, you are wondering if she has noticed the gowan! Has she not! She has watched for it for fifteen years! Speak, you fool! Don't keep staring at her bonnet! You dullard, Jessie must come to your rescue, and she does, "Is the sexton no' late this morning?" Jessie turned out of the gate as she spoke, snapping the latch with the right amount of care.

"Aye, later than usual," Jock agreed. (The sexton was never late in his life, and at that moment the bell rang out to give Jock the lie.) But Jock was so dazed, he would have agreed if she had said, "Let us choke the minister."

As they walked to the church, he meditated, "Evidently she never expected me to speer her, and she's never so much as glimpsed the gowan. I'll slip it out when we kneel in the kirk. But maybe I better sound her out first. It's gey and lonesome for a man biding by himself."

They were just turning round by the town hall where the rowan trees are red, when he said, "I had been thinkin' o' levellin' my rowan tree." Jessie's heart thumped. Here it came! (That was why he wouldn't move the peats.) But she wouldn't help him a foot of the road—she had waited too long—he must come every step himself.

"Oh, that would be a pity—it's a bonnie tree," she answered.

Not much help here, but he would try again. "I was thinkin' o' building."

"Building? My certies! What could ye be building so near the house?" this with some malice for all the fifteen long years. But you have gone too far, Jessie; he needs help.

"I—oh—I thought I'd build a shed for peats."

Thud! That was Jessie's heart you heard and that queer thin voice is Jessie's, saying, "I thought—ye were minded to leave the peats the other side o' the house."

"Aye, I am minded to leave them there—but a body canna hae too many peats."

And as they knelt in kirk, he slipped the gowan out—and Jessie did not need to widen her eyes to hold the tears this time. That sorrow was past, she would never weep over it again.

At home, she brewed her tea, looking round at her rag rugs and white tidies with pleasure. The tidy on the big chair was as white and smooth as when she pinned it there in the morning, and there was no mud to be carefully washed off the rug by the door. There was a certain contentment in knowing that it would never be; a certain exhilaration in knowing that next Sunday she could not be disappointed, because next Sunday she would not hope. She sipped her tea peacefully and smiled at the bonnet sitting so restful-like on the dresser, and at the tidy on the big chair so spotless and smooth, and thought, "Jock Sclessor would have been a mussy man to have about a house. I'm thinkin' his mother was over-lenient when she brought him up."

And Jock, at Skilly's was thinking, "I wouldna had time to build it anyway. Lambing is here—and that is too bonnie a tree to be cut down."

THE FISHER AND THE LADY

Jean White *The Sea Road*

At the corner of the main road where the Sea Road branched off to the right, she sat down to wait. The night was warm and scented, and she felt her breathing burdened as if the air was also heavy with thunder. She soon recognised his footsteps in the distance, a little unsure and stumbling.

There was not another soul abroad besides themselves, nor any sound at all to be heard but the gentle crooning of the sea. When he had passed her unawares and turned into the Sea Road, she called "Hullo, Rolly!" after him without moving, and speaking softly not to startle him.

Nevertheless, he was startled and stood still. She could only see him vaguely against the night sky, but she knew that he had turned in her direction and was searching the darkness for her. So she got up and went to him.

"What d'ye want?" he asked her gruffly.

"I minded on what ye said about not seein' in the dark, so I thought ye'd be none the worse o' a helpin' hand along the Linkshaugh road.* From the yitt to the steadin's a tricky road." She kept an elaborate calm which belied the wild beating of her pulse.

"I'll manage fine." But while he repulsed her he could not conceal a betraying uncertainty in his voice.

"Och, dinna be blate," she said more lightly, and took his arm with determination in hers.

"I hate bein' treated like a bairn," he grumbled, but made no further effort to resist her.

They went on without another word, he stumbling a little over the tussocks, till they came to the faint glimmer of the white gate on the left. Here he hesitated and would have turned in, but her firm pressure on his arm led him onward.

"I thought—isn't that the road?"

"No," lied Marty. "It's a good bit farther on."

She thought—she was not sure, but she thought—that she would go with him as far as his house. How much farther she would go she left to him and fate. She tried by her talk to divert his mind from the road, but her voice sounded squeaky and breathless, and she was constantly under the necessity of swallowing hard in order to moisten her throat. He made only monosyllabic answers to her high chatter, and she saw with panic the moment approaching when she would have to declare herself. That she must do so was the one thing she never doubted.

* Rolly has been partially blinded at the battle of Jutland.

139

He swung round on her so unexpectedly that she gave a smothered exclamation.

"Now then, nae mair o' this nonsense. Ye've told me lies, ye've led me past the Linkshaugh road, and now ye'll tell me what in God's name ye're tryin' to do wi' me."

He seized her hard by the elbows, holding her arms close to her sides.

"Rolly!" Her exclamation was an appeal to him to save her the embarrassment of explanations by kissing her at once. But he was adamant.

"Have you changed your mind since this mornin'?"

"Yes," she whispered.

He kept perfectly still as if he did not know what to do with this news. She was full of exultation at her own courage, but his silence was prolonged till dismay leapt upon her triumph and destroyed it. He was going to repudiate her; he loved Nellie best. She tried to hold out her arms to him in appeal, but he still held them as in a vice, and she was helpless. Not knowing their strength, he was digging his fingers cruelly into her flesh. She suddenly drooped forward in his hold with a sharp exclamation of pain.

"Let me go," she begged. "Ye're hurtin' me."

He dropped his hands at once and said, "I'm sorry, Marty," with humility which made amends for his hesitation.

"Never mind," she said, and went close against him and put her arms round his waist, laying her head on his shoulder. She loved his fresh smell of the sea.

He succumbed. His resistance fell away from him, no more potent than morning mist at the uprising of an ardent sun.

"Marty, my dearie," he murmured passionately against her hair, "my bonny, bonny doo! I've hardly been able to thole the day nor the night, I was so sore beset wi' wantin' ye." He found her mouth and kissed her long and fiercely, seeming to draw strength from a contact which drained all hers, for he continued in a loud defiant voice, "Marty, I've liked this ane and that ane, and whiles I've taken mair from them than I nott, but you're the only lass I've loved without divall,* without diminishment. I thought I'd fairly lost ye, and then I began to hae hopes again till the-day. I just couldna stand it. I was fair wild. If ye hadna got me away from Francie's, as sure's death I was up and away wi' Nellie. A terrible come-down from Marty Laird."

"I'm glad I was in time," Marty confessed, putting her arm up round his neck and hugging him with a shuddering sense at once of his bulk and his preciousness.

"God, ye're grand," he said, in a shaken voice; and they kissed again blindly,

divall cease

oblivious of night and stars and anybody who might be passing them either from the manse or from Linkshaugh.

The natural impulse of the spring, urgent, creative, indulgent, an overwhelming force from having been dammed back so long, flowed mightily over them and became irresistible from the certainty of their mutual love.

"Will ye come wi' me, Marty?" he said.

For sole answer she laid her hand in his. He should be left in no doubt about her absolute intention. He put his arm round her waist, and they walked on to the cottar house, but at a point just short of the Skail he turned aside to a dip between the cliffs. Here the sound of the sea came in more clearly on a sigh of expectant happiness. A faint star or two within the paler wedge of the slopes opened their eyes for a moment before Rollo moved and shut them out. As he took her in his arms the night too closed gently about her.

"Here's the place that I made for ye. I thought ye might come the-day, but I only hoped—I thought we'd sit and watch the stars for a bit." He had spread rushes and grass at the foot of the incline so that she could sit soft, and lean against the slope. He had let her go, and stayed a little way off, but with so much of the concentrated energy of the spring pulsing in a vivid current through and between them he was not to be curbed for long. He suddenly turned and loomed dark over her as he said in a fierce whisper.

"Marty, ye're nae only makin' a fool o' me, are ye? I mean, ye ken ye're bein' a sore temptation to me?"

"I'm tryin' terrible hard to be," she said, with a break in her laughter. She held him tight round the neck and slid down against the cliff, pulling him with her.

"Ye mean't?" He asked his last resistant question.

Her answer was plain, though it was not given in words.

It was a hard couch in spite of the rushes, but its very want of resiliency increased the abundance of fierce strength with which she was possessed. As they made ecstatic love, she defied with mind and body the soft emasculation of all feather-bedded pap-fed gentility. She went back and took Rollo triumphantly with her, to the strong and ruthless, cruel and utterly free and joyful life of wild nature. This love-making, which had been clamped and dumb and blunted by the imminence of an undesired husband and a stuffy room all muffled in darkness but for the presence of a few stars let in for the solace but in vain, was now under the open sky freely and furiously at one with the sweeping clouds, the wind tossing in the bents, the swift swoop of the night-bird, the surging gallop of the sea. Pagan, Maenad-haired, afire with the passionate impulse of sea-rovers and the lusty force of farm-folk, she gave up her voluptuous body to Rollo in an ecstasy of abandonment. "My love!" she said. "Oh, my love!"

She had not another word to utter, but an elemental song tore its way through the loosened bonds of the body and seemed soundlessly to lift her essential self to the uppermost edges of the cliff where it strained upward as from poising disembodied tiptoes, with its hair streaming among the stars. In spirit she sang in perfect harmony with the spheres.

"Ye're grand, Marty," murmured Rollo. "Ye're a star."

That was what she was; a star. She stepped down from her heaven to smile indulgently at the dark shadow of his head where it lay against her breast, and cupped it closer with her hands, full of her secret and her gratitude. Poor man, poor little wee man! When he woke to-morrow he would think he had been purposeful and overmastering and would be full of remorse for having betrayed her. But she knew well that the truth did not lie in that direction at all. It had been she who had proved too much for him and had tempted him to be her salvation. When he reached up to give her a final lax kiss she hugged him passionately to her with sudden wild joy that now, at last, they could go off happily together and live in his cottage and she would be for ever free of Robert Langside and all dark-garbed decencies.

*   *   *

She slept sweetly on her bed of rushes and woke neither to cry of bird nor slap of wind nor spit of passing rain, but only to the sly oncoming of the sun as it stalked her dazzled eyes. She turned drowsily to Rollo and did not find him. She put out her hand sharply and was as sharply full awake. She shook her tousled hair out of her eyes and ran to the top of the cliff, but the miniature mountain range of rock and dune stretched empty away before her, bleached white by the dawn, all the grasses combed one way by a small keen breeze. The whole seascape was vibrant with movement, aquiver with the myriad dancing of the dawn, diamond-pointed light and dancing shadow slipping and sliding from tip to trough, from trough to tip of the clashing waves, little white clouds so puffed up with themselves that they too were on the verge of dancing, seamews wheeling and glinting, momently ensnared by the light. Everything was gay and lovely and alive, but nothing in all this life was concerned with her. Rollo had escaped her. She considered his flight dispassionately and saw him in her mind's eye first awakening to his remorse and then quietly withdrawing his great clumsy figure to steal off homeward in the first light, stumbling now and then because he had no longer her arm to guide him. Her heart melted in pity for the helpless creature. Well, but he could wait. And she, though she was ravenously hungry, would keep him waiting.

She climbed lightheartedly as far down the cliff as she could, then slid to the beach, filling her shoes with sand so that she had to take them off. Tying them up with her stockings and laces in order to sling them across her shoulders, she set off running fleetly to dip her feet in the water, so happy that she clapped her hands like a child above her head as she ran. Once her feet had been the same golden colour as the sand, but time and the wearing of black cashmere stockings had turned them as white as flowers, a little exotic and un-Martyish. A short distance from the incoming tide she sat and ruffled her white toes to the wind, thinking gleefully how shocked Robert would be to see his wife behaving shamelessly like this. "Something of decency, if not of dignity, is due from my wife." She giggled at the memory of his empty pompousness and mentally flicked her fingers in his face. With this defiant imaginary gesture she was on her feet again, kilting her skirt to her knees, and was off running towards the spit of green where the cottar house stood. Her heavy shoes, a serviceable pair bought for her, bumped hard against her shoulder blades as if in loyalty to their purchaser they must helplessly register their protest. She was a flirt, a jade, and a randy—jab, bump, bang! She was a married woman who had run away from her husband and that husband a minister, but if only she would put on her shoes again and walk home in sedate contrition, confessing her sin or better still making up a good lie, she might yet learn to walk circumspectly in what paths Robert might choose for her.—Oh, joy, joy! If her hands had been free of the impedimenta of shoes and skirt-tails she would have clapped them once more because she was never again going to attempt to be restrained and calm and genteel unless she felt like that. She was walking with a laughable youthful swagger, conscious of having recaptured something of the spirit of her childhood, tossing her head. Her precarious hair fell from its few restrictive pins, and she shook it into the breeze. . . . Her feet faltered. Round the corner stood the cottar house, but she could not bring herself to go on. What was the good? Love was selfishness, subjugation, sorrow. She was not made for it.

Rollo would not remember her. "Ye're grand, Marty; ye're a star." But he would soon forget her. Silent and pensive, digging her toes into the sand and warming her cold chin on her shoulder, she considered her future, seeing with dismay that there was nowhere she could go to now if Rollo rejected her. This was a sad declension from her mood of high disdain, and it was a chastened Marty who rounded the cliff and picked her way carefully through the detritus below the bothy. A clear stream of sunlight filtered over a dip of the land and met her like a welcome.

She had never been so near Rollo's house in daylight before, and her spirits rose as she looked, it so obviously had need of her and would have so little power to hold her when she would away. . . .

But there was still enough left for him and her to do. He had not troubled to tear away the rotten gate which had to be lifted coaxingly to shut or open, nor to weed the overgrown path and dig up what had once been a garden but was now a rank harbourage for course sourock and docken and tansy and carl-doddy, nor to clear away an accumulation of rubbish, mostly empty tormented tins, in one sheltered corner where tinkers had lit their fires beneath the stars. He had not cleaned the windows nor washed the doorstep nor fenced his half-dozen white wyandottes into their own part of the garden. She was quite gay and assured again as she jumped the little burn, her shoes giving her one final jab as a vicious reminder that now at last she had taken a step which she could never retrace. She went straight into the kitchen.

"Hullo Rolly!" she said, dropping her shoes and stockings to the floor.

The place was cluttered with rubbish, but it was also filled with a refreshing smell of sea-stuff, a big piled plateful of newly picked dulse. Rollo was staying his morning hunger with tough mouthfuls of it, and she too put out a greedy hand; but his fist shot out and gripped hers.

"Let go, Rolly Yitts," she cried indignantly. "Ye're hurtin' me, ye great muckle sumph."

"Who told ye to come here?" he demanded, and pulled her forward till she stood close up beside him and he was glowering straight down into her face. She was taken aback at this cavalier welcome and made no answer, but gave all her attention to forcing herself free.

"Last night should hae taught ye better than that, lass," he said, encircling her wrist with thumb and forefinger in a bracelet of steel. "Come on. Sit down." With one humiliating tug he had her on his knee, and his arm was round her like a vice. "Now ye can tell me what way ye've come here after me. Do ye nae ken that I've had all I want from ye?"

She realised that by shedding his tenderness he was trying to outface his morning remorse. Sure that he would come to heel when she wanted him, she could afford to be careless.

"I winna say a word to ye if ye don't let me go."

"Let ye go? That's what I want to do, let ye go. That would be best for both o's."

"Imphm." She gave a casual grunt of assent.

"Ye dinna care?"

"Not a docken," she said saucily, ramming a handful of dulse into her mouth.

He looked at her with sudden fierce suspicion. "Ye've been up to tricks like this before, haven't ye, Marty Laird? Ye're gey weel-practised, aren't ye? Ye're nae better than the lave, are ye, my bonny lass?"

"No," she said nonchalantly. That would let him down easily, and for herself, now that she was "nae better than the lave", the answer lost her nothing.

"No? Just like that, ye jaud?" His grasp on her loosened in his wrathful amazement. "And so all this time I've been pinin' and dwinin' for ye, ye mean to tell me ye were just to my hand?"

"Imphm," she answered lightly, continuing to munch. She was so hungry that she stuffed dollop after dollop into her mouth.

"Oh well then!" He seemed reluctantly to discard an ideal. "If that's the set o't, what way have ye come here?"

"I've come to bide."

"Away wi' ye, what would your minister say?"

"That you and I were unrepentant sinners. And so we are. Oh, it's true—isn't it true, Rolly?"

She flung her lightness away from her, and so suddenly recaptured in that vibrant question the passion of the night that a flame in him sprang to meet hers, and he bent his head and kissed her hard on her white neck. They strained together in a long breathless embrace, then he held her back with a triumphant laugh.

"This is grand, Marty. I'm unco' glad ye've come to bide wi' me, my bonny dearie. Ay, but I'll keep ye fast and fairly this time, my wee white seamaw, and hell and damnation winna get ye away from me." He set both his hands about her neck and pressed back her head for another kiss.

"I dinna want to gang away, Rolly," she assured him contentedly, and rubbed her cheek against his rough one.

"There's just room for ye," he said. "I've twa chairs, though we'll only need ane—and a table and a puckle dishes. I'm a bit short o' blankets maybe, but from what I've seen we'll take nae harm from that."

He laughed, and so did she. She loved this natural coarseness in him. Far from discouraging it, she would join him willingly in any ruthless destruction of the conventions he liked, smash, shatter, utterly cast them down, and with them all Langsides.

"It'll be rare," she said and, getting up suddenly from his knee, leant forward and hugged him round the neck, then pulled him towards her by the ears till she had only to bend her head to kiss him. "Let's get some breakfast inside's, and syne we'll have a look round our gear."

"And—Marty, ye're sure ye dinna bear me no grudge?"

In the climbing light his face showed a little rosier than usual and the scar looked puckered and livid, so that her heart melted with the already familiar sense of pity which would always leave her defenceless against him.

"What d'ye think?" she counter-questioned with a sidelong look.

"Tell's, Marty."

"Then listen, Rolly. I'm not a light randy though I said I was. I've never, never—well, broken whatever Commandment it is. But now I'm proud and pleased that I've broken it. I've loved ye ever since I was a bairn and ye carried me over the Girnan; kind Rolly. No, listen to me; my speech isn't finished yet. I loved ye so much that I meant everything to happen just like that. I tempted ye, ye dear silly gype. Ay, and I will again."

"Ye nickum!" he said in amusement and admiration.

CHRIS'S WEDDING

Lewis Grassic Gibbon *Sunset Song*

It had left off snowing, Chris, dressing, saw from her window, a sunless day; and a great patching of clouds was upon the sky, the light below bright and sharp, flung by the snow itself; and the smoke rose straight in the air. Far over the braes by Upperhill where Ewan would be getting set in his clothes—unless he'd done that long before in the morning—the sheep were baaing in their winter buchts. Then Chris took off her clothes, and stood white again, and put on the wedding things, mother'd have liked to see them, mother lying dead and forgotten in Kinraddie kirkyard with the twins beside her. She found herself weep then, slowly, hardly, lost and desolate a moment without mother on her marriage-day. And then she shook her head, *Oh, don't be a fool, do you want to look a fright before Ewan and the folk?*

She peered at her face in the glass, then, fine! her eyes were bright, the crying had helped them. Pretty in a way, not only good-looking, she saw herself, dour cheek-bones softened for the hour in their chilled bronze setting. And she combed out her hair, it came far past her middle, thick and soft and sweet-smelling and rusty and tarnished gold. Then last was her dress, blue also, but darker than her under-clothes because so short was the time since father had died, she threaded the neck with a narrow black ribbon but round her own neck put nothing, her skin was the guerdon there.

So, ready, she turned herself round a minute, and held back the skirt from her ankles and liked them, they were neat and round, she had comely bones, her feet looked long and lithe in the black silk stockings and shoes. She found herself a hanky, last, and sprinkled some scent in that, only a little; and hid it away in her breast and went down the stairs just as she heard the first gig drive up.

That was the Strachans from Peesie's Knapp, Mistress Strachan fell long in

146

the face at first. But Chae soon kindled her up with a dram, he whispered to Chris that he'd look after the drink; and Mistress Melon said it was aye best to have a man body at that end of the stir. And before they could say much more there came a fair stream of traffic up from the turnpike, all Kinraddie seemed on the move to Blawearie: except the old folk from Netherhill, and they sent their kind wishes and two clucking hens for Chris's nests. The hens broke the ice, you might say, for they got themselves loose from the gig of the Netherhill folk and started a wild flutter and chirawk everywhere, anywhere out of Blawearie. Long Rob of the Mill was coming up the road at that minute, in his Sunday best, and he met the first hen and heard the cry-out that followed her, and he cried himself, *Shoo, you bitch!* The hen dodged into the ditch, but Rob was after her, grabbing her, she squawked fair piercing as he carried her up to the house, his fine Sunday coat was lathered with snow; and he said that such-like work would have been nothing to Chae, who had chased the bit ostriches out in the Transvaal, but he'd had no training himself. Syne he took up the dram that Chae had poured him and cried *Here's to the bonniest maid Kinraddie will mind for many a year!*

That was kind of him, Chris had been cool and quiet enough till then, but she blushed at that, seeing Rob stand like a Viking out of the picture books with the iron-grey glint in his eyes. Mistress Munro, though, was right sore jealous as usual, she poked her nose in the air and said, and not over-low, *The great fool might wait for the tea before he starts his speechifying;* she was maybe mad that nobody had ever said that *she* was bonny; or if anybody ever had, he was an uncommon liar.

Then the Bridge End folk came up, then Ellison and his wife and their daughter, and then the Gordons, and then the minister, riding on his bicycle, it looked as though he'd had a fall or two and he wasn't in the best of temper, he wouldn't have a dram, *No, thank you, Chae,* he said, real stiff-like. And when Rob gave him a sly bit look, *You've been communing with Mother Earth, I see, Mr Gibbon,* he just turned his back and made out he didn't hear, and folk looked fair uncomfortable, all except Long Rob himself and Chae, they winked one at the other and then at Chris.

She thought the minister a fusionless fool, and went to the door to see who else was coming; and there, would you believe it, was poor old Pooty toiling up through the drifts with a great parcel under his oxter, his old face was white with snow and he shivered and hoasted as he came in, peeking out below his old, worn brows for Chris. *Where's the bit llllass!* he cried, and then saw her and put the parcel in her hands, and she opened it then, as the custom was, and in it lay a fine pair of shoes he had made for her, shoes of glistening leather with gay green soles, and a pair of slippers, soft-lined with wool, there wouldn't be a grander pair in

Kinraddie. And she said, *Oh, thank you*, and she knew that wasn't enough, he stood peering up at her like an old hen peers, and she didn't know why she did it but she put her arms round him and kissed him, folk laughed at that, all but the two of them, Pooty blinked and stuttered till Long Rob reached out a hand and pulled him into a chair and cried *Wet your whistle with this, Pooty man, you've hardly a minute ere the wedding begins.*

And he was right, for up the road came walking the last two, Ewan and his best man, the Highlander McIvor, near six feet six, red-headed, red-faced, a red Highlandman that bowed so low to Chris that she felt a fool; and presented his present, and it was a ram's horn shod with silver, real bonny and unco, like all Highland things. But Ewan took never a look at Chris, they made out they didn't see one the other and Mistress Melon whispered to her to go tidy her hair, and when she came down again all the place was quiet, there was hardly a murmur. She stopped at the foot of the stairs with the heart beating so against her skin it was like to burst from her breast; and there was Chae Strachan waiting her, he held out his arm and patted her hand, when she laid it on his arm, and he whispered *Ready then, Chris?*

Then he opened the parlour door, the place was crowded, there were all the folk sitting in chairs, solemn as a kirk congregation, and over by the window stood the Reverend Gibbon, very stern and more like a curly bull than ever; and in front of him waited Ewan and his best man, McIvor. Chris had for bridesmaids the little Ellison girl and Maggie Jean Gordon, they joined with her, she couldn't see clear for a minute, then, or maybe too clear, she didn't seem to be seeing with her own eyes at all. And then Chae had loosed her hand from his arm and she and Ewan stood side by side, he was wearing a new suit, tweed it was, and smelt lovely, his dark face was solemn and frightened and white, he stood close to her, she knew him more frightened than she was herself. Something of her own fear went from her then, she stood listening to the Reverend Gibbon and the words he was reading, words that she'd never heard before, this was the first marriage she'd ever been at.

And then she heard Chae whisper behind her and listened more carefully still, and heard Ewan say *I will*, in a desperate kind of voice, and then said it herself, her voice was as happy and clear as well you'd have wished, she smiled up at Ewan, the white went from his face and the red came in spate. The Red Highlander behind slipped something forward, she saw it was the ring, and then Ewan fitted it over her finger, his fingers were hot and unsteady, and Mr. Gibbon closed his eyes and said, *Let us pray.*

And Chris held on to Ewan's hand and bent her head and listened to him, the minister; and he asked God to bless their union, to give them courage and strength for the difficulties that the years might bring to them, to make fruitful their marriage and their love as pure and enduring in its fulfilment as in its conception. They were lovely words, words like the marching of a bronze-leafed beech on the lips of a summer sky. So Chris thought, her head down-bent and her hand in Ewan's, then she lost the thread that the words were strung on, because of that hand of Ewan's that still held hers; and she curved her little finger into his palm, it was hard and rough there and she tickled the skin secretly, and his hand quivered and she took the littlest keek at his face. There was that smile of his, flitting like a startled cat; and then his hand closed firm and warm and sure on hers, and hers lay quiet in his, and the minister had finished and was shaking their hands.

He hesitated a minute and then bent to kiss Chris; close to hers she saw his face older far than when he came to Kinraddie, there were pouches under his eyes, and a weary look in his eyes, and his kiss she didn't like. Ewan's was a peck, but Chae's was fine, it was hearty and kind though he reeked of the awful tobacco he smoked, and then Long Rob's, it was clean and sweet and dry, like a whiff from the Mill itself; and then it seemed every soul in Kinraddie was kissing her, except only Tony, the daftie, he'd been left at home. Everybody was speaking and laughing and slapping Ewan on the back and coming to kiss her, those that knew her well and some that didn't. And last it was Mistress Melon, her eyes were over bright but carefull still, she nearly smothered Chris and then whispered *Up to your room and tidy yourself, they've messed your hair.*

She escaped them then, the folk trooped out to the kitchen where the fire was roaring, Chae passed round the drams again, there was port for the women if they wanted it and raspberry drinks for the children. Soon's the parlour was clear Mistress Melon and Mistress Garthmore had the chairs whisked aside, the tables put forward and the cloths spread; and there came a loud tinkling as they spread the supper, barely past three though it was. But Chris knew it fell likely that few had eaten much at their dinners in Kinraddie that day, there wouldn't have been much sense with a marriage in prospect; and as soon as they'd something solid in their bellies to foundation the drink, as a man might say, the better it would be. In her room that wouldn't be her room for long Chris brushed her hair and settled her dress and looked at her flushed, fair face, it was nearly the same, hard to believe though you thought it. And then something felt queer about her, the ring on her hand it was, she stood and stared at the thing till a soft whispering drew her eyes to the window, the snow had come on again, a scurry and a blinding drive from down the hills; and below in the house they were crying *The bride, where is she?*

So down she went, folk had trooped back in the parlour by then and were sitting them round the tables, the minister at the head of one, Long Rob at the head of another, in the centre one the wedding cake stood tall on its stand with the Highland dirk beside it that Ewan had gotten from McIvor to do the cutting. The wind had risen storming without as Chris stood to cut, there in her blue frock with the long, loose sleeves, there came a great whoom in the chimney and some looked out at the window and said that the drifts would be a fell feet deep by the morn. And then the cake was cut and Chris sat down, Ewan beside her, and found she wasn't hungry at all, about the only soul in the place that wasn't, everybody else was taking a fair hearty meal.

The minister had thawed away by then, he was laughing real friendly-like in his bull-like boom of a voice, telling of other weddings he'd made in his time, they'd all been gey funny and queer-like weddings, things that you laughed at, not fine like this. And Chris listened and glowed with pride that everything at hers was just and right; and then again as so often that qualm of doubt came down on her, separating her away from these kindly folk of the farms—kind, and aye ready to believe the worst of others they heard, unbelieving that others could think the same of themselves. So maybe the minister no more than buttered her, she looked at him with the dark, cool doubt in her face, next instant forgot him in a glow of remembrance that blinded all else: she was married to Ewan.

Beside her: He whispered *Oh, eat something, Chris, you'll fair go famished*, and she tried some ham and a bit of the dumpling, sugared and fine, that Mistress Melon had made. And everybody praised it, as well they might, and cried for more helpings, and more cups of tea, and there were scones and pancakes and soda-cakes and cakes made with honey that everybody ate; and little Wat Strachan stopped eating of a sudden and cried *Mother, I'm not right in the belly!* everybody laughed at that but Kirsty, she jumped to her feet and hurried him out, and came back with him with his face real frightened. But faith! It didn't put a stop to the bairn, he started in again as hungry as ever, and Chae cried out *Well, well, let him be, maybe it tasted as fine coming up as it did going down!*

Some laughed at that, others reddened and looked real affronted, Chris herself didn't care. Cuddiestoun and his wife sat opposite her, it was like watching a meikle collie and a futret at meat, him gulping down everything that came his way and a lot that didn't, he would rax for that; and his ugly face, poor stock, fair shone and glimmered with the exercise. But Mistress Munro snapped down at her plate with sharp, quick teeth, her head never still a minute, just like a futret with a dog nearby. They were saying hardly anything, so busied they were, but Ellison next to them had plenty to say, he'd taken a dram over much already and was crying things across the table to Chris, Mistress Tavendale he called her at every turn; and he said that she and Mistress Ellison must get better acquaint. Maybe he'd regret that the morn, if he minded his promise: and that wasn't likely. Next to him was Kirsty and the boys and next to that the minister's table with Alex Mutch and his folk and young Gordon; a real minister's man was

Alec, awful chief-like the two of them were, but Mistress Mutch sat lazy as ever, now and then she cast a bit look at Chris out of the lazy, gley eyes of her, maybe there was a funniness in the look that hadn't to do with the squint.

Up at Rob's table an argument rose, Chris hoped that it wasn't religion, she saw Mr. Gordon's wee face pecked up to counter Rob. But Rob was just saying what a shame it was that folk should be shamed nowadays to speak Scotch—or they called it Scots if they did, the split-tongued sourocks! Every damned little narrow dowped rat that you met put on the English if he thought he'd impress you—as though Scotch wasn't good enough now, it had words in it that the thin bit scraichs of the English could never come at. And Rob said *You can tell me, man, what's the English for sotter, or greip, or smore, or pleiter, gloaming or glunching or well-kenspeckled? And if you said gloaming was sunset you'd fair be a liar; and you're hardly that, Mr. Gordon.*

But Gordon was real decent and reasonable, *You can't help it, Rob. If folk are to get on in the world nowadays, away from the ploughshafts and out of the pleiter, they must use the English, orra though it be.* And Chae cried out that was right enough, and God! who could you blame? And a fair bit breeze got up about it all, every soul in the parlour seemed speaking at once; and as aye when they spoke of the thing they agreed that the land was a coarse, coarse life, you'd do better at almost anything else, folks that could send their lads to learn a trade were right wise, no doubt of that, there was nothing on the land but work, work, work, and chave, chave, chave, from the blink of day till the fall of night, no thanks for the soss and sotter, and hardly a living to be made.

Syne Cuddiestoun said that he'd heard of a childe up Laurencekirk way, a banker's son from the town he was, and he'd come to do farming in a scientific way. So he'd said at first, had the childe, but God! by now you could hardly get into the place for the clutter of machines that lay in the yard; and *he* wouldn't store the kiln long. But Chae wouldn't have that, he swore *Damn't no, the machine's the best friend of man, or it would be so in a socialist state. It's coming and the chaving'll end, you'll see, the machine'll do all the dirty work.* And Long Rob called out that he'd like right well to see the damned machine that would muck you a pigsty even though they all turned socialist tomorrow. And they all took a bit laugh at that, Chris and Ewan were fair forgotten for a while, they looked at each other and smiled. Ewan reached down and squeezed her hand and Chris wished every soul but themselves a hundred miles from Blawearie.

But then Chae cried *Fill up your glasses, the best man has a toast.* And the red Highlander, McIvor, got up to his feet and bowed his red head to Chris, and began to speak; he spoke fine, though funny with that Highland twist, he said he'd never seen a sweeter quean than the bride or known a better friend than the groom; and he wished them long and lovely days, a marriage in the winter had the best of it. For was not the Spring to come and the seedtime springing of their love, and the bonny days of the summer, flowering it, and autumn with the harvest of their days? And when they passed to that other winter together they would know that was not the end of it, it was but a sleep that in another life would burgeon fresh from another earth. He could never believe but that two so young and fair as his friend and his friend's wife, once made one flesh would be one in the spirit as well; and have their days built of happiness and their nights of the music of the stars. And he lifted his glass and cried *The bride!* looking at Chris with his queer bright eyes, the daft Highland poet, they were all like that, the red Highlanders. And everybody cried *Good luck to her!* and they all drank up and Chris felt herself blush from head to foot under all the blue things she wore.

And then Long Rob of the Mill was making a speech, different from McIvor's as well it might be. He said he'd never married himself because he'd over-much respect for those kittle folk, women; but if he'd been ten years younger he was damned if his respect would have kept him from having a try for Chris Guthrie, and beating that Highland childe, Ewan, at his own fell game. That was just Ewan's luck, he thought, not his judgement, and Chris was clean thrown away on her husband, as she'd have been on any husband at all: but himself. Ah well, no doubt she'd train him up well, and he advised Ewan now, from the little he knew of marriage, never to counter his wife; not that he thought that she wasn't well able to look after herself, but just that Ewan mightn't find himself worsted though he thought himself winner. Marriage, he took it, was like yoking together two two-year-olds, they were kittle and brisk on the first bit rig—unless they'd fallen out as soon as they were yoked and near kicked themselves and their harness to bits—but the second rig was the testing time, it was then you knew when one was pulling and one held back, the one that had sheer sweirty—and, that was a word for Mr. Gordon to put into English—in its bones, and the one with a stout bit heart and a good guts. Well, he wouldn't say more about horses, though faith! it was a fascinating topic, he'd just come back to marriage and say they all wished the best to Chris, so sweet and trig, and to Ewan, the Highland cateran, and long might they live and grow healthy, wealthy, and well content.

Then they all drank up again, and God knows who mightn't have made the next speech if Chae then hadn't stood up and cried *The night's near on us. Who's game for a daylight dance at Chris's wedding?*

THE GOWK

Jessie Kesson (previously unpublished)

You'd felt pity for the Gowk, when yourself was young. And he was a boy—debarred. Clutching the School Gates. Engrossed in the rough and tumble of the playground.

In Manhood, this on-looking compulsion was still with him. But you had outgrown pity. Revulsion, tinged with apprehension, had taken its place. Until you thought about it, and realised that maybe, maybe the half-witted dribbling boy was now imprisoned grotesquely in the flesh of Manhood.

But you didn't often think about that. And certainly the boys on the inside of the School playground never thought about it at all. Ettling always to get out, and within taunting distance of the Gowk.

> We saw Gowkit Jockie
> We saw him run awa
> We saw Gowkit Jockie
> And his nakit Bum and a'!

"Come *inside*, Rob! *And* you, Peter!" Jean Aitken shouted from her Kitchen window.

"And stop tormenting the life out of that poor bloody Gowk!" Her Father admonished, over her shoulder.

"That 'Poor Gowk' as you call him", Jean Aitken shrugged. "Should have been Lockit up and Away. A long time ago. Terrifying the life out of the bairns."

"Jockie's harmless enough". The old man defended. "He wouldna mind *them*. If they didna keep tormenting *him*!"

"You try telling Kate Riddrie that, Father. She's had her bellyful of the Gowk!"

"That's true enough." Her Father agreed. "But not until the Gowk's Father put the Wedding Ring on her hand!"

"And she's lived to regret *That*!" Jean Aitken pointed out. "Forbye, the Gowk was but a bairn, then. He's a Man. Full Grown, now."

". . . and the older he grows, the worse he grows." Kate Riddrie was complaining. "He's started to Abuse himself again. In broad day-light now! You'd think he hadn't got the wit for *that* even!"

153

"Maybe it's the *instinct* he's gotten." Hugh Riddrie said. "Even the Brute Beasts have gotten *that*."

He had long since found that words failed to justify to himself the existence of his Idiot Son. And was beginning to discover that they failed even to protect him.

"I could *cope*." His Wife claimed. "I could *cope* when he was young. But he's getting *beyond* me, now."

"You could never cope, Kate." Hugh Riddrie reached above the Dresser for his bonnet. "You could only pretend he wasna there at all."

"*Better*!" Kate Riddrie flared. "Than pretending he wasn't an Idiot *Born*! But then, of course, he's *your* Son."

"So you aye keep reminding me, Kate."

"And you *need* reminding! Do you know something?"

Hugh Riddrie shook his head. "No. But I know you're just about to *tell* me something."

"High Time Somebody did! You *puzzle* me." Kate Riddrie admitted. "Where other folk would try to keep a Gowk out of sight, *you* seem to like flaunting him in the face of the World."

"Letting everybody share the *shame*, like, Kate?"

"I don't know what you'd call it!" Kate Riddrie snapped. "But Nell Crombie was saying that she gets a Red Face, every time she puts her foot across this door!"

"She would." Hugh Riddrie agreed. "A very modest woman, Nell. Forever bragging that her Man has never seen her nakit. In his life. Come to think of it," he reflected, "neither have You! What the Hell is it makes you all so feared to *Look*!"

"Decency!" Kate Riddrie said. "Just plain *Decency*!"

"Is *That* the name they've gotten for't? Ah well. I'm aye learning."

"Not fast enough!" Kate Riddrie shouted, as he made for the door. "*Something's* got to be done. About the Gowk!"

"*Jockie*! *You* mean. Don't you, Kate?" Hugh Riddrie spun round on his heel. "*Jockie*!"

"I *meant* Jockie". She flustered. "It was just. . . . It was just that everybody else calls him. . . ."

"*THE GOWK*!" Hugh Riddrie finished the sentence for her. His quiet anger rising loud. Out of control. "What do You suggest I do with him, Kate? *Lib* the poor bugger! The way I'd lib a young Calf! Or would you have rather I had THRAPPLED him at *Birth*! With my BARE HANDS! . . . I've killed a Calf for less. For just being shargered. . . ."

... He could hear the School bairns taunting in the distance. Forcing his fore-fingers between his teeth, the shrillness of his whistle brought the taunting to a halt. And evoked the memories of the workers on their way home from the farm.

Old Riddrie. Whistling his Gowk, again. Poor Bugger. Other men had dogs to whistle for. Still. The man himself could be more sociable. Oh, but they minded on Riddrie, young. An other man then. An other man, altogether. That, of course, was before the Gowk was born. They themselves found little enough wrong with the Gowk! A pat on the head. A word in his ear, in the passing. A chew of tobacco slippit into his hand. And God! The Gowk was as happy as if he was in his Right mind!

... The shrill whistle halted their wives on their way back from the Baker's van. Myth and memory blending in a confusion of truth.

The *minute* the Gowk was born. The *instant* the Doctor set eyes on him ... "Poultice Jimmy" ... as he was known. For he believed that a Bread Poultice could cure anything from a Blind Boil on your Bottom to a Broken Heart. Though a Poultice was of little use to the Gowk. But at least the Doctor knew *something* was far wrong.

It was the Midwife, of course, that had let the cat out of the bag. In *confidence*, mind you! Though she should never have done the like. Not in a job like hers. According to her, the Doctor cursed and swore like a Tinker when he set eyes on the Gowk. Roaring away at the Midwife. To pay heed to the *Mother*. . . . The Midwife swore to the day she died, that Poultice Jimmy *knew*. That he hopit, if they paid no attention to the bairn, it might just dwine away. But the Gowk had survived. Never a day's illness in his life. To the great regret of Mistress Riddrie The Second.

Still. There was nothing on the *Women's* consciences. The Gowk, young, had never been debarred from *their* games as girls. Always willing to be "Poor Gracie" lying dead and in her grave. While they circled mournfully around him. . . .

> We planted an Apple-tree
> Over his head
> Over his head
> We planted an Apple-tree. . . .

... "Did you not hear me the *first* time? I'll comb your hair for you!" Jean Aitken threatened. "If you don't come *inside*. And stop crying after that Gowk!"

The gowk

"The Gowk was following our Liz." Young Rob dodged his Mother's upraised hand. "Liz didn't see him. That's why Peter and me was shouting. They were going down Sue Tatt's road."

"Sue Tatt's Road!" The information halted Jean Aitken's enraged intention.

"There you *are*, then!" Dod Aitken laughed. "*There's* something for you to pick your teeth on! We know Sue's not all that particular. But even Sue Tatt would draw the line at the Gowk!"

"Are you *sure*, Rob?" His Mother demanded.

"Positive!"

"*Certain!*" Peter added. Enjoying the effect the information had produced. "We was trying to warn Liz. That's why we was shouting."

"Our Liz." Jean Aitken remembered. "Should have been home by *this* time! The School Bus gets in at the back of five. What on earth would Liz be seeking down Sue Tatt's Road?"

. . . Liz Aitken, herself, knew what she was seeking. But was not sure whether it was to be found.

"Sue Tatt will know what to do." Chris Forbes had informed Liz. "They say she's had more men than we've had Suppers."

That had sounded reassuring enough, last night. But then night had always brought reassurance to Liz. Expecting its very privacy to produce the dark, quiet miracle. And herself waking up. To confirm it, in the morning.

"I've *often* been late" Chris had said. Sounding it like some special privilege. Rather than a comfort. "Sometimes a whole *week* late."

But then Chris Forbes had never been enticed up into the woods. How glad Liz had always been that she was herself. And not Chris Forbes. Never Chris Forbes. Now, she could have torn Chris right out of her skin. And gone inside it. To be safe. Like Chris was safe.

The rumours surrounding Sue Tatt were such that her house, itself, should have imparted an aura. Secret. Erotic. Its ordinariness disappointed Liz. But then the ordinariness of familiar things had begun to confuse her.

They should *know*. They should look *different*. The thing that had happened to herself. Should lie distorted. Reflected in everything she set eyes on. The skeleton of Rob's bike, stripped of essentials, lying out in the shed. The handles of her Father's old plough, curving high above the nettles.

But it was her landscape that was the ultimate traitor. Lochnagar couldn't *stand* there. The Dee it should Flood. . . .

> The Sky it should Fall
> Since I am with bairn
> Unwedded and all. . . .

... "This *Friend* ... This ... friend ... of yours, Liz" Sue Tatt asked. "About how old would she be, then?"

"Sixteen and a Half. Nearly *Seventeen*!" Liz extended her age, thinking somehow that it might advance her cause. "Chris Forbes said You could help!"

"Oh she *did*! Did she? It could be Nothing, Liz." Sue Tatt concluded, transforming her irritation with Chris Forbes into an attempt to reassure Liz Aitken. "That whiles happens to young lassies. Till they become Regular, like."

"But I *am* Regular!" Liz Protested. "I've always been Regular. Till *Now*."

"Oh Liz! Liz Aitken. Not *YOU*!"

The roof at home would have fallen in, under such an admission. It was the echo of its fall that sounded in Sue Tatt's voice.

"But you could *help*!" Liz urged. "Everybody says. . . . "

"Everything except their Prayers, Liz. The thing is", Sue stood pondering the paradox. "Everybody knows the cure. Till the ailment happens. Syne, they know nothing. For *myself*", Sue recollected, "I just fell back on the old Penny Royal. Quinine. And the skin of my legs peeling off in a pail of hot water and Mustard. Knowing they were all useless. But always just . . . hoping. Nothing ever budged mine an Inch! Not until they were good and ready to be born. But Cheer *UP* Liz! It *could* be a 'Wrong Spy'! And I've had my share of them! You might just waken up the morn's morning to find that everything's just fine, again. And Oh. Whatten a fine feeling *that* is, Liz, Stroking yourself under the sheet. As if your hands loved your body, again. And the sweat pouring out of you. With relief, just. And Thanking God. Even though you're not a Christian. Because you cannot think of anybody else to thank. And promising never to do it again. Not as long as you live. . . . But *of course* you'll do it again, Liz!" Sue Tatt bent towards her, laughing. Pressing her hands on Liz's shoulders, as if they might leap up, and dance together, to a bright reel of Sue's composing. ". . . Again. And Again, Liz! And it will be *right* then. And fine. For some lad will have *wedded* you! There's no chance of *this* lad wedding you?" Sue asked, as if the music itself had ended, and the bright bubble of hope drifted high up. Out of mind's reach.

"*None*!" That was a certainty. And Liz merely confirmed it. "He's sitting his Highers", she explained, "and I'm trying for a Bursary. I'm going to the University. My Mother's *set* on that. And my Father will kill me. You'll not TELL!" she urged. For, although hope had gone, secrecy still seemed essential. "You'll never Tell."

"*I'll* not Tell", sue Tatt promised. "But *you* should, Liz. Tell your Mother. And tell quick! Before *other* folk get in there first. That's what "gets" Mothers. Not having the time to get their faces ready. To look on the world again."

"It's my *Father*!" Liz rose to go. "He'll kill me. When he finds out."

"I *doubt* that, Liz. I very much doubt *that*!"

"You don't know my *Father*!"

Liz Aitken could well be right, Sue Tatt thought, as she watched Liz turn the bend of the road. But still Sue doubted. It was with the *Mothers* of the Parish, that she had a mere "Nodding Acquaintance".

"A fine night, again, Jockie!" Sue Tatt cried out to the Gowk, as he shambled past her gate. Poor silly Creature, he wouldn't understand a word she was *saying*. But he might just know that somebody was *speaking* to him. "Another fine night again, Jockie!"

The brambles down in the King's Howe were always the first to ripen. Liz Aitken stood amongst the bushes, caught up once more in a deceptive sense of security. The taste of childhood on her tongue. The colour of it staining her mouth. Savouring a fallacy.

The reeshling in the bushes behind her didn't disturb her peace of mind. It was the unseen hands that gripped her shoulders, that sent her cry rising across the Howe.

Such cries breaking the silence of the quiet Howe, were common enough. Easily enough analysed by listeners in the passing. A screaming rabbit cornered at last by the watchful weasel. A bleating ewe worried by a stray dog. The black sweep of the Hoodie Crow. And the rising protest of its victim. Distress traced easily enough to its unseen source. It was the Source, itself, that could always momentarily stop the listening heart.

. . . The Gowk was no solitary. Hugh Riddrie nearly always knew where to find him. The Smiddy, the General Shop, the Bus Stop. For Jockie liked to be amongst folk. A pity, that. For folk either ignored his presence. Or acknowledged it, the way they acknowledged old Moss, the Shepherd's dog. With a pat on the head.

In all the years, Hugh Riddrie had never got rid of the ache that caught at him, at the sight of his son, standing with, but not of, normal men. It was rare. But easier, at times like now, when they came upon each other, alone. In the nakedness of their relationship. When communication, though primitive, was natural. When tone of voice transcended interpretation. And monologue, comprehended by the listener, gave release to the speaker.

"*There* you are, Mannie! I've been whistling on you all night. What have you been up to, Jockie?
Riving head first amongst the Bushes!
Steady! Steady now! Till I get you wipit down.
Let's see your Mouth Now! You've been dribbling again!
The moustache of you's all slavers!
Steady now! Steady *on*!
Your Flies are wide open again! Will you *never* learn to button yourself up!
You know fine that drives her clean Mad.
She's gotten such a spite to Flies.
Especially Open Flies.
STILL!
You're *fine*, now!
In you go, then, Jockie.
Up the stairs. As nippit as you can!
Hold it! Hold it, Jockie. Till I get the boots off you.
That's *It*! *That's* it!
She'll not hear you, now.
We'll better her, this time!
Eh, Jockie? Eh, Mannie!
In you go, then! You're fine, now.
All Present and Correct!
NO! Jockie, *NO*!
Let my hand *go*.
I'm *coming* In! Right *behind* you.
Let my hand *go*!
Do you not *see*, Jockie?
You've got to go in *first*!
As if you'd been a *good* Mannie!
And come all the way home. By *Yourself*!
It's *easier*, that way, Jockie.
In you go then. We'll be all Right!

"It's all *Wrong*! All wrong, I tell you!" Jean Aitken insisted. "That Gowk should never be allowed to roam the country-side. Just look at the *state* Liz has come home in. Are you all *right*, Liz? What did that mad bugger of a Gowk *do* to you?"

"We tried to warn Liz." Young Rob remembered. "*And* Me!" Peter confirmed. "We was shouting after the Gowk."

The gowk

"Off up to your beds! The pair of you!" Jean Aitken commanded. "Are you *sure* you're all right, Liz? Are you *sure!*"

"Liz will be all right." Rob Aitken said. "She got a fleg just."

"She's gotten more than a fleg! She's looking *terrible*."

"He grabbed me." Liz explained. "And I didn't *see* him. *That's* what it was. I didn't *see* him. I ran all the way from the King's Howe. But I thought I'd never get out of the spot."

"What took you down to the King's Howe, like?" her Father asked. "That's bit out of your road, isn't it?"

"My Homework. I forgot to take it down. I went over to get it from Chris Forbes."

"I wouldn't bother about Homework the night," Jean Aitken advised. "You should hold straight on up to your bed. You've had a gey Shake-up."

"I'll be all right. I couldn't sleep if I went to my bed."

"Liz is right!" Her Father agreed. "Stop fussing her Woman!"

"Well then!" Jean Aitken turned in attack on both of them. "If she's all right, and can't go up to her bed, and can't sleep, she's *not* going to sit molloching *here* all night! She can just take herself through to the sink. And make a start to the Washing-Up!"

She would "tell them on Saturday". The decision taken, Liz leant against the sink, comforted by the postponement of time that lately she had begun to allow herself, when days could seem almost normal.

"I could have sworn I put Preserving Ginger down on the Grocer's List." Her Mother's voice drifted through to the Scullery. "I'm sure I noticed some at the back of the Press, the other day. . . ."

There *couldn't* be anything wrong with Liz! Her mother would *know*. She would never be worrying about Preserving Ginger, if there *was* something wrong. . . .

"But I think it's *last* year's Preserving Ginger that's in the Press. The strength will have gone out of it. . . ."

If there *was* something wrong, her Mother would stop going on about Preserving Ginger Forever. . . .

"I could be speaking to *Myself*!" her Mother was complaining to her Father. "I *told* you she would be better off in her bed! Standing through there in a dwam. She's had a bigger Upset than she'll admit. AND! If it's the *last* thing I do. I'll make Hugh Riddrie's ears *Blister*! Him and that *Gowk* of his."

. . . The Gowk, himself, was beginning to take on a subtle, new dimension, in the eyes of the Howe. A curious kind of normality. An ability to share in the venial sins of ordinary men. It was Liz Aitken who began to lose dimension to its inhabitants.

You could have "knockit them all down with a feather", they swore. Liz Aitken of *all* people. And her set to sit for the Bursary. She was just about the *Last*! Not that anybody was perfect, of course. But Liz Aitken was . . . .

"As Liable as the *next* one!" Teen Rait had snapped, in an attempt to keep her own image of perfection intact. God help *Whoever* was the Father, they agreed. It was bound to be Somebody. *That* was for certain. Though it had happened *once*. Just once. But that was two thousand years ago. And, though they were regular Kirk-goers, and believed in every word the Psalms uttered, they'd just never quite managed to "swallow *that* one". It was for Papes. Although, Cis Coutts, the simple creature, had tried it on when *she* was pregnant. And syne forgot. And admitted to the Doctor that she "had Pink Knickers on at the time." Still, and seriously, though, God help Whoever was the Father when Rob Aitken got his hands on him. He couldn't get a word out of Liz, *herself*. She wouldn't say a Cheep. There was a Rumour. Only a rumour, *mind* you! But then, there always was. They would have died without one. A "Speak". Oh! A *whisper* just. That it was—*The Gowk*.

"You haven't got Liz to *admit* it, yet, then?" Kate Riddrie asked.

"No." Jean Aitken shook her head. "But she will. The state Liz came home in, that night. Her jumper torn, her legs scratit. And herself, nearly hysterical. . . ."

"I can believe *that*! Your Liz would never have had the strength against a Brute-Beast like the Gowk!"

"Never a one for the Lads, Liz. Her head aye buried in some book, just. . . ."

"I was saying Liz would never have had the strength! Something will have to be done about the Gowk, *now*! And you've gotten Witnesses!"

"Aye some book, just. . . ."

"You've gotten Witnesses!" Kate Riddrie urged.

"Young Rob. And Peter. They were trying to warn Liz."

"WELL! THEN! That's *it*!"

"She never crossed the door at night. Except whiles. Down to Chris Forbes for her Homework."

"You've gotten *Witnesses*! All it *needs* now, is to Testify before the Board!"

"But Liz. Liz is so unwilling. So *unwilling* to do that! Do you think. Do You

Think, maybe. . . ." Jean Aitken hesitated, unable to put her own apprehension into words. "Maybe, it's because he is A *GOWK*?"

"That's where you've *got* him!" Kate Riddrie got to her feet, in triumph. "That's what I'm trying to *tell* you. It's Liz's word against a Gowk's word. And he's got none. At least none that anybody could make any *sense* out of. Forbye! The whole Howe can testify that the Gowk's forever shambling all over the place. *Exposing* himself!"

"You'll be satisfied *now* then Kate. You've gotten your will. You've gotten rid of Jockie, at last. . . ."

"*My* first job. The first fine day. Will be to get that stinking mattress of his outside. And set fire to it."

"*That* was what you always wanted, Kate. . . ."

"It stank the house to High Heaven."

"Wasn't it, Kate?"

"At least we'll get a bit of fresh air into the house, at last . . ."

"Speak! You *Bitch*! Or have you lost your *tongue*! A damned pity you didn't lose it in front of the Board!"

"It wasn't *Me* that got rid of the . . . *Jockie*".

"NO! But you said damn all to *prevent* it!"

"What could *I* say to prevent it? The Board could see for themselves. Liz Aitken's *belly* was getting big enough!"

"*Jockie* didn't make it so."

"You've got no *proof* of that."

"Nor of the *t'other*!" Hugh Riddrie concluded, making for the door. "All that Jockie ever wanted was for somebody to *speak* to him."

"*Speak* to him!" Kate Riddrie snorted. "What on earth can anybody say to a GOWK!"

"I'll tell you what they can say to a Gowk, Kate! I'll *tell* you."

Hugh Riddrie turned to face her. Searching dumbly for words, that could be put *into* words. *Knowing* them. Thousands of them. Words that often weren't words at all, but instincts. Transmitted by tone and touch. A language acquired and mastered in a confusion of pain and frustration.

"You can say *anything* to a Gowk, Kate!" The realisation took him by surprise. "Anything at all. That's the *best* thing about Gowks. They never *tell*. And that's the *worst* thing about them. They *cannot* tell. But I'll find somebody, Kate. I'll find somebody who *can* tell!"

Jessie Kesson

. . . Liz Aitken O Liz Aitken . . .

"Come on, Liz! Come on, lass" her Mother persuaded. "Moping around the house like this is doing you no good. No good at all. And it such a fine night. Why don't you take yourself off for a bit walk?"

"Because she's *Feart!*" Young Rob blurted out. Unable to contain his knowledge.

"*FEART?*"

"That's *right!*" Peter confirmed. "*Feart!*"

. . . Liz Aitken O Liz Aitken . . .

"Feart of *what*, LIZ!" It was her *own* fear that Jean Aitken probed. Convinced that such a fear had not touched her daughter. Oh, but the young were lucky. One danger at a time. Clear and cut. Over and done with. With little hindsight. And not very much foresight. If only the Father had been a *normal* lad. And not a Gowk. "Feart of *what*, Liz?"

"Nothing. Nothing, just."

. . . Liz Aitken O Liz Aitken . . .

"Well *then!*" Jean Aitken urged. "Off into the fresh air with you. Young Rob and Peter will go with you for company."

"Never *ME!*"

"*ME Neither!*" Peter echoed his brother's determination. "The other bairns will cry after us! 'Gowk's Bairn! Gowk's Bairn!' *That's* what they'll cry."

"Is that right, Liz?" Her Father asked. "Is *that* what they cry?"

"Sometimes. It's only the bairns, though."

163

The gowk
. . . Liz Aitken O Liz Aitken . . .

"I wouldn't let *that* worry you, Liz. Folk have always needed *somebody* to cry after. And they've got no Gowk, now."

"If only it had been some *other* lad. . . ." Regret slipped out of Jean Aitken's control. And sounded itself in her voice.

"Some *other* lad!"

Her Father's astonishment confirmed Liz's own certainty.

"*If* it had been some *other* lad, Liz would have been out of here. *Bag* and *Baggage*! What happened was no fault of her own. It took half a dozen of us, *Grown Men*, to hold the Gowk down, till they got him off to the Asylum."

"Come on, Liz. Up you get." Her Mother piloted her towards the door. "Just you take a turn round the Steading. I used to like fine a walk when darkness was coming down" her Mother confided, as they stood on the doorstep. "I suppose I felt ashamed in day-light. *Not* because I was carrying a bairn, Liz. But just I felt so ungainly. And ugly in myself. Still!" her arm found her daughter's shoulder. "Every creature's *bonnie*, when it's little, Liz."

A daft thing to say, Jean Aitken thought, as she watched Liz from the door. The wrong words sometimes came out. When you couldn't find the right *ones* to say.

"Just the length of the Steading, Liz!" She called out, reminding her Daughter. . . .

But the Gowk's Father roamed *freely* enough. On the prowl. Night after night. They said. Neither Gowk to whistle on, nor dog for company. His croft running to wreck and ruin. His oats rotting in the stack. And the Threshing Mill had gone long since past his road-end. His turnips neither howked nor stored for his cattle-beasts. And Winter nearly on top of the man. Bad enough when his first wife died, and the Gowk was born. Worse than ever *now* since they'd carted the Gowk off to the Asylum.

Come to think of it, they themselves missed the Gowk. You would never believe *that*! But, they'd just got used to him, like. Popping up here and there. And everywhere around the Howe. Still. It was an ill wind. And it had fair suited *Kate Riddrie*!

"I'm not so sure that it did!" Meg Tait informed them. "I'm not so sure at all! Kate Riddrie *herself* was telling me only the other day. . . ."

164

"There's no living with him. No living with him at all. On the prowl all night. And sitting amongst my feet all day. Never taking his eyes off me. And never opening his mouth to me. Just mumbling away yonder to himself. He aye maintained that his *first* wife was at fault for the bairn being born a Gowk. But I'm beginning to have my *doubts*. The way he sits mumbling to himself. He'd aye gotten such an *obsession* with that Gowk."

. . . Liz Aitken O Liz Aitken . . .

LIZ!

So it hadn't been merely in her imagination. Or, maybe it had been created out of her imagination.

LIZ AITKEN!

Strange how prepared she was. . . . "I'm in a hurry, Mr. Riddrie."
"Aye, Liz. You've been in a great hurry this past few weeks!
What is it that you're *running* from like?
Hold on, Liz! Just hold *on*, there!
You're not *feart* are you, Liz?
No! Of course you're not feart!
You know fine that the *Gowk* canna jump out on you the night.
No. He canna do that. He's far enough away, the night.
You made sure of *that*!
You *all* made sure of it. The whole bloody Jing Bang of you!
No! No! Liz! Hold *on*!
It wasn't *Jockie*? Was it, now?"

"I told the Board. . . ."

The gowk

"I know damned fine what you told the *Board*!
You try telling *ME*!
Struck sudden *Dumb* are you, Liz?
It's some late in the day for *That*!
It was never *Jockie*, Liz. *Never* Jockie.
You see Liz, he wouldn't even have kent *where* to *PUT* the bloody thing.
But *I* ken, Liz.

I ken *for* him."

THE SOCIAL HOUR

The Social Hour

THE GAMES

John R. Allan *Farmer's Boy*

The day of the games dawned modestly but cleared up to a brilliant noon, with the heat of the unclouded sun tempered by a gentle wind from the sea. The old people and I drove over to the games field in the gig and as we came through the wood we could see the tents on the level haugh beside the river, the bright colours of the dresses and the fantastic tower of a merry-go-round high over the heads of the crowd that were already gathering about an oval in the centre of the field. We unyoked the pony under a vast beech tree, hitched her to a post and went over to join our friends. I wish I could set down on paper, as I can see so clearly in my mind, the rural company who met that day, so secure in the enjoyment of their pleasant world and who were never to meet again in that or any other place this side of death*. . . .

This is the old world as I remember it—farmers like Dungair and Thomas, slow footed and bent under a weight of years; my grandmother and Aunt Scott in black bonnets and black-trimmed capes, like pyramids in mourning, with wisps of white hair breaking from behind their velvet bows; young men like Uncle Sandy, in high waistcoats and higher collars, rather dashing in a clumsy way and smelling of hard yellow soap; handsome girls like Sally in yellow blouses and long skirts that swept the grass with incomparable and unconscious grace as they ran about in threes and fours; farm boys in their very tight Sunday trousers which made their legs seem quite inadequate for their slouching shoulders and their clumping feet; servant girls snatching a nervous pleasure by flirting with the men before the faces of their employers; and children everywhere, from babies to hulking brutes in knickerbockers. Some leaned against the ropes, some sat on forms, some lay in the grass, some walked slowly up and down, constantly stopping to greet a friend or pass a joke. A murmur of gossip and laughter, mingled with the shouts of the children, rose on every hand, while the sellers of candy and apples sang a song of "three a penny" and the merry-go-round turned a sweet sentimental tune into acid drops of melody.

* This scene takes place just prior to the outbreak of the First World War.

The games

Three large tents stood in a shady corner of the field. One was for the Committee, one for the competitors, and the third for refreshments. As the Old Man was on the Committee we went to the first at once and the Old Man began to revive the glories of the days when he could toss the caber further than any other man in three parishes. Such memories were dry work. They demanded the refreshment of many drams, which led to a contest in another rural art, the drawing of the longbow. The old men would have argued all afternoon, but time was passing and, after the secretary had run himself almost off his feet, he managed to get the Committee out of the tent and the first competitors on to the field.

The next three hours saw a desperate but intimate struggle among the young men of the parish. They ran, leaped, threw hammers, tossed cabers, wrestled and cycled against each other, while their friends cheered them or shouted dry but not unkindly criticisms when they failed. To our great delight Tom threw the hammer a prodigious distance; "Donal' Dinnie couldna a deen better in his sleep, man"; and won the first prize with yards to spare. He and the other prize-winners became the heroes of the afternoon and, as soon as they drew their prize money from the Secretary, they made straight for the refreshment tent and the stalls, where they spent it on drinks all round and fairings for the girls. They owned the world that afternoon, and as evening came on the swagger of their shoulders told old men like Dungair that a new generation had taken their place and that there was nothing left for the old but a seat at the fire and then good-bye.

The games finished between five and six and those who had bicylces went home to supper. Those who had not, or who could not bear to leave the field, ate sandwiches in little groups under the trees or bread and cheese at the refreshment bar, and all washed down their meal with bottled beer. Many of the young fellows were already a little drunk and their careless spirits kindled a recklessness in the girls. Little squeals rose from the parties under the trees and some of the wenches even made so bold as to drink a few mouthfuls of beer out of the bottles, to the accompaniment of choking and laughter. Meantime the Old Man and his friends had some settling-up to do in the Committee's tent while my grandmother and the other ladies were accommodated with port wine and shortbread in the now empty competitors' marquee. When the Secretary had made sure that every cork had been well and truly drawn and when some of the Committee were beginning to stagger under the load of their responsibilities, the Old Man collected my grandmother and myself and we went off to tea with a friend nearby. As we left the field in the gig, the young people were returning from supper, ready for the evening's fun. A dancing board had been laid under the beeches and a small band consisting of a fiddle, two cornets, a clarionet and drums, was tuning up for an eightsome reel. Meanwhile the sun was casting long shadows over the field and its light was tinged with a faint gold in transit to the rose, as afternoon passed into evening and the fiddle's thin music grew upon the air.

We visited the field again on our way home, for the Old Man could not pass the place where he had drunk so often and so deeply. The evening was very still and the music, augmented by the incongruous sounds of the merry-go-round and the drummling of the river, came loudly across the field while the feet of the dancers beat a heavy insistent rhythm on the board. That was a night to remember the old world by. The sun had gone down. Shadows were drawing in from the wood. Flares hung before the booths and lit a constellation of stars among the bottles in the refreshment tent. The young people and some who were not so young had gathered in well-defined blacks of shadow about the rings of light of the merry-go-round, the dancing board and the stalls, while some maintained a traffic to and fro between the entertainments, or stole away arm in arm into the privy wood. Others who had drunk wisely swaggered about with wide sweeping motions, now trying a snatch of song, now roaring out a challenge to the world, masters of their fate for this one night; while a few who had drunk too well lay fast asleep where they had fallen. It was a pagan festival, dedicated to the old traditions of the countryside, and it centred around the dancing board, for the oldest game of all was being played out there. The technique may have varied, but the spirit was the same. Whether it was a tall young farmer with his black hair falling over his forehead as he whirled his partner masterfully round while his eyes burned above her upturned face, or a ploughman butting his wench in the clumsy motions of the waltz, like the movements of a rude stone idol, they had only one thought,—that they were young and the night was short, while the girls could only remember as desperately as they could that life is long and honour fleeting. So it had always been: so it would always be.

We did not leave the gig but drove to the whisky tent where the Old Man took a dram, then we made a round of the side-shows and finally drew up beside the board. I was all exclamations of wonder as I noticed dancers I knew and my grandmother talked to someone who was standing by. The Old Man did not speak at all. He sat very square in the gig, listened to the music of the country band and looked at the board where the couples circled round and round. I wonder what he saw there. Perhaps the shapes of the dancers dissolved and re-formed as they might have been when he was twenty. Perhaps he felt the bitterness of age when youth is at its lusty pleasures. Or he may have thought that they would sometime be as old as he and that they were wise to enjoy themselves while they were able.

Now the shadows were growing darker. It was time for us to leave. The Old

Man picked up the reins, called to the pony and we bumped away over the grass towards the road. As we turned the corner of the wood I saw the games for the last time—the black figures against the lights, the gaudy lanterns on the merry-go-round and the dancing on the board. Then a tree occluded them and they were gone. The pony trotted quietly along the mossy road. The sound of the games fined away into a remote music that died into the muted undertones of the river.

COUNTRY DANCE

Amy Stewart Fraser *The Hills of Home*

The fiddles tuned up, the smoky wall-lamps were forgotten as the Master of Ceremonies made his opening announcement . . ."Gentlemen, take your partners for a Highland Schottische!" At once there was a sound like a stampede of cattle on a Western ranch; skidding across the intervening space, each man made a dash to secure the partner he had marked when looking the girls over. He crooked his arm, offered it to her with a bow and mumbled "May-I-have-pleshur-of-this-dance?" At once, she took it and they joined the Grand March, conversing politely as they moved round the room. When there was enough couples in the parade the signal was given for the dance to begin, and when it ended the lady was escorted back to her seat, her partner bowed low and left her. Soon the dance was in full swing, the piper with one foot thrust forward tapping in time with his music, and the toes of seated folk tapping in appreciation. There were reels, waltzes, quadrilles, and lancers, when the men delighted in whirling their partners off their feet. There were "The Flowers o' Edinburgh", "Petronella", "The Triumph", and "Rory o' More", besides the Circassian Circle and the Waltz-Country-Dance, a restful slow dance for four to the tune of "Come o'er the stream, Charlie". There was gaiety and friendly chaff. The strident music, provided in turn by fiddles, bagpipes, melodeons, and mouth-organs, the odour of sweat and paraffin, the smoke from many pipes of Bogie Roll, the stamping of heavy boots that made dust rise from cracks in the floorboards, the clapping in the lancers and the hooching in the reels . . . all contributed to an atmosphere of abandonment and enjoyment; even the elderly birled on the floor, the old men hooching as loud as any, while all laughed and twirled to Kafoozalum, Cawdor Fair and Tullochgorum.

Fizzy lemonade in green glass bottles, and ginger ale in stone bottles were available, and conversation lozenges. Jock could buy his Jenny a tuppeny poke of sweeties that cost sixpence a pound. From time to time it would be announced that Miss J. or Mr B. would "favour the company with a song". A lass would produce the sang-book she had in readiness, or a farm-lad would consent to render a bothy ballad. Sitting on the end of the big desk, with arms folded and feet swinging in the true tradition of the corn-kisters (who drummed their heels on the corn-kist in time to the music) the lad would sing in a nasal, indifferent tone, quite unlike his usual robust voice, one of the songs of the land . . . of ploughing matches, of feeing markets, harvesting, courting, and all the other occupations that made up the life of the countryside. One I remember well was the ballad of Johnny Raw, a guileless loon up from the country for a day in town, who was left literally holding the baby. All joined in the jeering refrain, "And I wish ma Granny saw ye". We had a different version at school which said:

> Johnny Raw shot a craw
> Took it hame tae his Ma-maw,
> His Ma-maw ate it aw
> An' left the banes for Johnny Raw.

The ballads which the farm-lads sang are now well-known, having been collected, published and publicized, but when I was a child they were handed down by word of mouth from one ploughman to another, and were lengthy and uninhibited in sentiment.

Everybody at the dance was on their best behaviour, at least until midnight, when the Manse party, having joined in heartily said "Good Night" all round and went home by the light of the fully-risen moon. I would not say that our presence had cramped the style of any of the young men, but it was whispered that after we departed the atmosphere became somewhat rowdy. Wilted collars were removed and dancing continued into the wee sma' 'oors. We had not seen any whisky-bottles but it was suspected that some were circulating among the men in the darkness of the playground. Their conduct became wilder as the night wore on; we heard rumours of bare-knuckled fights which took place to decide who should convoy a popular lass to her home.

At four o'clock, when dawn was breaking, after singing "Auld Lang Syne", the revellers went home, changed into their working clothes, and went straight to their work in byre or stable. Yokin' time was 6.30, and men and horses had to be fed before that. Balls were not so frequent that they could not afford, once in a while, to lose a night's sleep.

FISHER FOYS

Catherine Gavin *The Hostile Shore*

"Aye, it was in m'father's day they had the great *foys*," said David. "When the Greenland boats gaed oot in the spring, there was naebody sober in the Broch. They held royal, for twa-three days at a time, in the inns aside the hairbour—"

"And the women was as bad's the men, in some wyes," interrupted Kirsten. "I aye mind m'mother used to tell's aboot gaun to Peterhead wi' m'father ae time he signed on in the *Alibi*. She was a young lass, barely twenty, and Davie was just the baby on her airm. She was fisher-bred, ye ken, and had never been awa' frae Pitullie—Peterhead was a gey metropolis to her. Weel, the *Alibi* was ready to sail, when the word gaed aboot that her skipper didna like the look o' the weather, and wasna gaun to cross the bar. And, or ye kent o' yoursel, a' the wives in Peterhead cam' skirlin' doon to the harbour, some wi' shawls round their heids and some wi' their hair lowse and fleein', a' yellin' and shakkin' their fists, orderin' the skipper to put out to sea!"

"But why?" asked Kai. "Were they not glad that their husbands should have another night in port?"

"Nae fears!" said Kirsten. "Divn't ye see, they couldna draw the half-pay till the ship had sailed? That was what they were concerned aboot. When you've been mairrit a while and has a hooseful i' litlins, it's the siller ye have to spend through the day and nae the smoorichin' through the nicht that ye think aboot. But ma mother was fair terrifiet at the Peterheid wives. Terrible folk the Blue Moggins! And I daursay they were nae quaeter in the Broch."

"*I* was tellin' them aboot the Greenland *foys*," said David, rather nettled at being interrupted in the middle of his story. "In fact I was mindin' a sang m'faither used to sing aboot the whalers," continued the old man, and beating time with his pipe stem, he began in a husky bass:

> "Once more to Greenland we are bound
> To leave you all behind,
> With timbers firm and hearts so warm
> We sail before the wind.

Aye, those were the sangs," said David. "Those were the days! And the *foys* they held when the Greenlandmen gaed oot were naething to the rants when they cam' safely back again. When the *Enterprise* and the ither boats were sichtit, the hale toon was down at the harbour. The schools got a holiday, and wives and litlins, and young lasses, were rinnin' like widdifu's* to get on their braws. And

widdifu's madmen

174

when they were near at the bar, the skipper gied orders for the Garland to be hung. It was made o' coloured ribbons. The lads wove it on their outward voyage—sittin' up there in the lamp-licht aneath the ice-cap, wi' the bears and the whales wallochin' amon' the floes round aboot them," continued David graphically. "Then it was put awa', and when they were near into harbour the skipper had it hung in the maist dangerous part o' the riggin'—atween the foremast and the mainmast. Then the crew lined up at ilka side o' the deck, and when the boat gied in atween the pier-heids the skipper gied the signal, and they a' flew up the riggin' like monkeys. Aye, there was broken bones whiles, ower the heid's o't, and twice a broken neck. But the lad that was the swackest and the maist darin' cairried away the Garland. He wore it round his neck when the crew gaed ashore, and a' the folk cheered him and clappit him on the back, so that he was a kind o' hero o' the day."

A RURAL REFEREE

Dufton Scott *Humorous Scots Stories*

They say the aulder a body gets the mair young they growe. An' I think that's the wye wi' me. Man, I made a richt cuddy o' masel' yesterday. I hardly like ta tell ye aboot it.

Ye ken this while back Glenscutterach's been gyaun a' ta potterneeshun wi' fitba'. A' the young fowk aboot the place is fitba' mad. They ca' themsel's the Glenscutterach Fleers, an' they flee aboot wi' strippit wirsit jerseys an' breeks 'it's far ower short for them efter a ba', an' kick aboot at it like a lot o' young laddies. I reckon ye'll unnerstaun a' aboot the game yersel', bit I ken vera little aboot it, tho' I likit fine ta gang doon an' see them playin' noo an' then. Bit it wis this yesterday's caper I wis gaun ta tell ye aboot.

Ye ken the Fleers hid on a match wi' the Heuchsiccar Gallopers, an' there wis great excitement ower the heids o't. So fat wid hinner me ta gyang doon an' see them playin'?

I mention't the maitter ta the wife. I telt 'er I wis maybe gyaun doon the length o' the village in the evenin'. Af coorse I didna say I was gyaun ta a fitba' match, or that wid fairly hae put a damper on't. Oh, it's nae 'it I couldna gang masel' whether she wis pleas't or angry, bit there's nae eese raisin' din if ye can avide it.

Rural referee

So fin she spier't fat I wis gaun ta dee there, I said I was gaun ta get some intment for shot jints. Nae 'it I hiv ony shot jints, bit a body niver kens fan they *micht* hae, an' it's a handy thing ta hae in the hoose. At ony rate that wis the only thing I could think on at the time.

But if *I* wisna needin' muckle, *she* wis needin' plenty. Man, it's a queer thing, bit I can niver gang fae hame bit I hiv ta tak hame a great string o' eerans wi' ma. This time she said as lang's I was the wye I could gyang inta the merchant's an' get marmalite, an' fitenin', an' raisins, an' floor, an' yalla haddocks (if they waurna ower dear), an' spice, an' black threed, an' spier the price o' coal, an' a cut o' grey wirsit ta men' sox, an' gyang inta the souter an' see foo he didna gie's a calander at Christmas, an' the awfast rigmarole ye iver heard the like o'.

Fin I heard the lang lingie I began ta think I micht manage withoot the intment, an' wid bide at hame; bit I hid aince made up ma min' 'it I wid see that fitba' match, an' fin I mak' up ma min' it'll tak' mair than the wife ta mak' me cheeng't. So I said I wid *get* the eerans.

Bit fat a job I hid ta min' on them a'. A' the wye doon I keepit sayin' them ower ta masel' for fear I wid forget them. I reckon the fowk 'it met ma on the road thocht I wis dottl't—me gaun wi' ma haun's ahin' ma back an' ma heid hingin' doon, mutterin' ta masel': "Marmalite, an' fitenin', an' black threed, an' a cut o' grey wirsit ta men' sox, an' spier the price o' coal—." I tell ye I wis thankfu' fin I hid gotten them a' gaither't thegither. I landit ower at the fitba' green wi' ma airms an' pooches stuff't fu' o' a cargo o' stuff 'it wid stockit a shop.

It wis past the time for startin' afore I got in aboot, bit they warna yokit. There wis a brakdoon in the arrangements. The captain o' the Heuchsiccar lads objectit ta Peter Tousle, the referee; said Peter widna gie a fair deceesion because he hid an ill-will at their goalkeeper. It seems 'it the goalkeeper hid aince said 'it Peter couldna play the fiddle, an' Peter said he wid pey 'im back for't the first chance he got.

Oh, there wis a great hullabaloo aboot it. Bit ta squar up maitters they decided ta get anither referee, ane nae connectit wi' ony o' the clubs. An' lookin' roon for a substitute, fa should they licht on bit *me*!

Noo, I kent aboot as muckle o' fat a referee wis suppos't ta dee as a hen kent aboot plooin'. In fact, the only athletic game 'it iver I gaed in for wis the dominoes. So I wisna on for the job ava. Bit, man, baith the sides priggit wi' me ta tak it on, till I said ta masel', "Oh weel, it's jist fun; I micht as weel be in the hert o't." So I gaed ower an' gaed the goalkeeper ma parcels ta haud, an' I wis plankit in the middle o' the green like a stalk o' rhubarb an' a fussle in ma haun'. Foo we got startit I could not say, bit it wisna lang afore they war jumpin' roon aboot me like a lot o' puddocks.

I wis beginnin' ta enjoy the fun masel', an' wis watchin' a chance to get a kick at the ba' fin a' at aince I wis knockit flat on ma face an' ma nose dirdit aboot an inch an' a half inta the grun. Which o' them did it I could not say; for they war up an' efter the ba' withoot sayin' as muckle's "Excuse me," an' left ma ta howk fat wis left o' ma nose oot amon' the dubs.

I wis in a perfect rage. I got on ta ma feet, an' blew ma fussle an' stoppit the game.

They a' croodit roon me, spierin' fat wis up, wintin ta ken if it wis a foul or a touch or a corner-kick, or fat. I couldna exactly say fat kin' o' a kick it wis, I says, but it wis a nesty kick, an' I wint ta ken fa knockit me ower. Bit, man, nane o' them wid tak wi't. They tried ta mak oot it wis an' accident, an' they manag't ta pacify me amon' them, so we got startit again.

Bit och, it wis nae meenits afore I wis in anither snorrel. The ba' happen't ta come stottin' my wye, so I loot fung at it wi' ma fit, an' sent it richt throw the shafts o' the Gallopers' goal. An' I thocht I hid scor't a goal for the Fleers, but they widna admit it wis a goal—said the referee's kickin' didna coont. As if it made ony difference fa kickit it, as lang's it gaed throw.

They a' startit ta lauch at me. Oh, little wid 'a gart me throw the fussle at them. Bit fin ance I hid taen the thing in haun' I wis determin't ta see't ta a feenish. Only I hadna the same interest in't after that. Ony mair o' their squabbles I telt them ta sattle themsel's, 'it I wisna lookin'.

They were in the middle o' ane o' their rows fin I min't a' at aince I hid forgotten ta buy a scrubbin' brush. So I jist laid the fussle doon on the grun an' slippit awa' ta get it, thinkin' I wid be back afore they miss't ma.

Weel, I wisna awa' mair nor a quarter o' an oor, an' fin I cam' back there wis another lad in *my* place struttin' up an' doon as tho' the hail place belang't ta 'im. Fin he saw me comin' in aboot he made a face at ma, bit och, I niver min't 'im. I jist made ane at him, an' that wis a' 'it past atween's.

I thoucht I had gotten eneuch o't. So I gaed awa ta the goalkeeper ta get ma parcels, an' fin I cam' in sicht o' 'im there's the goalkeeper sittin' wi' a jar atween his haun's, up ta the e'en amon' my marmalite, an' aboot a dizzen loons fechtin' wi' ane anither for ma raisins.

I creepit quaetly up ahin' the goalkeeper an' dabbit his nose up ta the reet inta the jar, an' says, "Tak' a guid lick as lang's ye'er at it, ye hungry hun!"

Man, ye should a' seen his face fin he took it oot o' the jar! It wis a' clartit wi' ma guid marmalite. Bit I wis in that great a rage 'it I couldna lauch. I took up the paper bag o' fitenin' an' I jist took 'im fair—.

Man, the sicht o' 'im efter that pat ma in a better humour. I loot the loons gang wi' the raisins, liftit up fat wis left o' ma parcels, an' gaed awa hame.

An' fin I gaed inta the hoose—the wife—. Eh, man, man! Are ye mairriet yersel'? Ye are? Oh well, ye'll unnerstaun' a' aboot it than.

OUR CLASSIC MOTOR RUN

Hunter Diack *That Village on the Don*

The simple and straightforward idea of a picnic at the Bullers o' Buchan was gradually submerged in the "seeing somebody" syndrome. There was a whole string of acquaintances and connections we could "see" on the way to and from the Bullers o' Buchan. Not much more than a mile from the Bullers themselves was the farm of Longhaven where the Forbeses lived; we could hardly be so near as the Bullers without "lookin' in past" the Forbeses. But long before that we'd be passing through Whiterashes where Alec Troup and his wife lived; either father or mother thought it would hardly be the thing to do to drive past their door without looking in. Then of course there was Auntie Bella at Peterhead. Before her widowhood, she had lived at Pictillum on the Kemnay-Inverurie road. We'd be only a few miles from her and I am fairly certain it was mother's idea we should call on her. It was not only that Auntie Bella would be delighted to have news of Kemnay; there was also Auntie Bella's tendency to be offended. That we had been so near Peterhead without paying her the compliment of calling! On the other hand it was no doubt father's idea that we should show our faces at the Rev. Albert Diack's house, also in Peterhead. Then on the way back by the other route we'd be driving past the very garden gate of the house where more Forbeses lived. Finally, Nellie had a claim to visit Agnes Helen Ironside with whom she had shared digs in Aberdeen. The Ironside farm wasn't exactly on the road, but we'd be driving right past the end of the accommodation road that led to it.

To all these somebodies letters or cards went out in the course of the week. On the day before the run there was some preparation. Lilian made her speciality—meat loaf; eggs were boiled hard to save time with the eggs-and-lettuce sandwiches in the morning, and various other eatables were got ready for the Bullers o' Buchan picnic. In the morning I was got out of the way by being told to watch for the car coming. A watched kettle never boils, but this watched car arrived at Benview in time. We packed into it and off we went.

Mrs. Duncan, the blacksmith's wife, was under the net in her front garden filling a basket of strawberries; she gave us a wave from under her straw hat. We waved to Willie Riddell in Gordon's horse-drawn van as we swept past him, and we waved to somebody who didn't see us as we flashed past the cart-entrance to Pictillum; it hadn't been thought necessary to send a post-card to cousin Alfie there telling him that if he kept a lookout that morning he'd get a wave from us as we drove past.

My father, sitting in front, kept up an intermittent conversation with Dod, the driver, but occasionally turned round to point out something of special interest—the Bass o' Inverurie a great mount of grass-covered earth at the confluence of the Ury and the Don, thought for a long time to be an ancient burial-ground but now accepted as the remains of a Norman castle in earth-work; an old Quaker meeting-house at Fintray; "Ye're brother Jim used tae bike doon here sometimes for the service."

A moment of solemn silence recalling the eldest, dead.

In this commenting way, we came to our first house of call—the Troup's at Whiterashes. . . .

"Ye'll be ready for a cup o' tea?"

There wasn't a time of day when my mother wasn't ready for a cup of tea. She drank it scalding hot without milk or sugar. There was cake with this cup of tea. There was also strawberries and cream.

"They're fresh fae the gairden. Alex picked them special—this mornin'."

After a reasonable time for the adults and an unreasonable eternity for me, not being allowed to eat more strawberries because I had "to leave room for the picnic", we set out on our way again through the broad, tree-less acres of north-east Aberdeenshire.

It could not have taken an hour to reach the Bullers o' Buchan from White-rashes. In a sheltered hollow within hearing distance of the rumbling of the swell in the Pot, we had our picnic of meat-loaf, egg-and-lettuce sandwiches, and what else? I don't remember. Certainly not tomatoes; you couldn't get them at that time of the year then. But we had enough of whatever there was. After scrambling among the rocks for a short time, we got into the car again and set off for the Forbes's farm. I am not at this time-distance certain whether there was something special on at the farm; in those days farmers helped one another with rush jobs as a matter of course and there might well have been a rush of hay-making. Anyway there seemed to be a great many people at Longhaven farm that day, so many that three long trestle-tables had been set up in a large clean airy barn, one to hold some of the food, and two laid for eating.

Farm helpings of food are necessarily substantial, but so soon after our picnic it was difficult to enter into the spirit of the thing when a great plateful of cock-a-leekie soup was placed in front of you to be followed by roast chicken with oatmeal stuffing—with onions in it that didn't please my father—and boiled potatoes and mashed turnips, and that again to be followed by dishes of straw-berries, fresh-picked from the garden, and great jugs of cream, fresh from the cow.

"Ye must be hungry comin' a' the wye fae Kemnay!" And since we must be hungry, it had been thought necessary to reinforce the strawberries and cream with cream trifle, and, to complete the whole set-up, there was a kebbock of farm cheese, a few square feet of thick oatcakes, and mountains of butter.

To this meal we did as little injustice as we could in our tightened circumstances.

Both my parents could be very serious-looking people when the occasion demanded. In the mere absence of smiles or laughter the corners of my mother's mouth showed a tendency to droop. The line of my father's mouth was hidden by his moustache, but when anything went wrong, the line of his jaw, something about his eyes, and the very set of his head were all expressive of the burden he had to bear. It was a solemn party that packed into the car again at Longhaven farm.

Father forced himself near enough to the edge of his pre-occupation to say to Dod.

"I hope ye've got reasonably strong springs in yer car."

Then his mind came back to what was troubling him.

"I'd like tae ken what ye wrote tae a'body," he said. "Droppin' in for a bite tae eat, or something like that?"

"Nonsense!" mother replied. "We jist said we'd be lookin' in past."

For all that I was but a little growing boy, I had begun to feel the weight of things. The sun was still shining, but the edge had been taken off the sunshine. I even turned away from the sight of a woman picking strawberries in her garden. There was no lively comment now on anything we passed except Peterhead Prison. That red-granite building was grim enough to be mentioned without interfering too much with the mood that had settled among us.

"That's Peterheid Prison," my father said. "A grim-lookin' place, isn't it?"

But no grimmer than his look.

And in no time at all we were in Peterhead. Father had the idea we might have a look at the harbour before we went to Auntie Bella's.

"She'll be expectin's by this time," mother said.

"We'll be a' the better for a short walk onywye," father said, and down to the harbour we went and could hardly see the boats for the smell of the fish. Back to Auntie Bella's house. Father sniffed the air at the gate suspiciously.

"There's something cookin'," he said. He sniffed again. "And it's CURRY!"

There were one or two things that he could not come within a hundred yards of if he could help it. Curry was one of them.

"And I widna be surprised if there's nae ingins there an' a'."

It did not take him seconds to make up his mind that he'd go straight round to the Rev. Albert's. Then the thought struck him.

"D'ye think there's a denner waiting for's at Albert's an' a?"

The serious look on my mother's face was a reasonable answer to that.

"I'll walk roon' tae Albert's," he said. "I'll be back by the time ye've finished yer denner."

He didn't step over Auntie Bella's threshold, staying no longer than it took to say how d'ye do.

Auntie Bella was a square-built, hairy chinned dogmatic woman who pressed food upon you and would brook no refusal. We had hardly got inside the house when we were plonked down at the table.

"Ye maun be hungry comin' a' the wye fae Kemnay an' yer denner's been waiting for ye mair nor an oor."

Minced steak done in curry—was there soup before that? I don't know. I can remember only the brown and yellowish mess on my plate, the ineffectiveness of my protest. "A'm nae verra hungry!" as two big boiled potatoes were put on my plate, and a fire in my throat when I tried to put down what seemed determined to come up. I have a vague recollection of strawberries not from the garden but from the shop, but in my recollection those strawberries are not swimming in cream but in curry sauce. The very walls of the room seem now to have been distempered with curry sauce. I have no consciousness now of the existence of anyone but myself during the period of that visit.

There were no signs that our visit was an open disaster, but there was nothing that could have turned it into a success. Auntie Bella's easily offended nature—she'd be "real offended" if she heard that—put any easing of the situation quite out of the question. To tell her that we'd had a picnic at the Bullers o' Buchan that had taken the edge off our appetites would have been like telling her that we thought her so mean that we couldn't trust her to give us a bite to eat. To say we had just had a substantial meal at Longhaven was the same as telling her we didn't think much of her cooking. Even if in her letter mother had said, as perhaps she might, that Auntie Bella wasn't to put herself about or make any special preparations, that would have done not the slightest bit of good. It would merely have had the effect of setting her off on the making of special preparations in order to produce the impression that that was the standard of her everyday cooking and household management.

After, I suppose, about three-quarters of an hour of the kind of torture suffered by geese in the production of paté de foie gras, we staggered out to the car. Father was already there.

"Well, ye've been tae Albert's?" mother asked.

"Aye," he replied solemnly. "They were expectin' the lot o's for denner."

"I'm nae gaun," I said. "I canna eat ony mair."

"Nor can ony o' the rest o's" mother said. "But what did ye dae?"—to my father.

"Tell't them the truth," father said. "If ye canna tell the truth till a minister, fa can ye tell the truth till?"

"How did Maggie tak' it?"

"Nae that ill," father replied. "What else could she dae? Onywye I promised her we'd look roon' past, but nae get oot o' the car."

We trundled along the causewayed streets and even now I seem to feel the dirdin' of the wheels in the stretched muscles of my stomach.

I did not look forward to this arrangement about lookin' roon' past the Rev. Albert's. I had long before learned not to believe adults when they stated their intentions of coming or not coming, going or not going, staying or not staying, coming in or staying out.

"No, I winna come in," someone would say on the doorstep and half a minute later she'd be sitting in front of the kitchen fire.

"A'll come in, but jist for a minute," another would say, and thirty minutes later her tongue would be clash-prattling away.

Or it would be: "Well, I'll need tae be awa' noo. My gweed-man'll be winderin' faur I am." That would be at eight o'clock; at ten o'clock she'd be saying it for the tenth time.

So the arrangement father had made seemed to me to indicate that a few inviting words would be said and we'd all troop into the Rev. Albert's and sit there in swollen misery for an hour or so. My foreboding was wrong. In spite of the smell of curry that hung around the car, father stuck to his arrangement and after a brief exchange of embarrassed greetings we set off on our rounds.

Our next stop was at Longside, eight or nine miles from Peterhead. Having escaped Auntie Bella's curry, father was reasonably cheerful and even tried to lighten our spirits. But there was a great heaviness upon us, especially, I feel, on me. It is no small thing for a growing boy to be in a condition when he can honestly say he never wants to see food again. "I have seen guys on their way from the condemned cell to the hot seat," wrote Damon Runyon, "but compared with Harry the Horse at that moment them guys was laughing." Compared with me as we drove along from Peterhead to Longside, Harry the Horse was laughing.

There was none of the faith that can remove mountains in my father's voice when in an attempt to make us see the brighter side of things, he said:

"By the time we reach Longside, it'll be past their denner-time and nae near time for their tea. Maybe they'll jist offer's a fly-cup."

"I could maybe jist manage a fly-cup," mother said, but added. "I doot if the Forbeses are the kind o' folk that'll lat's awa' wi' naething but a fly-cup."

The Forbes's house at Longside was a pleasant cottage with a substantial hedge round it and behind the hedge a fruitful bed of strawberries.

At the door we were greeted with:

"O, hello! It's awfu' fine tae see ye! Ye'll be hungry comin' a' the wye fae Kemnay!"

At the same time there drifted into my nostrils an orchestration of smells that made my stomach turn a silent somersault. This blunt statement is no reflection on the cook. I have no doubt that if there could be devised a coefficient of savouriness the mingled odours that met us would have ranked very high. To a man only normally hungry these combined smells would have seemed as savoury as an ordinary meal would to someone who had just come back from climbing Cairn Toul, Braeriach, Cairngorm, Ben Macdhui, Benn a Bhuird and Ben Avon all in one day. And when the big steak and kidney pie was brought through to the room where the table was set even my eyes, bloated with prejudice could not help registering the fact that the high brown puff-pastry was the result of rolling and folding, rolling and folding, folding and rolling with expert and loving care.

Hysterical behaviour was something completely unknown among us. We wept when there was a time for weeping—as in the shadow of the graveyard—and we laughed, sometimes uncontrollably, when something that struck us as really funny happened. We sometimes laughed until we cried, of course, but never till we sobbed; and we never cried till we laughed. The first time I ever saw hysterics was in a film and I didn't understand what was going on. Yet I think now that when that steak and kidney pie was put on the table among the oatcakes, the pancakes, the scones, the bread and butter and home-made jam, with, on a side-table, a great dish of strawberries, a milk-jug of cream and a sister kebbuck of cheese to the one at Longhaven, then if any one of us had let out a half guffaw we'd all in a matter of seconds have been rolling on our chairs or on the floor in a cackling hysteria. But such behaviour was unthinkable—all the more unthinkable because ahead of us loomed the shadow of another farm-house to visit, only nine or ten miles away.

"Ye're jist pickin' at yer tea, laddie. A growin' loon like you has tae eat ye ken."

Old Mrs. Forbes was as kindly a person as you could meet, but never were kind words so steeped in unconscious cruelty. The thought that if I managed somehow to clear my plate of the reasonable helping of steak and kidney pie another helping was likely to land on it!

We had begun our meal with a grace. In silent communion with my portion of steak and kidney pie, while the older folk were pretending by their talk that this was a normal and highly agreeable visit, I said another grace silently: "For what I have received I am truly thankful, but, please, if I can finish this, dinna lat ony mair come on ma plate, for Jesus' sake, Amen—And," I added, "I dinna even want strawberries and cream."

That visit dragged itself to a close. Dod, the driver who had not eaten since Longhaven, welcomed us back to the car. He had been invited to eat at Auntie Bella's and Longside, but had not found it difficult to thank himself out of it.

"Have ye had onything tae eat?" father asked him.

"Nae the last twice," he said, "but there's time yet. Ye've mair folk tae look in on yet, haven't ye?"

"We have that," my father replied dolorously.

"A'll maybe hae a bite tae eat there," Dod said.

Time had marched far enough on by this time to denude us of any hope that at the next house of call we'd be let off with anything as light as a fly-cup. There was another fact that weighted heavily on our already over-burdened minds. We were now to visit Nellie's friend, Agnes Helen Ironside, and somebody on the way there brought out to the light of day the fact that Agnes Helen had recently completed a course at the Aberdeen School of Domestic Science and had become the holder of a diploma which testified, among other things, to her expertise as a cook. You may think that I am laying this on a bit. It seems too much of a good thing that, without the aid of artistic imagination, the events of that day of astronomical gastronomy should work up to the climax of a meal prepared with the skill and enthusiasm of a cook on whose brow there had been so recently placed the laurels of the "Dough School". But, with my hand on the best haggis that the Dough School of Aberdeen ever produced, I swear that this is the truth and nothing but the truth.

What I cannot remember about the highest of high teas at the Ironside's house is what the real peak of the meal was. All the usual accompaniments were there— the scones, oven and girdle, pancakes, oatcakes, home-made jams and jellies, sponge cake, sandwich cake, a kind of Dundee cake home-made, a home-cured ham, a kebbuck of cheese, and a great dish of strawberries. I have an idea that there was a cheese souffle and the word "kedgeree" hovers uncertainly on the threshold of my memory. Certainly there was a meat dish fit for people who must be hungry comin' a' the wye fae Kemnay.

Dod had a glorious time. Father, who now that I think of it never showed middle-age in his figure and may indeed have had a small capacity stomach, got out of it altogether by pleading that he did not feel altogether well and sat apart from the table looking out of the window with a faraway look in his eyes. The rest of us made what little show of it we could—which was not very much. That ordeal, too, passed and at last we set out with a clear run to Kemnay.

"Ye left the key o' the hoose wi' Nellie Imlach, of coorse," father said.

"Yes," mother replied. "She had tae get in for the hen's meat."

"Ye dinna suppose she'll tak' it inta 'er heid that we'll be hungry comin' sic a lang wye tae Kemnay," he said.

"Nae for a minute," mother replied. "She's jist pittin' a match tae the fire and haein' the kettle bilin' for a cup o' tea."

"Sounds ominous," father said.

"There's nae need tae worry," mother replied. "Naebody can force us tae eat in wir ain hoose."

The tension was eased by that. By the time we had reached Oldmeldrum the countryside was beginning to smile in the evening light and by the time the Quarry Hill appeared as we came over the Bogfur Hill the world was swinging rapidly back to normal.

Nellie Imlach had done precisely what she was asked to do. She had fed the hens and lit the fire.

"I was winderin' if ye'd be hungry comin' sic a lang wye," she said, "but I thocht maybe ye'd have had a bite tae eat wi' some o' yer freens?"

"We had that," said father.

"Well, the kettle's bilin'," said mother. "I'll jist hae the fly-cup I'd have liked at Longside. Onybody else wint ane?"

There were no takers.

Appendix

NORTHEAST SCOTS AS A LITERARY LANGUAGE

David Murison

Literature, we may say, begins with a free and creative use of language, when it is used in a way beyond mere factual communication, when the associations of ordinary speech are exploited to their full and extended in figures and images to give new associations, emphases, excitement, and colour to what is being said. Language is a social phenomenon and grows out of the historical background of the community and changes with it, and the literature grows naturally out of the language; so while the writer can mould and refashion the language according to his ability, he has first to take it as he gets it as part of his native inheritance. We shall see how this pattern works out in the Northeast.

The Scots language developed from the Northumbrian dialect of Anglo-Saxon, already distinct from the dialects south of the Humber by the eleventh century, by which time it had absorbed a large element from Norse brought into Northern England by the Vikings. Then in the mid-eleventh century French came with the Normans and drastically modified the structure and vocabulary of Anglo-Saxon. Out of this amalgam arose Middle English, the precursor of the English of today and probably best known from its use in literature by Chaucer. All these influences made their way with the feudal system into Scotland and by the thirteenth century a form of speech had established itself in Lowland Scotland much alike to Northern English and closely associated with the independent nation that spoke it. In the fourteenth century, in fact, it became the national language of Scotland used for all purposes—law, government, trade, historical record and literature. As it happens, our first piece of Scottish literature, and an impressive piece at that, comes from the Northeast: Barbour's historical romance on Robert the Bruce. There is nothing specifically Northeast about the language, however, which is what we must assume to be the speech of the Scottish Court, for Barbour was a churchman and a government official as well.

Here is a prosaic passage about how King Edward was called in to adjudicate on the succession to the Scottish throne in 1291:

On this maner assentyt war
The barownis, as I said yhow ar;
And throuch thar aller hale assent,
Messingeris till hym thai sent,
That was than in the haly land,
On Saracenys warrayand.
And fra he wyst quhat charge thai had,
he buskyt him but mar abad,
And left purpos that he had tane;
And till Ingland agayne is gane.
And syne till Scotland word send he,
That thai suld mak ane assemble;
And he in hy suld cum to do
In all thing, as thai wrayt him to.
But he thoucht weile, throuch thar debat,
That he suld slely fynd the gate
How that he all the senyhowry,
Throw his gret mycht, suld occupy.

By the middle of the sixteenth century the Town Clerk of Aberdeen was writing up his minutes as follows:

> The said day James Allane and Marjorie Bryane his spous wer convickit and put in amerciament of court for the strublens, striking and blae-making of Marjorie Pattoun, indualler of Monymusk, under sylens of nicht, within the toun of Futte, and for the wrangous reiffing, awaytaking fra hir of ane plyd, ane petticoitt, twa curchis, ane collar, ane buckram approwne, ane stomak, ane preyne cod and saxteen pennies thairin.

And a year or two after, at the time of the Reformation, the baillies report

> Certain strangearis and sum nichtbours and induallers of this burgh hes enterit to the blak freiris and quhyt freiris of this toun and spulyeit thair places, and takin away the geir and gudis of the samen with the tymmir wark and insicht, togidder with the leid of the kirkis, and now are enterit upon the ruiffis of the kirkis and biggings, and takand away the sklaittis, timmer and stanis thairof, applyand the samen to thair ain particular uses.

Again there is little or no sign of the local dialect, the language being formal and official, though no doubt the clerk himself pronounced the words in the

Northeast manner. But in 1560 the Reformation took place in Scotland and its leaders hastened to place the Bible in the hands of all who could read it and set up a parochial school system to teach those who could not. Unfortunately there was no Scots translation of the Bible in existence and the nearest available was the version made in Geneva by English refugees from Mary Tudor's regime in that very year. It was this English version that had sole currency in Scotland for fifty years till superseded by King James's Bible of 1611. This at once gave English a spiritual status in Scotland it has never lost—the status of solemnity, sacredness, and the dignity of the Word of God. When you spoke to your children or your friends about the ordinary, domestic or sentimental things of life, you used Scots; when you began to speculate about the higher mysteries or abstract moral values, you had the English of scripture to formulate your thoughts.

Then in 1603, the Scottish king and his court took off for London, and started to conform to the speech standards of the new capital. The King's Scots was replaced by the King's English which became the pattern for all Scottish courtiers and officials who had business there. English thus acquired a social or class prestige which it still enjoys throughout Scotland, not least among the working folk who normally speak a kind of Scots. In the course of the seventeenth century we can trace in state and local records, in private correspondence, and in literature, a rapid anglicisation in the language as literary usage becomes more and more dissociated from spoken. Here is an extract from the Aberdeen Burgh Records in September 1644 during the Civil War, a mixture of Scots and English:

> It is to be remembrit, but nevir without regrait, the great and heavie prejudice and lose quhilk this burghe did sustaine by the cruell and bloodie feicht and conflict, quhiche was fochtin betwixt the Crabstane and the Justice Mylnes, upoun the threttein day of September, instant, betwixt ellevin houres befoir noone, and ane eftir noone, occasioned be the approaching of James, Marquis of Montrose, with thrie regimentis of Irishes and some others, thair adherentis . . . the magistrates and counsell did refuise to rander the toune, and dismissed the commissioner and drummer, with answer to the said demand. Bot as they wer passing by the Fyffe Regiment, the drummer was unhappily killed by some on or uther of the horsemen of our pairtie, as wes thocht, quhairupoun the feicht presentlie begane, and eftir tuo houres hote service or thairby, the Fyff regiment, with our haill tounes men and otheres of the schyre wer forced to tak the retrait, quhairin many of the regiment wer killed.

Appendix

In 1700 the famous case of the fiddler MacPherson was reported thus:

John Shand deponed that at St Ruffus' Fair wes nyne years, ther came three women and took possessione of his kill and he being at work he sent word to his wife to put them off but they would not, and told that Peter Broune was coming to take up quarters with them; and that he came and stayed ther with his company for a moneth, and took nothing but peats from him; and that Peter Broune went sometymes to Elchies and played on the wiol; and deponed that they coft milk and cheese with their own money, and no more than ane leg of mutton. . . . They are holden and repute as Egiptians; and that he has seen them in bands; and that he has heard the women that followed the pannalls speak a particular language, which he knowes not; and that he seed about twelve men, with a piper come in to Kieth whereof the pannalls were a pairt; and that McPherson came into his house and spilt his ale and stobbed the bed, seeking the deponent.

Granted that the witnesses would have spoken Banffshire dialect, the Sheriff Clerk has translated it carefully into officialese, in effect the Scottish-English of the day.

Finally in 1707 with the Union of Parliaments the speech of the new legislature simply took over as the official language of the United Kingdom to be used for all formal purposes. Scots had ceased to exist as a national language and could only survive as an informal means of communication between, be it noted, fewer and fewer of the upper and educated classes. This process continued throughout the eighteenth century and indeed elocution classes came into vogue in the Scottish cities for the purpose of acquiring the correct grammar and pronunciation of English. By the end of the century conservative old ladies in Edinburgh who clung to their Scots were looked on as rather quaint and *passées*. The Edinburgh of the Enlightenment was very definitely opting for English, at least in its writing, and when Johnson passed through in 1773 he noted that "the great, the learned, the ambitious, the vain all cultivate the English phrases and the English pronunciation".

But all was not lost. Already at the beginning of the eighteenth century Scots poetry, which had been kept alive through ballad and folk-song, had a second flowering under Ramsay and Fergusson, and in the Northeast Skinner and Ross. Above all, there was Burns, who really established Scots as one of the poetic languages of the world and laid the foundations of a linguistic tradition which still continues, not least in the Northeast, as the anthology *Poetry of North-east Scotland* shows. But by 1700, Scots prose had ceased to be written except as a

David Murison

tour de force. Specimens of this are rare, but it is noteworthy that most are from the Northeast. A Buchan man, Robert Forbes, who had taken up business in London, tried his hand at translating passages of Ovid into verse and wrote an amusing account of a coach journey from London to Portsmouth all in the braidest Buchan. Obviously he was an enthusiast for his native tongue:

First an foremost there wis three i the coach forby me; the first was a leiftenant o a ship, a gawcy swack young fellow an as guid a pint-ale's man as eer beeked his fit at the coutchack o a browster wife's ingle; he was well wordy o the gardy-chair itsel or een to sit ben wi the guidman upo the best bink o' the house, I believe an honester fallow never brack the neuk o' a corter nor cuttit a fang frae a kebbuck wi a futtle that lies i the quinzie o the maun ooner the claith. The second chiel was a thick settrel swown pallach wi a great choller ooner his cheeks like an ill-scrapit haggis; he's noo gane back tae London, an I'm seer gin ye'll tak the pains to fin him out and flay him belly-flaucht, his skin wad mak a gallant tulchin for you. He did geylies confeerin, only he connacht a hantle o' tobacco; for deil belicket did he the hale gate bat feugh at his pipe; an he was sae browdent upon't that he was like to smore us a' i the coach wi the very ewder o't; bat yet he was a fine gabby auldfarran carly, an held us browly out o' langer by the rod.

This is, of course, dialect at double strength. The metropolitan standards of Scots had gone with the removal of the Court to London, and with the setting up of English schools in place of the old grammar or Latin schools in the eighteenth century, Scots disappeared from the curriculum. There was no longer any model to go by and each writer could only fall back on the speech of his native place, a colloquial and regional variety of what had once been the King's Scots. But it had at least the quality of naturalness and spontaneity, it was the language of the heart, so to speak, as opposed to the English of the school and the book—which is of course why it was the natural medium of poetry. When Scott came along with the historical novel as the vehicle for his phenomenal knowledge of Scottish manners and traditions, he said, "Burns by his poetry has already attracted attention to everything Scottish and I confess I can't see why I should not be able to keep the flame alive, merely because I write Scotch in prose and he wrote it in rhyme." But the cases were not entirely parallel; Burns was following a tradition of popular poetry that had descended in an unbroken line from the Middle Ages and had got a new lease of life at the beginning of the eighteenth century. With prose, as we have seen, it was a different story; the prose tradition had died two centuries before and the recreation of a full canon of all-purpose Scots was

191

beyond even Scott's skill, nor did he attempt it, except, perhaps, in the magnificent *Wandering Willie's Tale*. He took the only course open to him, of writing his narrative in English and using Scots only for those who, given their social class, would still be speaking it: daft Davie Gellatley in *Waverley*, the gipsies and Dandie Dinmont in *Guy Mannering*, the Headriggs in *Old Mortality*, Edie Ochiltree and the fisher-folk of Musselcrag in *The Antiquary*, Andrew Fairservice in *Rob Roy*, the Deanses in *The Heart of Midlothian*, Meg Dods, the innkeeper, in *St Ronan's Well*, and so on.

This procedure gave reality to the Scots characters whose ways and ethos it was Scott's main purpose to portray, and the author in his best English, which lumbered along rather badly at times, did little more than lay out the setting for the action and act as impressario for the characters as they played their roles. There were, of course, Scots characters in his novels who did not speak Scots, whose status in life had already cut them adrift from their native speech—the lord and lady, the soldier, the churchman, the lawyer and other professional types; and they speak their various kinds of English much as they do today. By their speech they distance themselves from their fellow-countrymen as the mouth-pieces of a different culture and outlook, as one can see for instance in the cliff scene on Fowlsheugh in *The Antiquary* when a common deadly peril brings Sir Arthur Wardour and his daughter together with Edie Ochiltree and it is the Scots of Edie and the fishermen that takes the dramatic weight of the situation.

It is a truism that Scott's Scots was better than his English, and *a fortiori* his Scottish characters are better conceived than his English or Anglo-Scots because they grow naturally out of their native idiom. They describe themselves out of their own mouths; they are what they are in saying what they say. And it was Scott's felicity in conveying character and action through their Scots speech that inspired his imitators for the next hundred years—Susan Ferrier, Hogg, MacDonald, Stevenson, Barrie, Crockett, Alexander, George Douglas, and John Buchan. The tradition of narrative in standard English and dialogue in various degrees of dialect has been the usual procedure since (and of course English novelists from Fielding through George Eliot and Bennett to Hardy and Lawrence have done likewise).

In Scotland at least, the use of the native and historic speech for what is emotional and hameower and practical has always been in contrast with the alien import for complex, abstract and conventional utterance, and the Scots have had a schizoid attitude to language in consequence. Further complications have arisen. The alien speech has increasingly been encroaching on the domain of the native and has in some cases ousted it altogether. Yet the consciousness of the distinctions, often associated with class attitudes, is still there, and it has probably been accentuated by a growing awareness of the threat to the existence of Scots. If we accept at the outset the actuality of distinct historic communities like Scotland or even the Northeast by itself and the appropriateness, to put it no higher, of their having a literature which interprets their way of life, their attitudes and values, their ethos, then the use of the language which is a very characteristic and conservative one in the Northeast, becomes of considerable importance to a writer in his efforts to communicate the Northeast to his readers and it will on the whole be the Scots-speaking characters who will take on the burden of the job.

There are three alternatives at hand for the Northeast novelist. The first is to abandon the linguistic problem altogether by writing in English throughout with perhaps a few apostrophes thrown in as a concession to the "sub-standard" type of speech known to be used in the area. This of course cuts out one of the most basic elements in the background of his fiction, though one may argue with some truth that this is in accordance with what is actually happening under the attrition of school and television English. But in our modern psychological novel in which the author is more interested in his characters' deep motives and emotions than in the ordinary plot of the action and tries to describe them in their own words and not his, there is some danger of giving the impression that he has not really made himself at one with his characters, that he is talking down to them as his stock-in-trade, his "cases"; in modern jargon there is a lack of empathy between the creator and the created. There may lurk a suspicion that the author has detached himself from the culture he is trying to interpret; he has gone over to the other side, as it were, and writes his report on the area like one of those school inspectors of the 1890s who were responsible for so much of the trouble. The traditional reverence for book-learning in the Northeast does tend to foster this sort of cultural ambivalence.

This last, indeed, arising out of the history of the Scots tongue and its gradual displacement by English, has been a hair in the neck of Scottish writers since the seventeenth century. We have seen Scott's solution and the alternative of ignoring the problem altogether and letting it go by default, which is no solution. But Scott's contemporary Galt sought a third alternative, that of devising a compromise style where the narrative is in a rather subtly scottified English and given verisimilitude by being told by an old-fashioned character whose speech it may well have resembled, like the old minister in *The Annals of the Parish*, or the provost in Gudetown, or the last of the Lairds. Galt continued his experiments right till the end of his work and his example was followed by Moir, Latto, and Mrs Oliphant in her earlier novels. But the Kailyarders who mainly descend from this school reverted to Scott's practice, and we see no more of it until the general ferment of the Scottish Renaissance after the Great War when language problems came again to the fore (as in many other countries besides Scotland) and the Lallans movement was founded with Hugh MacDiarmid as its chief exponent. Lewis Grassic Gibbon was for some time involved in this and in his *Scots Quair*, the greatest novel of the Northeast in the twentieth century, he explicitly faced up to the language problem with its three alternatives—everything in synthetic Scots (Lallans), everything in English, "so that, names apart, the story might well take place in Cornwall. The third method is what I myself employ, writing everything, descriptive matter and all, in the twist of Scottish idiom but not in the actual dialect except for such words as have a fine vigour or vulgarity and no exact English equivalents."* In his foreword to *Sunset Song* he puts it somewhat more formally: "If the great Dutch language disappeared from literary usage and a Dutchman wrote in German a story of the Lekside peasants, one may hazard he would ask and receive a certain latitude and forbearance in his usage of German. He might import into his pages some score or so of untranslatable words and idioms—untranslatable except in their context and setting; he might mould in some fashion his German to the rhythms and cadence of the kindred speech that his peasants speak. Beyond that, in fairness to his hosts, he hardly could go—to seek effect by a spray of apostrophes would be both impertinence and mistranslation. The courtesy that the hypothetical Dutchman might receive from German a Scot may invoke from the great English tongue."

Leaving aside some begging of questions in this statement, Gibbon is essentially following in the footsteps of Galt. He will mingle in a few of the dialect words and idioms and try to make his adopted speech echo the tune patterns of his own native tongue. In other words, he will adopt a kind of compromise speech which will not be authentic dialect—but a basic English interwoven with enough of the vernacular to give it a sense of locality and the sound and stot of the Northeast voice. "Chris's Wedding", from the present anthology, is one of the more successful passages in this vein. This is not what the purists and whole-hoggers like, but curiously enough it may result in something more like a classical Scots prose than the dialect *tours de force, Johnnie Gibb* or, even more, *Eppie Elrick*, excellent as they are. The method Gibbon in fact adopted avoids the impossibilities of the first alternative, the falsity of the second, and by obliterating the distinction between narrative and dialogue, bridges the gap of empathy between the author and his creation.

Whether Gibbon was entirely successful is another matter. He was obviously anxious about his English market and although he toned his Scots down to the minimum, so that the "spray of apostrophes" became unnecessary, his cadences

---

* See his letter to Cuthbert Graham in 1933 quoted in D. F. Young, *Beyond the Sunset* (1973), p. 82.

can all too easily turn into a kind of incantation where sound takes over from sense, not unlike Lawrence. But there can be no doubt that the experiment was well-founded and it seems that if a Scots prose is ever to be recreated it is by such methods as Galt and he employ.

Index of Authors

Alexander, William
9, 113, 127

was born in Chapel of Garioch in 1826. He began life as a farm-servant but an accident caused him to have a leg amputated and this diverted him to journalism. His most famous work, *Johnny Gibb of Gushetneuk*, was published in *Aberdeen Free Press* in serial form 1869-70. He became editor of the *Free Press* and died in Aberdeen 1894.

Allan, John R.
17, 31, 67, 89, 169

was born at Udny in 1906 and graduated MA at Aberdeen University in 1928. He served for a time as a sub-editor of *The Glasgow Herald* and in 1935 published his first book *Farmer's Boy*. This was followed by *Summer In Scotland, Down On The Farm, Northeast Lowlands of Scotland,* and *The Seasons Return*. For many years he farmed at Little Ardo, Methlick, but now lives in retirement in Lincoln.

Anson, Peter F.
38

(1890-1975) author and marine artist, he left behind him many books on fishing life and religious orders. For fourteen years a brother in an Anglican monastery, he moved over to the Cistercians in the Roman Catholic Church. Coming to the Moray Firth he spent six years with the fishermen of Buckie and twenty years at Macduff. His most famous book is *Fishing Boats and Fisher Folk on the East Coast of Scotland,* but his *Fisher Folklore* is also a standard work.

Diack, Hunter
178

(1908-1974) was born in Kemnay and graduated from Aberdeen University. He taught at Gordon's College and then in the University of Nottingham Institute of Education where he became an expert in the teaching of reading. He will probably, however, be best remembered for his two autobiographical books *Boy in a Village* and *That Village on the Don*.

Dieth, Eugen 123

(1896–1956) linguist and dialectician. He was Lecturer, and later Professor, of English Language at the University of Zurich, and one of the editors of the *Idiotikon,* the standard dictionary of Swiss German. He was appointed as an assistant in the German department at the University of Aberdeen in the early 'twenties, and started on his Zurich PhD. thesis, a linguistic study of Northeast Scots. Parts of this were later published as *A Grammar of the Buchan Dialect,* Zurich 1932.

Fraser, Amy Stewart 98, 172

was born at Ballater in 1892 and brought up in the manse at Glengairn. She was educated at Esdaile College, Edinburgh, and at Dunfermline College of Hygiene and Physical Training. She devoted herself to voluntary public service and was awarded the WVS Long Service Medal. Now retired, she lives in Carlisle but still returns to Glengairn for part of each year, and it is there that she returns in her books *The Hills of Home, Dae ye min' Langsyne,* and *In Memory Long.*

Gavin, Catherine 47, 174

was born in 1907 in Aberdeen and educated at the High School and Aberdeen University. She lectured for a time in the History Department and then became a War Correspondent with Kemsley newspapers. She writes mainly historical fiction dramatising such events as the Russian Revolution and the battle of Jutland. Married to an American, she lives partly in London and partly abroad.

Gibbon, Lewis Grassic 3, 56, 121, 146

was the pseudonym of James Leslie Mitchell, born in 1901 in Auchterless, and brought up in Arbuthnott in the Mearns. He became a journalist in Aberdeen and Glasgow and then served in the Army and the RAF. In 1929 he became a full-time writer and settled in the south of England. Between then and his death in 1935 he published seventeen books the best of which, e.g. *Sunset Song* (1932), *Scottish Scene* (in collaboration with Hugh MacDiarmid 1934), take him back to his roots in the Northeast.

Gordon, Alexander 19, 112

was born in 1857 at Boharm near Keith. He was apprenticed to a draper in Keith, but then moved to London, where he was attached to the Mission for Deep Sea Fishermen, and also worked as a journalist. His stories of Carglen first appeared in *The Gentleman's Magazine:* "Carglen is a purely imaginary world, though, let us hope, wonderfully like the real."

Kirk, Rothael 43

was the pseudonym of William Leslie Low, born at Inverurie 1840. He graduated MA from Aberdeen in 1862 and became a minister of the Episcopalian Church, at Kincardine O'Neil, Cruden, Largs, and in 1890 Canon of Cumbrae. His novel *By The North Sea Shore* was published in 1891.

MacDonald, George 74, 109

was born in Huntly in 1824 and educated at Aberdeen University. After a short and stormy career as a minister at Arundel, where his unorthodox religious views led to his dismissal, he turned to fiction as a means of teaching, and produced over fifty books, many of which are set in his native Aberdeenshire. Before his death in 1905 he had become a most esteemed figure in London literary life.

Mackenzie, R. F. 112, 122

was born at Lethenty in Aberdeenshire in 1910. He was educated at Turriff, Gordon's College, and the University of Aberdeen. He travelled widely on the Continent and in America, and established a reputation as a progressive educationist in such books as *A Question of Living, Escape From the Classroom, The Sins of the Children*. He was headmaster at Braehead in Fife, and subsequently at Summerhill Academy, Aberdeen. His book *The Unbowed Head* is based on his Summerhill experience.

Mackie, Alastair 57, 69

was born in Aberdeen in 1925. He was educated at Skene Square School, Gordon's College, and Aberdeen University. He became a teacher of English and has taught at Stromness and Anstruther. He is best known for his poetry in Scots and his selected poems *Back-Green Odyssey* were published recently.

Macpherson, Ian 94, 101

was born at Forres in 1905, moved to the Mearns, and was educated at Laurencekirk, Mackie Academy, and Aberdeen University. After two years of lecturing in the University, he gave it up to do a multitude of odd jobs, finally taking a farm on the edge of the Dava Moor. His first novel *Shepherd's Calendar* is set in the Mearns and was published the year before *Sunset Song*. Macpherson was killed in a motorcycle accident in 1944.

Milne, W. P. 12

was born at Longside in 1881, and educated at Peterhead Academy, Aberdeen Grammar, Aberdeen and Cambridge Universities. He was Professor of Mathematics at Leeds University from 1919 to 1946, and President of the Buchan Club from 1940 to 1948. His attachment to the Buchan dialect is most evident in *Eppie Elrick* which was published in 1956.

Moon, Lorna 135

was the pseudonym of Helen Low, born in Strichen 1886. She emigrated to America and wrote scripts for Hollywood. *Doorways in Drumorty,* a collection of short stories, was published in 1926, followed by *Dark Star,* a romantic novel in 1929. She died at Albuquerque, New Mexico, in 1930, but her ashes were returned to Buchan and scattered on the summit of Mormond Hill.

Murison, David 187

was born in Fraserburgh in 1913, and educated at Fraserburgh Academy, and at Aberdeen and Cambridge Universities. He was lecturer in Greek at Aberdeen University for a time and then succeeded Dr. William Grant as editor of the Scottish National Dictionary in 1946. This life-work was completed in 1976. Now retired, he lives in Fraserburgh.

Paterson, Neil 34

was born in Greenock in 1916 and educated at Banff Academy and Edinburgh University. He has written a great deal for the cinema. His novels include *The China Run* (1948), *Behold Thy Daughter* (1950), *And Delilah* (1951). He now lives in Perthshire.

Patey, Tom 88

was born in Ellon in 1932, and educated at Ellon Academy, Gordon's College, and Aberdeen University where he graduated in medicine in 1955. He worked for a time on the staff of Inverurie General Hospital before joining the Navy, finally becoming a GP in Ullapool. He was internationally renowned as a climber, taking part in Alpine and Himalayan Expeditions, but never lost his affection for his native hills. He died in a climbing accident in Sutherland in 1970.

Robbie, William 58

was born in Aberdeen in 1829 and worked most of his life as an accountant in the city. As a historian he is known for his *Aberdeen: its Traditions and History,* 1893, and as a novelist for *The Heir of Glendornie,* 1880, and *Mains of Yonderton,* 1928. He died in Aberdeen in 1914.

Scott, Dufton 175

was born in Forgue in 1880 and started life as an ironmonger's assistant in Huntly. He moved into the city of Aberdeen and became a full-time professional entertainer, specialising in comic monologues and readings. In 1911 he settled in Inverurie and died in 1944.

Shepherd, Nan 85

was born at Peterculter in 1893. She was educated at the High School for Girls and Aberdeen University, and was for many years a lecturer at Aberdeen Training College (now Aberdeen College of Education). In addition to her evocation of the Cairngorms, *The Living Mountain*, she has published poetry and the novels *The Quarry Wood*, *The Weatherhouse*, *A Pass in the Grampians*. She died in Aberdeen in 1981.

Singer, Burns 41

was born in New York in 1928 but moved to Scotland when he was four. He was educated in Glasgow but evacuated to Maud in Aberdeenshire during the War. He spent a few years at the Marine Biology Laboratory in Aberdeen and this provides the background to his description of the fishing industry in *Living Silver* as well as some of his poetry. He left Aberdeen for London and died in 1964 in Plymouth.

Toulmin, David 116

is the pseudonym of John Reid. He was born in 1913 at Rathen in Aberdeenshire. He left school at fourteen to work on farms and spent most of his life in that way. More recently he moved into Aberdeen where he now lives in retirement. Though he has written all his life, his first collection of short stories *Hard Shining Corn* was published only in 1972. Since then he has published further collections and a novel *Blown Seed*.

Victoria 93

Queen Victoria first visited Scotland in 1842. She and Albert were so taken with the country that they set out to acquire a home of their own there. They came to Balmoral in 1848 and re-built the castle some distance from the old house. She and Albert spent their happiest days there and she later recalled those times in her *Leaves from the Journal of our Life in the Highlands* (1867).

White, Jean **139**

was the married name of Jean Will who was born at Tyrie in 1892, daughter of James Will the schoolmaster of New Pitsligo. She was an Aberdeen University graduate and published two novels *The Moss Road*, 1932, and *The Sea Road*, 1935. She died at Camberley in Surrey in 1960.

Acknowledgments

The editors and publishers thank the following for permission to print copyright material:

John R. Allan and Robert Hale Ltd for *The fisher communities, Peacock's Close* and *Bloodsports on Deeside,* from *NORTHEAST LOWLANDS OF SCOTLAND* John R. Allan and Longman Group Ltd for *The life of the ploughmen* and *The games,* from *FARMER'S BOY*

J. M. Dent & Sons Ltd for *Religion and superstition* by Peter Anson, from *FISHING BOATS AND FISHER FOLK ON THE EAST COAST OF SCOTLAND*

Mrs Elsie Diack and Ray Palmer Ltd for *Our classic motor run* by Hunter Diack, from *THAT VILLAGE ON THE DON*

W. Heffer & Sons Ltd for *Two Tongues* by Eugen Dieth, from *A GRAMMAR OF THE BUCHAN DIALECT VOL. 1*

Amy Stewart Fraser and Routledge & Kegan Paul Ltd for *Life in Glengairn* and *Country Dance,* from *THE HILLS OF HOME*

Catherine Gavin and Methuen & Co Ltd for *A man from the sea* and *Fisher foys,* from *THE HOSTILE SHORE*

Hutchinson General Books Ltd for *The two Chrisses* and *Chris's wedding* by Lewis Grassic Gibbon, from *SUNSET SONG*; and for *The land* and *Aberdeen* from *SCOTTISH SCENE,* now available in *A SCOTS HAIRST*

Cuthbert Graham and Robert Hale Ltd for *Royal domain,* from *PORTRAIT OF ABERDEEN AND DEESIDE*

Jessie Kesson for *The gowk*; Jessie Kesson and Chatto & Windus Ltd for *Term days and term nights,* from *GLITTER OF MICA*; Jessie Kesson and Paul Harris Publishing for *The lane,* from *THE WHITE BIRD PASSES*

R. F. Mackenzie and Edinburgh University Student Publications Board for *Changed days?* and *Acceptable speech,* from *THE UNBOWED HEAD*

Acknowledgments

Alastair Mackie and the Lallans Society for *Building a city* and *Tenements,* both from *My grandfather's nieve* published in *LALLANS*

Elizabeth Bremner and Methuen & Co Ltd for *I to the hills* by Ian Macpherson from *SHEPHERD'S CALENDAR,* and for *To meet the Queen,* from *PRIDE IN THE VALLEY*

P. Scrogie Ltd for *Mains goes to war* by W. P. Milne, from *EPPIE ELRICK*

Rev. David Ogston for the passage quoted in the Foreword

Neil Paterson and Curtis Brown Ltd for *Revival mania,* from *BEHOLD THY DAUGHTER*

Victor Gollancz Ltd For *Cairngorm Commentary* by Tom Patey, from *ONE MAN'S MOUNTAINS*

George Scott for *A rural referee* by Dufton Scott, from *DUFTON SCOTT'S HUMOROUS SCOTS STORIES AND SKETCHES,* Collected Edition

Nan Shepherd and Aberdeen University Press for *Man and mountain,* from *THE LIVING MOUNTAIN*

Dr Marie Singer for *Trawling* by Burns Singer, from *LIVING SILVER*

John Reid (David Toulmin) for *Playing truant* from *HARD SHINING CORN*

John Murray Ltd for *The fisher and the lady* by Jean White, from *THE SEA ROAD*